YEARS IN A MIRROR

VAL GIELGUD

Years in a Mirror

THE BODLEY HEAD

LONDON

For

my sister

ELEANOR

with admiration,

gratitude and affection

How wonderfully has the day gone by!
If only when the stars come we could die
And morning find us gathered to our dreams:
Two happy solemn faces, and the sky.
Richard le Gallienne

© Val Gielgud 1965
Printed and bound in Great Britain for
The Bodley Head Ltd
10 Earlham Street, London WC2
by C. Tinling & Company Ltd, Liverpool
Set in Monotype Ehrhardt
First published 1965

Contents

ACKNOWLEDGMENTS

The Publishers are grateful to Odhams Books Ltd for kind permission to quote the passage on page 208 from *My Early Life* by Sir Winston S. Churchill, and to Jonathan Cape Ltd for kind permission to quote the passage on page 198 from Carl van Vechten's *Tiger in the House*.

Foreword

IN 1946 I published a volume of autobiographical reminiscences under the title of *Years of the Locust*. In 1949 this was followed by *One Year of Grace*, in which I gave some account of a year of release—by mutual agreement—from my service with the B.B.C.: a year spent for the most part in the United States of America.

Both these books are now out of print, because, I assume, in the sound opinion of their publishers they are out of date.

On April 28th, 1963—my sixty-third birthday—that service with the B.B.C., which began at Savoy Hill thirty-five years ago, came to an end. And various people, among whom Mr Eric Partridge must accept responsibility for having been the first, suggested to me that there should be enough material in my diaries, my note-books and my memory to justify a third volume in which the letter 'I' is bound to recur with deplorable frequency.

This book is the result. I fancy it is bound to disappoint a number of people who have grown used to former members of the Corporation's staff spending unwonted leisure in biting the hands that fed them. 'Auntie B.B.C.', as she is termed by a popular press uncertain whether to patronise or more actively to denigrate an organisation which it cannot destroy, and which never—on a principle that personally I deplore—retaliates, may have her faults. I hope to examine some of them in these pages. But an aunt—no matter what her fads, idiosyncrasies, or shortcomings may be—remains a member of one's family. And I am so old-fashioned as to dislike the washing of family linen in public.

I cannot claim to have written an autobiography. Chronology has been largely neglected. A considerable amount of personal material has been omitted, out of regard for other people's feelings, and incidentally for my own. I have done my best to write about the things, the characters, and the places that have most interested me, in the hope that at least some of them may interest others. And if the result is something of a scrap-book—well, I have known a great many less popular programmes.

Should anyone consider the performance monstrously exhibitionist, I can only remind him that I was an actor before I was a broadcasting producer, and that the vanity of the latter often exceeds that of the former, because it has less opportunity for display in the course of his normal business.

Explanation is not excuse. But there it is.

I should perhaps add that the title has been chosen according to the accepted theory that no mirror exists which does not to some extent distort.

V.G

CHAPTER ONE

From an Armchair in Brook Street

THE CHAIR has no pretence to elegance. It is not even particularly comfortable. It is set on the left-hand side of the fireplace in what is called—in the parlance of the Club—the Sandpit. (Why it is so called I have no idea. Nor have I ever found any member, however aged, who could tell me.) Shabby from much sitting, it is upholstered in ochreish yellow now fading to snuff colour. It is perhaps appropriate that it should figure at the beginning of this book, for it was while seated in this chair that Eric Partridge, his pipe as ever gurgling between his teeth, was so rash as to urge me to write it. And I am unlikely to forget the evenings I have spent in the semicircle facing it, while Compton Mackenzie—so like the Don Quixote idolised by Michael Fane in the early chapters of *Sinister Street*—proved himself a prince among *raconteurs*; the most engaging among exhibitionists who somehow failed to make their platform of the Stage.

But there is another reason for the introduction of that armchair. I never sit in it myself without being most vividly reminded of my father. It was my queer privilege and satisfaction—queer because according to Edwardian tradition it was the father who introduced the son to membership of a club—to propose my father, when his own club had been severely damaged during the Blitz. He much appreciated his election, though he tended to prefer silence and the morning-room to the atmosphere of the Sandpit, where a tradition of uninhibited laughter produced an atmosphere almost unique in a West End club. But on occasion he would be found in that armchair beside the fireplace, grey-moustached, thin, distinguished in the slightly foreign way that betrayed his Polish blood, and speak of his boyhood memories of Paris under the Second Empire. He had never forgotten the beauty of the Empress Eugénie as she passed in her carriage down the Champs Elysées. It never failed to

9

give me a certain thrill to realise that he had actually seen her. In that recollection I appreciated that historical personages had been visible flesh and blood.

Sitting in that chair, I find it easy to remember the time when those magical words 'the Club' made an ineffaceable impression of the picturesque, almost of the glamorous, upon the mind of a small boy. 'Katie,' my father would say across the Sunday morning breakfast table, 'I shall take Val to the Albert Hall concert this afternoon. We shall have tea at the Club.'

The announcement implied several things, all of them, in my view, desirable. It meant an early luncheon. It meant leaving the concert before the playing of the final programme-item. And while on the whole I enjoyed my education in Wagner and Beethoven, I felt at the age of twelve or so that enough was enough. It meant a brisk walk eastwards through Kensington Gardens, and my father's invariable joke about the Albert Memorial—the only doubtful joke I ever heard from his lips. Above all it meant hot buttered toast, or crumpets, with China tea in Dover Street, surrounded by impressive-looking figures who seemed immensely old and frighteningly genial, though I am sure that in reality most of them were merely civil and middle-aged.

Everything was so quiet, so certain, so warmly dedicated to the masculine ideal: the respectful yet majestic hall-porter; the glimpse of the card-room through the half-open door, with Fred Terry beaming cheerfully across a table; the curving staircase over which hung—and hangs—the large portrait of (I believe) Mrs Pat Campbell in *The Second Mrs Tanqueray*; the silent-footed, deft-handed servants—all of them of course male; the low hum of voices; the smell of good cigars; the occasional celebrity of the artistic world, revealed on close inspection as astonishingly, almost disappointingly normal in appearance; the deep armchairs; the blazing fire; the amazing depth of butter on the hot toast. A comment, agreeably ironical, upon the idiosyncrasies of human nature was the discovery of a copy of *La Vie Parisienne* concealed between the eminently respectable covers of the *Illustrated London News*.

It was all ordinary enough in the London of the years immediately preceding the First German War, but it made up a scene very different from the circumstances of childhood in South Kensington:

the routine of daily round and common task: mealtimes, school and holidays, relatives, my toy soldiers and my brother John's toy theatre; and a background that somehow was predominantly feminine. For, while my father had always something withdrawn and consequently formidable about him, my mother's was the predominant personality in the home. It was wonderful to sit in one of those deep chairs, in front of that blazing fire, munching toast—if truth be told, sometimes licking a buttery finger—and dream of the time when I too should go to 'the Club'; when I should have a sanctuary of service and comfort and pleasant company; when I should smoke cigars, and summon with enormous casualness a servant to bring me a glass of sherry or a whisky-and-soda upon a silver tray. There were other dreams, coupled with such names as Lord Roberts, and Sherlock Holmes, and Rupert of Hentzau; but the dream of 'the Club' persisted. And, unlike the others, in the fulness of time it materialised; if not in Dover Street, at least in Brook Street.

It was, I suppose, only to be expected that reality should fail to live up to the dream. Most Edwardian dreams died with the autumn of 1914, as Ruritania now surely lies behind the Iron Curtain with other unhappy satellite states. I do not mean that, when I was elected to my club in 1929, I felt anything but privileged and grateful. I am no more the born clubman than I am the born pubman. I have always been far too fond of women's society to be either one or the other. None the less my club has been for almost thirty years the nearest possible equivalent of 'a home from home'. It has given me 'laughter and the love of friends'; it has given me peace and quiet; it has provided me with innumerable excellent stories, which happily I can never remember and so can hear over and over again with undiminished pleasure. I enter its doors with consistent anticipation, and leave them with equivalent regret. But I must confess that about that vanished long room in Dover Street (now happily rebuilt) there was an aura, an atmosphere, that Brook Street has never quite been able to capture—though I am inclined to think, when I look at the picture of our old Piccadilly premises above the fireplace in the Sandpit, that it is the fault not of the Club but of 'the times in which we live'.

Like the English Theatre—which has been supposed to be on its deathbed for as long as I can remember—London club life is generally publicised as being on its way out. The modern young man cannot afford it. The modern young man insists on a cocktail-bar and the company of young women. The modern young man is not interested in the conversation of his distinguished elders. The modern young man has better things to do than sleep in armchairs. And so on and so forth. The indictment is sufficiently comprehensive.

I can only speak for one club. (It is true that in the old days I should probably have been able to be a member of two or three.) The situation in Brook Street has seldom been more prosperous. Despite an increased subscription there is no lack of young members. The social centre may have shifted from the billiard-room to the bar, but there is little tendency for cocktails to replace the sherry or whisky-and-soda of tradition. It must be admitted that waitresses have come to enliven the dining-room, possibly at the expense of its quiet. We shall not, alas, see the like again of the old wine-waiter with his bald head and drooping moustache who could remember Robert Louis Stevenson and Rudyard Kipling as members. Was it lack of observation or, as I believe, professional discretion which confined his memories of such giants to the discreet comment that R.L.S. was 'rather a strange gentleman'; that Kipling was 'a nice enough gentleman, but rather quiet'? Nor can there be adequate replacement for the hall-porter, reputed the original protagonist of the story that when a lady rang up the Club and enquired for a certain Mr X., his immediate riposte was to ask whether she might be Mrs X. The caller asserted, not without asperity, that she was certainly Mrs X.

'In that case, madam, Mr X. is *not* in the Club.'

Such courage is not to be met with in this day and age.

However, the basic tradition of a masculine fastness remains, stemming from a member's assertion long ago that 'a man must have somewhere, other than his bathroom, where he can be secure from interruption by a woman.' Not long ago, in fact, there was serious dissension among members regarding the propriety of celebrating a considerable anniversary with a Ladies' Night. By many it was considered as a sinister end to a wedge, however thin, and an ensuing proposition that ladies might be admitted to meals over week-ends went down to condign defeat.

12

Nor have I noticed any diminution of eagerness to join the circle whenever one or other of the Club's admitted and admired 'characters' is on form and 'in the chair'. Compton Mackenzie, with his beard, his twinkle, and his unrivalled collection of personal reminiscences; Eric Linklater, with the hint of a baleful flash behind his spectacles; Herbert Agar with his elegance and wisdom; Lionel Hale and Denzil Bachelor—these are only a few among Brook Street notables to preserve the fine flower of intelligent conversation.

It may be that in this regard the Club holds an almost unique position. I know of no other so dependent upon a persisting environment which is sociable without being oppressively hearty, distinguished without being oppressively pompous; no other in which bursts of laughter—indeed of uninhibitedly loud laughter—are the rule rather than the exceptional occasion of scandal. On the other hand it is fair to record that when members were the guests of the Guards—at that time their Brook Street neighbours—and a member of the Brigade was invited to express an opinion, he was heard to remark, 'They seemed nice enough fellows. A pity that they all seem to make their own trousers!' It is true that Brook Street lacks the sartorial distinction of St James's, as it lacks the ecclesiastical and academic distinction of Waterloo Place.

But has, in fact, the club life of today degenerated vastly in contrast with that of the great era of King Edward VII? Taken by and large, I do not think so. The prevailing standards of creature comforts are not so high. In this respect there has merely been a movement appropriate to a changing, an increasingly uncomfortable, general background of existence. Meals are more simple. The wine-list is not so long. Service in clubs, as in hotels, has suffered inevitably from the consequences of the Catering Wages Act, which would seem to have been designed for the promotion of the greatest possible discomfort among the greatest number of people. It is probably true that during a life progressively more real and more earnest there is a tendency to use the club more as a convenience than as an essential luxury; more as a substitute for the intolerably expensive restaurant, as a haven of temporary release, and less as an integral of civilised existence.

None the less, the English club—like the English public school, which has likewise been included by many authorities as one of the inevitable casualties of the Welfare State—persists, because apparently it satisfies something peculiar to the English character. The American club, despite its unrivalled hospitalities, has not the same roots. Over its very existence hangs the persisting menace of a country wedded, and, as far as can be judged, happily wedded to matriarchy. And to women, and to managing women in particular, a club is a mixture of exasperation and menace for obvious reasons. It may well be that the American is right when he retorts that the English club is just one more instance of ineradicable English snobbery. The tie that other people may not wear, the house into which other people may not go, the society from which one may hope to exclude other people, the members' enclosure, the table reserved for third-year men, a dumb yearning for the exclusive— without these things England might well be less class-conscious, less forbidding to the foreigner, less smugly self-righteous, less susceptible to the influence of what has become known as the Establishment. She would also be unrecognisable: just one more of those well-scrubbed, dull democracies, like Holland or Switzerland or pre-Munich Czechoslovakia, notable for little apart from certain industrial aptitudes and great commercial integrity. The Club has meant to England very much what the Road meant to Rome.

In the days when I visited Dover Street with my father, we walked through Kensington and its Gardens. When I walked from my London flat to Brook Street, the way lay across Leicester Square and the purlieus of Mayfair. Travelling along this latter route, and musing nostalgically of the former, it is easy to draw comparisons. It is remarkably difficult to do so in favour of the decade in which I write.

Not that I pretend to regret for 'the snows of yesteryear'. In spite of traditional Christmas cards and Mr Bing Crosby the 'white Christmas' even in my childhood was more a legend, owing much to Charles Dickens, than a reality. And snow in London has less affinity with Hans Andersen than with slush and wet feet. But there is for me a genuine melancholy in the knowledge that I shall never again hear the bell of muffin-man or hansom-cab; never see another lamplighter, nor fire-engine rampant in brass and scarlet behind galloping horses; never experience the queer shock of realising that straw had been laid down outside the house of one of my parents' friends, and that in consequence the Shadow of Death must be presumed imminent. Upon those streets and squares dedicated to the living of the Edwardian professional class there would seem now to have descended that atmosphere of progressive seediness which comes to afflict all districts in which large private houses have been transformed into private hotels and boarding-houses, unless—like my own old home—they have disintegrated into flats whose bathrooms have to be sought in unlikely corners, whose ceilings are too high for their partitioned rooms. The shops also have suffered change. They have broken out into a rash of neon lighting. The family-type butcher and fishmonger seem almost to have disappeared as the chain-store and the Co-op have moved in. My own two favourite toy-shops have been replaced respectively by a wine-shop and a retailer of radio and TV sets. And the perambulators are pushed not by neat nursemaids, nor by nannies obviously modelling themselves upon conceptions of Queen Victoria's court, but by harassed-looking young mothers wearing trousers and make-up for the most part too carelessly applied.

About half-way between the house in which my family lived in the Old Brompton Road and the Gloucester Road Underground station two buildings faced each other at a street junction, which in some sort epitomised for me the period and background of my boyhood. One was a most hideous jumble of soot-grimed scarlet bricks rather than a house. It was my day-school, and it remains in my memory for its ugliness; for the faded blonde good looks of the headmaster's wife, who was rumoured to be consumptive and made me think of Beauty and the Beast when in the company of her husband, who had the fierce moustache and coarsely virile good looks of an opera singer; for the exciting presence of the youthful Jevan Brandon-Thomas, who seemed to me far more representative of theatricality in those days than my Terry relatives; and for the fact that there for the first time I made an intimate friend of about my own age.

He lived in the big house on the other side of the road, facing the school. He was nearly two years my elder, the younger son of a wealthy merchant from Hamburg, naturalised in this country for many years. His mother was Austrian. Both were of generous build, hospitable, and greedy. I fancy—though I never knew for certain—

that one or both of them came of Jewish stock. I felt they must be rich, because their house was much bigger and more comfortable than ours, and because I saw there for the first time a lift in a private house, a billiard-room, and a gramophone. It was Cecil who showed me how to handle a cue. (I only wish I could have been a greater credit to his teaching.) It was Cecil who introduced me to recorded selections from *The Count of Luxemburg* and *Gypsy Love*. It was with Cecil that I first smoked cigarettes with his father's amiable connivance and under a smoke-screen of his father's excellent cigars. (Cecil stole one of the latter one afternoon. We bisected it with care in the Botanical Gardens, and I almost burst with satisfaction to find that I could smoke it without a qualm while it turned him deadly sick.) It was with Cecil that I first spoke embarrassedly, and altogether inaccurately, of 'the facts of life'.

What brought us together it is hard to say. He was my intellectual superior, and inclined to patronise. He was anything but attractive physically, being thick-set and stooping, with steel-rimmed glasses even bigger than my own. We shared a dislike of athletics in any form, and a passion for reading and conversation about subjects which we did not understand. But I remember my occasional revulsion against symptoms of mingled sentiment and brutality so typically German; my satisfaction, most carefully concealed, that my father's origin was not German, like Cecil's, but Polish. It may have been that our intimacy was somehow stimulated by an atavistic mutual instinct of racial hostility.

After the first two or three years our friendship persisted rather as a habit than anything else. We went to different private schools in the country, and later still to Winchester and Rugby respectively. We wrote to each other. We met in the holidays. But we were growing apart, normally and painlessly, always with the expressed idea that somehow later—probably at the university—we should come together again. Then came the First German War. It must have been early in 1917 that I heard from Cecil that he had managed, in spite of his poor eyesight, to get a commission. Some six months later I had a letter from him, extolling the merits of his regiment, the Rifle Brigade, and demanding that when my own time came I should apply for the same corps. It was my last word from him.

He had not been a week in France when he was killed, possibly by a sniper, more probably by a stray bullet. For the first time it entered my head that there might be another side to the medal inscribed *dulce et decorum est pro patria mori*; that war could be futile and wasteful as well as necessary and glorious. The killing of that German boy of nineteen by a German bullet shocked and saddened me inexpressibly. And its irony is increased by the conviction that, had Cecil lived, our antagonisms would have increased, our friendship almost certainly perished. But the gods loved him, and he died young.

It must have been in the days when Cecil and I were tentatively exploring the West End of London, and peering through big spectacles at what we fondly believed to be 'life', that I first became conscious of that Leicester Square which for many years I crossed daily on my way to Brook Street or to my office. In those days Leicester Square had an unquestioned glamour to offset its legendary disreputability, and soon it was to be linked strangely and immortally with a remote Irish place-name in a tune that will live as long as British soldiers die. That Leicester Square was the Leicester Square of *Sinister Street*, of Stagg & Mantle, of the promenades of the Empire and Alhambra theatres. It had atmosphere, if not an air. If that atmosphere was vicious, it was also picturesque. And, if the vice was flagrant, it was also full-blooded, almost demonstrative, like the temperaments and hats of the 'ladies of the Town'. The exotic architecture of the Alhambra in particular provided a background sufficiently and appropriately unreal, and I am inclined to date the decadence of the Square from the day when the Alhambra was exchanged for the shiny black synthetic blocks of the Odeon Cinema, and Daly's ladies were replaced by Warner's films.

Oddly enough, I found myself personally involved in the death-throes both of Daly's and the Alhambra.

It was during the run of Edgar Wallace's famous play *The Ringer*, in which I understudied and played—improbably and without conviction—the part of a policeman, that I first met Ronald Squire. Leslie Faber, that most brilliant and too-little-appreciated of actors, was among the first in the profession to foresee what the future might hold for my brother John. Largely on the latter's account he was extremely kind to me during that year at Wyndham's Theatre, overlooking my incompetences and encouraging me to persist in my first tentative efforts towards the writing of plays. On occasion he would take me to supper at the Garrick Club, where I would sit tongue-tied, curious, and bewilderedly happy while Faber, Seymour Hicks, and Ronald Squire exchanged gossip and competed in tall-story-telling. Could I ever have qualified as an actor, the experience of such company must have made me one. It was fascinating to listen to Leslie Faber asserting that the last act of *The Liars* was the final word in dramatic construction; to hear Ronald Squire's confession that his unrivalled technique owed everything to his having under-studied Charles Hawtrey and watched Gerald du Maurier at close quarters throughout the run of *Bulldog Drummond*; to try to follow the flashing inconsequence of Seymour Hicks through the maze of relating the art of English acting to the craft of modern French comedy-writing.

Some years later, when I had joined the B.B.C. and realised—as the result of my experiences with Henry Ainley and Miss Dorothy Dickson—that the more distinguished and more talented the actors, the easier and more agreeable it was to work with them, I persuaded Ronald Squire to reproduce on the air his triumph as the dis-illusioned and escapist stockbroker in Somerset Maugham's play *The Breadwinner*. He seemed both astonished and gratified to be assured that his timing, his oddly attractive nasal laugh, even—improbable though it may sound—the roguish twinkle in his eye, had surmounted with success all the apparent handicaps of micro-phone representation. I hope that it was the broadcasting producer rather than the wide-eyed audience at Garrick suppers whom he remembered when he gave me my first opportunity to produce a play in the 'live' theatre, and I found myself directing Yvonne Arnaud and Ronald Squire in *Tread Softly*, which was the last play performed at Daly's Theatre before its demolition and reconstruc-tion.

My connection with the last phase of the Alhambra, while also owing inception to a broadcasting episode, was a considerably more exotic experience. Sebastian Shaw had worked with me in a broad-cast of one of Shakespeare's plays. Subsequently he was engaged by Sir Alexander Korda to take a leading part—with Gertrude

Lawrence and Miss Miriam Hopkins—in a film which, though a modern story, included a sequence from the final act of *Othello*. The chosen director, as so often in the British film industry, was not British. He had achieved a great and deserved reputation with elegant, frothy, Viennese comedy subjects. His command of English was, however, limited. His approach to Shakespeare was definitely continental. He was amiable enough to raise no objection when Sebastian Shaw suggested to Sir Alexander that he would be happier if the *Othello* sequence could be embellished by the services of an English dialogue director, and that I was the man for the job. The B.B.C.—too often stigmatised as an organisation without humanity or bowels—raised no objection. I found myself accordingly immersed in the quicksands and shallows of the Denham studios, fascinated by the discovery that at any rate where the film industry was concerned truth was certainly stranger than fiction.

All of which may seem, and indeed was, a considerable distance away from the Alhambra, already doomed to destruction at the builders' hands. But the aforesaid *Othello* sequence had been designed to be played on the stage of a theatre, not in the studio; and so for its last performance—and I imagine for the first time—the Alhambra presented Shakespeare on the boards sacred to memories of *The Bing Boys*, the great dynasty of music-hall artists, the ballet, and the promenade.

It was not perhaps out of keeping that a number of the ingredients of the production should have been out of the ordinary. The Willow Song, for example, was accompanied by a full orchestra. (This may have been due to the need, acknowledged with typical charm and sense of humour by Gertrude Lawrence, of 'cover' for her top notes, but it was also due to the fact that the director had a queer passion for the Coleridge-Taylor setting, and would sit smiling happily in the stalls while it was played over and over again for his especial benefit.) Again, Miss Lawrence played Desdemona in a night-dress of sheer black chiffon liberally bespangled with golden stars, recalling Charlot or Cochrane rather than Cyprus or Venice. Not for London Films were the modern austerities of production at the Old Vic or Stratford-on-Avon.

For the most part I had extremely little to do, apart from enjoying

19

a new experience—not difficult in the company of Gertrude Lawrence and Sebastian Shaw—and keeping my eyebrows reasonably horizontal, which was quite a job. However, towards the close of the final day's shooting a crisis developed. The climax of the film's not too original story occurred when its hero, the actor playing Othello, in a spasm of genuine as opposed to theatrical jealousy did his best to strangle his wife, who was of course playing opposite him as Desdemona. This emotional metamorphosis was perceived, a trifle improbably, by a young lady in the gallery of the theatre, who was involved in some complicated emotional relationship with the actor, and proceeded to scream out what she believed to be happening at the top of her voice. Whereupon the curtain was rung down, and shortly afterwards the Stage Manager appeared before it to explain that tragedy had, after all, been averted.

An elderly actor of experience and reputation had been engaged to play the Stage Manager. For some reason—probably sheer nerves—he proved incapable of remembering the few lines of his speech. Again and again the scene before the curtain was rehearsed. Again and again the 'take' resulted in a dismal dry-up. The day ended with the scene still untaken, in an atmosphere of general discomfort, irritation and embarrassment. Just as I was leaving, the production manager drew me aside, enquired whether I possessed a dress-suit, and, if I did, whether I would mind coming down in it to the next day's call. It appeared that, if the difficulty persisted, I was considered suitable to step into the breach.

I still remember how acutely conscious I felt of an appearance of raffish disreputability, as I walked from Long Acre to Leicester Square, wearing a white tie and tails, at half-past nine in the morning: how unbelievably more embarrassing it seemed to me to have to make a speech to an audience of some hundreds of extras than it had been in my time as a repertory actor to face the audiences at the Oxford Playhouse. Nor can I forget the lined greyish face of the actor displaced, as he wished me luck, and then stood watching from the wings with grimly masochistic determination. Those few lines of mine were the last ever spoken from the Alhambra stage: one small disaster symbolising, suitably perhaps, a larger tragedy, a veritable end.

It is easy, and by all means more pleasant, to consider Leicester

Square in such nostalgic terms. Its present-day realities are depressing, when they are not simply squalid. The prevailing impression is a dissolving view of crew-cuts and pony-tails, of painted nails and unwashed hands, of denim jeans and duffel coats, of the furtive eye and the swaggering, insolent walk. It may not be without significance that when I have crossed the Square late at night on my way home I have been accosted, in nine cases out of ten, by a man, not by a woman. The London of Compton Mackenzie has given place to the London of Graham Greene. Where the Romantics once drank champagne on credit, the Angry Young Men borrow the price of another beer—only too often from the Intellectual Young Women. I cannot be persuaded that the change is for the better.

American friends have confirmed my comparison of contemporary Leicester Square and Coventry Street with the reaches of Broadway round and about Times Square. There is viciousness without vitality, vulgarity without conviction, laziness without elegance, the crowd's jostling stupidities without its good-humour, the superficialities of entertainment presented to the impotent and the crass. Eyes are dull. Expressions are apathetic, at best envious. A flashy shabbiness prevails. For the most part the professional beggar has departed. The milk-bar has arrived. So much can be claimed by civilisation advancing.

Maybe late middle age is always jaundiced. Maybe through that dark glass alone the summers of the years before 1914 are seen as perpetually sunlit. June always flamed, and life went by rose-crowned and carefree to the music of the waltz. Maybe the real tragedy of age is simply its failure to adapt itself to inevitable change, its conviction that change must mean decay.

I wonder all the same. I remember what John Galsworthy wrote of the old Forsyte aunts in the Bayswater Road, who might not have opened their minds or their windows, and yet preserved a fastidiousness of standards and behaviour for whose loss the world is poorer. I remember the exasperated admiration with which I received my father's grim rebuke, when he heard from his bank that I had overdrawn my allowance—to the extent of twelve pounds: 'In fact you have obtained money under false pretences.'

Today nations inflate their currencies in terms of millions, and individuals overdraw their accounts almost on principle, and justify

CHAPTER TWO

Presentment of Two Brothers

1. Lewis Evelyn

I WAS born second into a family that consisted of three boys and a girl. On occasion I have felt that in this I was a little unlucky. In terms of inheritance and family pride there has never been any doubt of the advantages of primogeniture. On the other hand I read in the fairy tales that it was always the youngest son—very frequently the third into the bargain—who fulfilled the quest and married the princess. Both in life and fiction it seemed to me that second sons were at something of a discount. Even bastardy, however much it might be conventionally deplored, seemed to have a good deal to be said for it and even more written about it. From the heroic offspring of Zeus, through Cesare Borgia and Dunois, to Morny and Horatio Bottomley and Ramsay MacDonald, the record of illegitimacy appeared frequently distinguished and almost always picturesque. But second sons? King William Rufus, James Forsyte, Hamlet's wicked uncle, Claudius—hardly encouraging. The depressing thought sometimes crept into my mind that by and large the second son was little more than a form of insurance against the possibility of disaster affecting the eldest.

This must not for an instant be held to imply that I felt myself unwanted, or that I was treated by my parents in the least unfairly. It merely served as explanation—and, I fear, excuse—when I realised that I was considerably less talented than either of my brothers. And I think I can say honestly that it diminished neither my admiration nor my affection for them; especially for my elder brother Lewis.

Lewis was six years older than I, and I fancy that I became acutely conscious of his individuality about the time when he went to Eton in the glory appropriate to the second scholar of his year. A good deal has been written about Eton during the past few years

23

—most of it the denigration by second-rate and ill-natured persons of a system of education which they envied, and which might well have improved their manners. There have of course been nasty Etonians, just as there have been nice Etonians; stupid and hide-bound Etonians, just as there have been liberal and distinguished Etonians. (One of the two Etonians who shared an Army cadets' hut with me during the First German War invariably slept in his shirt.) I only know that if my brother Lewis could be considered as at all representative of Eton, it seemed to me during my years of adolescence that Eton was greatly to be admired; that its civilised sophistication was by all means preferable to the cheerfully philistine brutalities of Rugby, where we may have worked harder but certainly 'made more row'.

It is hardly necessary to add that Lewis became my idol: the idol upon whose behaviour and example I tried my best to model myself with notable lack of success. From him I learned what to wear and when to wear it, what to eat and where to eat it. From him I learned the delights of Sherlock Holmes, of translations of Greek plays, of minor military tactics, of keeping a diary.

It is, however, impossible to try to emulate an idol without inevitably forcing other people to draw comparisons. This, from my point of view, was unfortunate. At the age of twelve Lewis was the head of his private school. The following year he became a King's Scholar at Eton. From Eton he won a demyship at Magdalen. And I remember the incredulity with which the news was received at the family breakfast-table that he had only gained a Second in Mods, and not the anticipated First. It was rashly assumed that I would follow in his footsteps, but three public schools in succession rejected me as a scholar, and a minor history scholarship at Trinity, Oxford, did little to restore the balance.

Personally I was not in the least surprised, and I think I can claim that my natural envy was uncorroded by any odious jealousy. It would have been both improper and embarrassing to have found oneself on a level with one's idol. In any event all such considerations became of no account when the First German War interrupted Lewis's university career at the end of his second Oxford year. As one of the Second Hundred Thousand in Kitchener's Army he became a subaltern in the King's Shropshire Light Infantry, and in the autumn of 1915 was seriously wounded in one of the actions subsidiary to the Battle of Loos.

What sort of soldier he made I have no idea. He was never inclined to satisfy my natural curiosity on the subject. But I fancy that he would have been pleased could he have known that after his death, nearly forty years after Loos, a former private in his platoon wrote me a letter of sympathy concluding with a tribute almost Spartan: 'Mr Gielgud was a good officer.'

Two letters survive describing the high-lights of his experience in the field. One tells how he was buried by a shell in a dug-out with another officer under about three tons of earth. The other officer was killed, and Lewis only survived because of 'an extra stout piece of corrugated iron, and an Irish corporal who just stopped the rescuers from pulling down the wall which was keeping everything off me'. His only comment was to the effect that his luck was in that day, which to someone like myself who suffers from claustrophobia seems a considerable understatement. In the second —written from hospital at Le Touquet, where he was on the danger-list for three weeks—he wrote of the sensation of being wounded as 'exactly that of finding oneself in the path of a cricket-ball flung with great violence' and mentioned a bully-beef-tin-opener, which was found in his leg together with two fragments of shrapnel, as the cause of gangrenous complications. Most of it, however, referred to the nostalgic joys of the last New College Ball, with a wistful query as to the likelihood of his ever being able to dance again. In fact, as a result of his wound he was to walk with a slight limp and to suffer intermittent pain for the rest of his life. He seldom mentioned the pain—never except in terms of slight discomfort. And if his dancing style remained obstinately that of 1914 he could always manage to do himself credit on a floor, even in his late fifties.

Up to the end of the First German War Lewis might have been considered—he certainly considered himself—as exceptionally fortunate. His academic career had been well above the average. He had served, not ingloriously, with his battalion, and subsequently with credit when attached to one of the various military missions in Paris. During this period he took such advantage of a natural aptitude as to become for practical purposes bilingual—though he was delighted to be able to tell against himself that Parisians considered his accent to be Roumanian! This part of his military life ended with the close of the war, while he was attached *en liaison* to General Haller's Polish Army in France. Both posts had called for qualities diplomatic rather than soldierly, and a way of life with which he found a natural sympathy. His success in this field—he achieved a staff captaincy and a Military Cross—was one of the factors which induced him to sit for the Foreign Office examination in the hope of making a career in the Diplomatic Service.

The sequel was undoubtedly the greatest blow of his life. It was generally agreed that his chances of success were excellent, and in the examination itself he gained second place. He was, however, informed—with appropriate regrets—that he would not be accepted for the Service because by blood he was half a Pole. It was apparently of no account that he had shed a sizeable proportion of that blood in battle against the King's enemies; that his family had been naturalised British for three generations; that his grandfather Adam—Polish on both sides, and born in Koenigsberg as a refugee from the Russians in 1832—had worked as a clerk for many years in the War Office in Whitehall. Lewis would tell the story in terms of ironic comment upon bureaucratic absurdity. But he was in fact bitterly disappointed in his ambitions, and hurt in his *amour propre*. I believe that the rest of his working life, most of which was spent with distinction on behalf of the League of Red Cross Societies, was always in his own mind something of a second-best. It was a good second-best. It offered opportunities for travel from China to Peru—and he enjoyed travelling. His headquarters were in Paris, a city which he loved. But the supreme thing had been withheld for no conceivable fault or shortcoming of his own. And I think he went back into uniform to work, like his grandfather, for the War Office in the Second German War with a wry relief, a consciousness of a wheel coming full circle.

He always comes back most vividly to my mind when I remember an experience which we shared in the summer of 1920 at a frontier station between Poland and Czechoslovakia. Lewis had been working with the American Red Cross mission in Warsaw, and, with his invariable instinct for doing what would please me most, had suggested that I should join him during the Oxford Long

Vacation. My journey was complicated by various factors: a curious attempt to involve me in helping to smuggle a consignment of Army boots through the Gdynia customs—which is another story; the slowness and overcrowding with returning refugees of the steamer which ultimately landed me at Danzig; the inevitable difficulties of motor transport across a country barely restored to freedom and already engaged in a life-and-death struggle for survival against Bolshevik Russia.

My arrival in Warsaw coincided almost to the day with the collapse of Pilsudski's offensive against Kiev, and it became only too obvious that my holiday was liable to rapid truncation, if nothing worse. We saw Weygand and his French mission arrive to help the Poles' morale. We watched Haller take the salute as the last reserve divisions marched off to the crumbling front. (The men who made up those columns wore a fantastic mixture of British khaki, French *bleu-horizon*, and German *feldgrau*, and passed the cathedral in the great square with four mounted trumpeters at their head wearing the cavalry uniforms of 1831. The vast crowd that watched them was quite silent, except for the women who could not hold back their tears.) Music had been banned in the cafés. The Polish mark was falling like Vallombrosa leaves, so that the rate of exchange was chalked up in restaurants to show the difference between the beginning and the end of a meal! For the best part of a week we would go down from Lewis's office, where we had been trying to discover from unpronounceable place-names mentioned in the communiqués the progress of Tukachevsky's and Budenny's offensives, to sit after dinner on a terrace overlooking the Vistula and listen to the thudding of the guns far away to the east.

Ultimately the mission was ordered to leave in a train specially reserved for foreigners. With the order came the hint, studiedly unofficial, that the fall of Warsaw was considered inevitable. And I experienced what it must feel like to be a deserter.

We reached the Czech frontier a little after midnight. Czecho-Polish relations were rather worse than normal, with the Czechs showing their regrettable propensity to look to the apparently rising sun. No doubt they would have behaved less odiously if they could have foreseen the outcome of that battle of the Vistula, which has been called so justly a miracle. Instead of showing the slightest

27

sympathy or forbearance towards people who were travelling under conditions of extreme physical discomfort, many of whom had been compelled to abandon much that they valued, and more of whom were in considerable distress of mind, the Czech frontier guards were brutal, bullying, and bloody-minded. We were herded like cattle up and down the platform for hours. We were offered neither information nor food. Finally, with the exception of an imperturbable King's Messenger, who sat firmly in his carriage with his bags —and incidentally my sister-in-law's jewellery—and declined to move in any circumstances, we were stripped to the skin and searched by grubby-fingered officials while sentries stood over us with fixed bayonets. What they were looking for no one seemed to know. What they took was every small personal possession that might conceivably have value. (It took Lewis all of six months, and every ounce of pull he had in the circles of diplomacy, to get back our watches and cuff-links.)

Naturally enough the travellers' reactions were unamiable. The Americans were furious, and made no bones about showing it. They cursed, they threatened, they demanded the presence of higher authority, and in default of that free access to the telegraph office. They were extremely noisy—and quite ineffective. The French were, if possible, worse, aggravating their situation with several cases of feminine hysterics. Most of the British confined themselves within the bounds of a sort of sullen apathy, which only found expression in being as rude as possible to other nationals unaware of the privileges expected automatically by members of 'this happy breed'. Personally I cannot remember ever having felt so angry, so inclined, in spite of every sort of distaste for physical violence, to punch the nearest Czech on the jaw as hard as possible. I looked automatically to Lewis for my cue. He stood there quite impassive among the hubbub and confusion, leaning on a stick to spare his leg and smoking one cigarette after another. With his coat torn half off his back and his linkless shirt-sleeves fluttering untidily, he still managed to preserve the debonair 'form' whose ensign was his Old Etonian tie. He spoke when he was spoken to. He answered such questions as he could. He neither swore nor raised his voice. He was the embodiment of simple good behaviour. I wish frequently that some of those persons who inveigh so glibly against public schools and Oxford and Cambridge, who in times of crisis are so prone to ill-mannered hysteria and an acutely self-conscious determination to look after Number One, could have been present with me on that ill-lit station platform in eastern Europe.

To his perhaps most outstanding quality of all—his genius for friendship—other people, who may well have known him better and whose pens are infinitely more gifted than mine, can bear more telling and more touching witness, among them Aldous Huxley and Naomi Mitchison. The former was his contemporary at private school, at Eton, and at Oxford. To the latter and her family I know that he felt he owed much of the enchantment which Oxford always meant to him, enveloping his spirit in memories of bells and spires and long shadows falling across immemorially tended lawns. It was in that setting that England lived for him, for after 1915 he was never more than a visitor in his native country until the first two years of the Second German War. And he died in Paris, which had been his home and held so much of his heart.

Undoubtedly he could have made a fine actor. His occasional performances as an amateur were something quite out of the common run. He could have been a writer of parts. His translations of Horace and the *Pervigilium Veneris* have been acknowledged for their combination of grace, accuracy, wit, and delicate perception. Indeed he touched little that he did not adorn.

But there was something missing, which prevented him from achieving that sustained effort, that whole-hearted conviction, which marks out the professional from the gifted dilettante. It may have been the result of ambition blunted by the Foreign Office fiasco, or of the ultimate break-down of his first marriage, which I believe to have been deeply and almost desperately regretted both by his wife and himself. It may have been that his wound permanently affected more than his left leg, leaving invisible scars upon a personality sensitive beyond the normal. In 1915 the 'trick-cyclists' had not yet come into their own to find explanations for such things, and in any case Lewis would have been the last man to indulge in what he would have considered vulgar exhibitionism.

He was charming and intelligent, affectionate and generous to a fault. His untimely death was the greatest personal grief and loss that I have known.

I think he deserves to be remembered if only for his translation of the key couplet from the *Pervigilium Veneris*:

'For they shall be lovers, who never were lovers;
And they who were lovers be lovers again.'

2. Arthur John

It was typical of my mother's generosity of disposition that she should have given her eldest son, as his second name, the name of her husband's first wife. She was an American, to whom he was devoted, and she died tragically young. At the same time I cannot believe that there was ever much genuine hope or intention on my parents' part that 'Evelyn' should ever be adopted for current use. So indeed it proved. On the other hand it was a matter for real distress to my mother that her third son was always known in his extreme youth as Jack and thereafter invariably as John. Although he was deeply attached to her, nothing could induce him or his brothers to swallow 'Arthur'. The *Idylls of the King* were wallowing in that trough which so frequently follows hard upon the crest of popular literary reputation. And for all three of us boys Arthur Lewis was no more than a legendary figure greatly loved and revered by our mother, and a bearded portrait in the dining-room.

(As an odd footnote to the effect of best-sellers upon nomenclature it can be revealed—it is, alas, too late to upset him by the revelation—that Lewis as a small boy was known as Budge after the elder of the two brothers in *Helen's Babies*. He bore this cross with fortitude. I record with satisfaction that I was not afflicted with 'Toddie'. I have had enough trouble, heaven knows, with Val, which has almost invariably been assumed, erroneously, to be Valentine abbreviated. I confess that I would have found 'Toddie' unendurable.)

John was born at 7 Gledhow Gardens in South Kensington on April 14th, 1904. I have heard him spoken of as 'dedicated to the theatre' from his earliest years. There may have been, there almost certainly was, no doubt in his own mind about his future. The theatre, the inevitable aura of the Terry dynasty, lay all about us in our infancy (it should not be forgotten that on the Gielgud side

of the family there was a Polish great-grandmother, Aniela Asper-
gerowa, in her time as well known in her country as Ellen Terry was
in Great Britain). A toy playhouse, pillared and elaborately gilded,
was the pride and joy of our nursery. My sister was, and remains,
the most faithful and indulgent audience for her brothers' exhibi-
tionisms. We were made familiar with both sides of the curtain
before we went to school. And Marion, Fred, and less frequently
Ellen herself surrounded the annual Christmas tree in our drawing-
room.

But John owed his career to nothing but his own persistence. Our
parents looked distinctly sideways at the Stage as a means of liveli-
hood, and when John showed some talent for drawing his father
spoke crisply of the advantages of an architect's office. One of his
more managing aunts even extolled the Navy and the white tabs of
the youthful cadet.

John made no scenes on the subject and caused no crises in the
home—apart from doing his best to die on the nursery table on
which he had to undergo an operation for sudden acute appendicitis.
Adequate performances as Humpty-Dumpty and Mark Antony
did nothing to disturb the conventional years that followed as a
scholar of Westminster School. However, when the question of his
going to a university came up his decision was quietly but firmly
negative. He said that he wanted to go on the Stage, and that he was
going on the Stage. Accordingly he went.

His natural advantages were, in those days, hardly apparent.
Irving is reported as having once said wistfully to Ellen Terry that
'for someone with no face, no voice, and no legs' he had done pretty
well. John could claim regular features and youthful charm beyond
the average. His greatest asset, a voice unparalleled in his generation
of players for beauty, expression, and range, had to be developed
and proved by long experience. His legs—as he would be the first
to admit—were deplorable: a considerable handicap for the finest
'costume' player of his time, who started his career spear-bearing
at the Old Vic, played Romeo as his first leading part, and made two
of his greatest successes as Hamlet and Benedick. What he possessed
beyond question was singleness of heart and mind, together with a
remarkable capacity for hard work. When he was not acting in the
theatre, going to the theatre, or talking about the theatre, he was to

31

all intents and purposes not living. And to this day I am inclined to doubt if he ever experiences genuine happiness except on the stage, or in his dressing-room.

He has been called arrogant. I fancy that, as in the case of Cyrano de Bergerac, the nose has something to do with it: the big, bony, Polish nose down which—according to detractors—he is inclined to look in his less amiable moments, the nose whose abrupt lifting is one of his easily recognisable mannerisms. It is true that he does not suffer fools gladly, that he is liable to talk more easily than he listens, that his opinions are expressed both positively and fluently. While he is the best and most hospitable of hosts, he can simultaneously seem curiously withdrawn, and by innate temperament he is almost paralysingly shy. To this shyness he owes a reputation in the profession for the dropping of devastating 'clangers'—generally excused in that they produce entertainment more than they hurt feelings.

Supreme unselfishness as an actor he has never been denied. He has never felt the inclination to choose baser metal against which to display his own bright gold. The all-round excellence of casts with which he plays, or which he produces, is proverbial. To this quality can be attributed the pleasure he has achieved in smoothing the path for others in whom he has discerned quality, regardless of their possibilities as rivals. Sir Alec Guinness is not alone in his acknowledgment of a debt to John's help and encouragement at a time when these things made all the difference.

Can his approach and his technique justifiably be called old-fashioned? There is little doubt that it may seem so to the devotees of what Mr. Noël Coward has labelled with characteristic precision the gospel of 'mumble-and-spit'. And while I have heard John refer to 'the Method' with a mixture of enquiring curiosity and bland interest I very much doubt his making use of a technique originally designed to teach Hollywood 'clothes-horses' how to act.

Certainly he uses what is vulgarly called 'the grand manner' both in the speaking of verse and the wearing of costume. Considerable experience of other actors employing lesser manners has not convinced me that he is wrong. In contemporary clothes he is less happy, and he tends—in my opinion—to underestimate his capacity to play contemporary parts. This stems from a weakness which he shares with most actors. While an excellent judge of a part, he is less reliable in his estimate of a play. Hence his prejudice in favour of classic drama—though he has done few things better than his performances in *Musical Chairs* and *A Day by the Sea*. He is extremely aware of the audience's contribution to any acting performance. This accounts for his mistrust of the media of the cinema, television, and sound radio, where the audience's reaction cannot register, and where the actor's problems are complicated by the demands of complex technical machinery. Of recent years this apprehension—at least as far as the microphone is concerned—seems to have been largely overcome. No one would quarrel with the decision that has preserved his broadcast performances of *Hamlet*, *Richard II*, and *Oedipus at Colonus* among the archives of Broadcasting House.

As actor and producer he admits that he owes most to Harcourt Williams, with whom he worked so happily and fortunately at the Old Vic; to Leslie Faber, an actor whose talent was never adequately appreciated; to Komisarjevsky, who introduced him to Chekhov's plays; and to Michel St Denis, whose production of *The Three Sisters* with John as Colonel Vershinin at the Queen's Theatre in 1938 was a definite milestone in British theatrical history.

He is supposed to worry more than a little about his future. On the face of it there would seem little to attract him in 'kitchen-sink' drama, pieces designed to promote proletarian culture, or plays of 'non-communication'—yet he expressed the greatest admiration for *The Caretaker*. Excellent character-actor though he has proved himself to be—for example as Prospero and Gaev—he shares neither the inclination nor the talent of Sir Laurence Olivier for identifying himself with the seedier types of the English lower-middle class.

He believes, very sensibly, that once he is fifty an actor should realise the folly of continuing to play the young and romantic roles in which he has made his name. And once *King Lear* has been successfully tackled, what acting worlds remain to conquer? When he played Othello at Stratford-on-Avon in 1961, he did so less because he saw himself heaven-sent as the Moor than because it was the one remaining great Shakespearean part which he had never tried. The result was not a success. But the story might have been a different one, had the producer realised that to cast Othello and Iago from two diametrically opposed schools of acting technique was to invite disaster. To my extreme regret I have failed dismally to persuade him that the part of Coriolanus might have been written for him. He finds politics both confusing and tedious, and he can only see *Coriolanus* as a political play.

Most probably his activities will tend more and more away from acting, more and more towards direction. The time has long passed since, as a producer, he was liable to make of other actors' performances unsatisfactory carbon copies of his own. He has always possessed the essential qualities of the good producer: patience, consideration, imagination, a tireless application to detail, and a capacity for hard work only equalled by his love for the medium in which he is engaged.

Also—and this is vital to good direction—his general background and interests are by no means confined within the bounds of a single idea. He has considerable knowledge of music, and plays the piano by ear with enviable facility—an accomplishment which helped him considerably both in *Musical Chairs* and *The Constant Nymph*. He is an intelligent amateur connoisseur of pictures. He has studied theatrical design, with particular reference to his cousin Gordon Craig. He has travelled widely. And when he travels he is an inveterate sightseer, leaving no church unvisited, no museum or gallery unscoured. These things combine to give him the aesthetic perspective, the feeling for atmosphere and period, the basically civilised know-how without which the theatrical producer tends to bombinate in a vacuum of his own devising.

Restless—he can seldom sit still for long—lively, fantastically generous, in essence he is almost certainly unsatisfied. The face is a little gaunt, the eyes quick and intelligent, the fingers eloquent and mobile. He has played no games since he left school. His knowledge of mechanics is nil—he does not even drive a motor-car. He is the life of any party, yet usually somehow rather aloof. He is a far better writer than he knows—the first half of his *Early Stages* could hardly be better. In his clothes he inclines to dandyism. No one gives his friends better food and wine, while caring so little himself what he eats and drinks. He knows more of luxury than of comfort.

Finally, I would claim for him what he would certainly never dream of claiming for himself: that he is the greatest actor of our time.

34

Is the estimate too flattering? As with the case of most other cele
brated actors John's work and personality have been put beneath
a number of microscopes of criticism and appraisal, among them
that of Miss Marguerite Steen in her book *A Pride of Terrys*. I read
A Pride of Terrys with natural curiosity, much pleasure, and considerable admiration. I was flattered by the agreeable references in
it which she made to me personally. And I was grateful for the
consideration she showed me in letting me read the book in proof.
It was, however, a stage at which from the point of view of publishing economics it was impossible to contemplate making more than
the simplest alterations. Miss Steen was good enough to raise no
objection to the suggested erasure of two matters of fact. But two
impressions—which could not have been removed without considerable rewriting and resetting—inevitably remained with all their
implications, and struck me, when I re-read the book carefully
after publication, as even more misleading than they had seemed
when they first struck me. There was no question of any deliberate
distortion of the truth, still less of malice. My own belief is that the
trouble arose from information, probably given in all good faith,
having been inadequately cross-checked: a shortcoming comprehensible enough, considering the complexities of the story and the
personalities involved.

These two impressions concerned respectively my grandmother,
Kate Terry, the eldest of the famous family, who married Arthur
Lewis; and my brother John.

I hope Miss Steen will not take it amiss if I suggest that she is
primarily a novelist rather than a historian, that her strength lies in
colourful writing rather than in research. Writing of this kind
certainly tends to make easier reading. And for a born story-teller
and a trained and experienced author of fiction the history of the
Terrys must have presented an overwhelming temptation towards a
treatment to some extent after the fashion of the family saga. Such
sagas require a strong central story line with its appropriate heroine.
In this case the heroine was ready-made in the person of Ellen
Terry. No one could quarrel with the selection. She alone of the
singular clan had genius. But as white demands black to establish its
perfect radiance, so a heroine requires a contrasting villainess. And
for this part Miss Steen chose Ellen's sister, Kate.

Even Mr Darlington of the *Daily Telegraph*, most amiable and long-suffering of dramatic critics, raised an indignant eyebrow at what he conceived to be a case of serious miscasting of a leading part. He pointed out that it was hardly a case for reproach that Mrs Arthur Lewis had taken all possible pains over the bringing up of her four daughters to take their appropriate places in the contemporary society into which they had been born. To contrast such behaviour unfavourably with Ellen's quite incredibly casual and unpractical attitude towards her children was surely a little unfair. Exemption from normal codes is the prerogative of genius. No one would have wished the flame of Ellen's acting dimmed by the demands of domesticity. And if Edith and Gordon Craig were unduly penalised by being given a father to whom their mother was not married, three successive step-fathers, and the peculiar relationship with Sir Henry Irving, not to mention Ellen Terry's complete inadequacy in all the mundane details of looking after a home, they also received considerable compensation in being dearly loved—in Gordon Craig's case hardly this side idolatry—and in inheriting personalities of a quality to sustain a bohemian existence not only with fortitude but with satisfaction. Miss Steen draws an effective picture of four prim little Victorian misses on the well-kept lawns of Moray Lodge—where, incidentally, Arthur Lewis held his oyster feasts for his artist friends with no sort of protest from his wife—carefully guarded from the infection of the companionship of Edie and Ted, living their tenuous existence in unfashionable Earl's Court.

I believe the truth to have been considerably less dramatic. Considering the time in which she lived—and the accepted manners and morals of that time cannot in this context be ignored—Ellen Terry 'got away with murder'. Her private life was acknowledged her own affair by her family and friends, who gladly submitted to the famous charm and delighted in the acting genius. Her love-life was tactfully buried in oblivion. Until stated as a proven fact by Miss Steen the liaison with Irving was invariably denied as mere gossip—even by Mr Laurence Irving in his biography of his grandfather.

With her marriage Kate Terry abandoned the theatrical *ambiance*, uniquely for one of the profession at the very height of her achievement and career, and at a time when she was infinitely better known than Ellen. I cannot feel that she had less right to do so than had Ellen to persist in the casual, unpractical bohemian existence which suited her refusal to be bound by conventions. It is right and comprehensible that the outlaw should get sympathy and admiration: sympathy for hardships borne with fortitude, admiration for courage in refusing to conform. But such an attitude should not proceed to adorn the law-abiding citizen with horns and a tail. And, while it is probably true that Kate must have seen certain complications as likely to arise from the association of the Craig cousins with her own daughters, it is equally fair to assume that the Craig cousins would have, as likely as not, recoiled in horror from the conventional domestic disciplines of Moray Lodge: the regular meals, the lessons, the governesses, the formula, accepted as utterly normal by the Lewis children, of speaking when they were spoken to and doing as they were bid.

In my own experience my grandmother was certainly a formidable character. I have often thought that she would have been ideally cast as Lady Bracknell. But she lacked neither human charity, common sense, nor reasonable breadth of mind. Her only flagrant vice was the inability to realise just how badly she played bridge—a game to which she was devoted, and which she insisted on playing for stakes so low as to make it almost dull. There was certainly no hint in my mother's attitude to the Craigs of any tradition of hostility established at Moray Lodge. It is a fact that she did not care for Edith Craig. She felt, not without some justice, that Edie and her intimates, out of a mistaken devotion only to be described as fanatical, isolated Ellen Terry from many of her friends and complicated her life needlessly and hurtfully. But whenever Gordon Craig paid a visit to this country he was a guest at Gledhow Gardens (I remember him vividly arguing with my father, with whom admittedly he never got on) and my mother always spoke of him both admiringly and affectionately.

I feel that Miss Steen made a mistake in drawing so sharp, so uncompromising, a line between what she seems to label the 'reputable' and the 'disreputable' sides of the family, with her sympathy so definitely slanted in favour of the latter. Kate Terry was a good deal more than a tubby-figured matron, hopelessly prejudiced by domestic proprieties and snobbishly wedded to the ideal of bettering herself through her husband and her children. In the days when her own parents were still 'strolling players' she took on her shoulders a good deal more than her fair share of economic and practical responsibility for the family as a whole—including Ellen. She was admittedly a fine, if not a great, actress in her own right, being the first to make the Terry name famous. She adapted herself with skill and success to the completely different circumstances of her husband's world. And when that husband lost his fortune she adapted herself again with dignity and good-humour to an old age spent in the unpromising environment of the West Cromwell Road.

It is possible that in her heart she could not altogether approve of Ellen's 'goings-on'. I doubt if either sister lost that mutual affection which dated from the days when they had skipped along the streets of Bristol, each holding one of their father's hands, on their way to the theatre. What had happened was that fate had decreed that they should inhabit different worlds: worlds with frontiers which could not be crossed successfully without the help of something more than affection.

Miss Steen has made a rather similar mistake in writing of my brother John. She refers again and again to the advantages which he had in starting his career compared with his relatives of the same generation on the less 'reputable' side of the family, such as, for example, Anthony Hawtrey. I have already mentioned that John went on the Stage rather against my parents' wishes and hopes. He flatly declined to make use of the Terry name, or to exploit his Terry relations with their established theatrical position. That apart, there was nothing in his home-life to justify the implication of any silver spoon. His background was almost painfully middle-class, his father being a not particularly successful stockbroker. Certainly he was never ignorant of whence his next meal would come, nor of where to look for a bed. But the bed was inclined to be hard, the meals were the reverse of elaborate, the bath-water was almost always cold. (I record this point from experience and with feeling.) His public-school education, like that of his eldest brother, was paid for by a scholarship. He may not have come up a particularly hard way, but he was certainly not pampered.

Anthony Hawtrey, on the other hand—I personally found him

most attractive, and worked with him most happily on several projects during his management of the Embassy Theatre—in spite of the illegitimacy which on occasion he was distressingly inclined to flaunt, took for granted his prescriptive right to a way of life that could fairly be termed luxurious. Not for him the chilly bath-water, the rice-pudding, the régime of punctuality for meals and abhorrence of debt. He was extremely talented both as actor and producer, but his failure to go a great deal farther than he did was not due to his being deprived of advantages which John had been handed on a plate at birth. It was due to the fact that a favourite race-meeting, an opportunity to go fishing, or the charms of an attractive woman, were liable at any time—even when a production was in actual rehearsal—to distract his interest to the point at which he would vanish into the blue and be unavailable for days at a time.

That he has his faults and his shortcomings John would be the first to admit. Unfair exploitation of a flying start is not among them. It is a pity that Miss Steen, who has paid him handsome tribute in many other pages of her book, should have been misled in this particular regard.

I feel it due, almost as much to her as to John, to put the record straight.

CHAPTER THREE

Blank Cartridges

I WAS born at 36 Earl's Court Square in South Kensington London, on April 28th, 1900. Almost three weeks later Mafeking was relieved, and that dusty South African township provided the English language with a new term. I have occasionally wondered whether it may have been some queer pre-natal influence associated with the war in South Africa which implanted the fascination which things military have always had for me. This is probably fanciful. At the beginning of the present century militarism was not yet a dirty word. Small boys automatically played with toy soldiers or 'at being soldiers', without fear of psychological corruption. And, when at the age of four I first learned to read, the books that I remember most vividly—the works of Beatrix Potter always excepted—were an edition of *Don Quixote* with the Gustave Doré illustrations and the vast red volumes of *With the Flag to Pretoria*, only to be properly enjoyed when spread out on the floor of the library. I must admit to having been mightily impressed by the attempt to save the guns at Colenso, the overrunning of the rearguard of yeomanry at Braken-laagte by mounted Boers shooting from the saddle, the charge of the Devons led by Ian Hamilton outside Ladysmith, as presented through the imagination and the pencil of Caton Woodville. And favourite units of my own leaden army were the City Imperial Volunteers and the New South Wales Lancers.

That leaden army's first parade-ground and field of manœuvre was the top of a bare kitchen table. This gave little scope to the aspiring strategist. But fortunately—or perhaps in the eyes of anti-militarists unfortunately—with the addition of my brother John to the family it became necessary to exchange Earl's Court Square for a larger house in Old Brompton Road. On that house's top floor there was one room besides those occupied by the servants. It was sizeable, and neither furnished nor carpeted. It became our equivalent of Aldershot and Salisbury Plain combined. And across its bare boards, diversified with shifting scenery composed of cardboard villages, a model railway, trees made of sponge and matchsticks, we fought battles, and at a later stage campaigns that lasted for a week or more, with troops that amounted—at the end of 1918—to nearly 700 men, eighty odd officers, and twenty-nine guns.

I am not pretending that there was anything exceptional about this childish activity. Sir Winston Churchill is on record as stating that he drew up fifteen hundred toy soldiers for his father's inspection and that 'those toy soldiers changed the current of my life' by suggesting to Lord Randolph's mind that the best career for an apparently stupid boy might be the Army. One of the consolations of my disagreeable existence at Rugby was the discovery in my House of another boy whose hobby was toy soldiers. Needless to say, we kept this mutual interest strictly to ourselves. Nor was it possible to contemplate the introduction of leaden warriors within the confines of the study of a public school. However D., like many other fat boys, was remarkably deft with his hands. He would draw large imaginary *terrains* on sheets of cartridge paper, and make tiny representations of squadrons and battalions with slivers of painted wood. This ingenuity enabled us to spend many pleasant hours engaged in amateur *Kriegspiel*, while our little playfellows busied themselves with the infinitely more important activities of stump-cricket in passages, gossip on the subject of athletic personalities and prospects, and preparation for the next day's lessons. D. had the advantage over me of coming from a county family with a house in the country. He roused a hideous envy in my breast by telling me how he conducted his miniature campaigns during the holidays in one corner of a large garden, where manœuvres could be held on a really large scale against a background of lawn, flower-beds, and an artificial lake, with all the elaborations that such embellishments implied. Partly for this reason, partly also, I fear, because I found him physically quite repellent, our intimacy was confined to *Kriegspiel*, and withered when his increasing weight made him a valuable forward in the House XV. However, I remain grateful to him because it was he who in 1913 introduced me triumphantly to a copy of H. G. Wells's *Little Wars*. After that one possessed an

41

invincible retort to people who sneered at toy soldiers as being no more than 'childish things' which it was quite time to put away.

As with the majority of my generation, Wells, together with Kipling, Arnold Bennett, Galsworthy, Conrad, Anthony Hope, Rider Haggard, and Conan Doyle, had the most formative influence upon my adolescence. I never dreamed that the author of those books which I had taken with such regularity from a shelf in the House library might one day acknowledge me as his fellow clubman during the last years of his life. There was an occasion when, greatly daring after an unusually good lunch, I found myself in the Sandpit daring to argue with him over some fascinating generalisation and to provoke that curiously squeaky voice to be pitched higher than usual with indignation over what was no doubt my youthful impertinence. When it was all over and he was leaving the Club I followed him into the hall and stammered some halting apology for such temerity. In the hope of gilding the pill I added how much I had enjoyed his *Little Wars* so many years before, and explained how I had used the rules of his war-game to improve mine. The expression behind his spectacles seemed to me a combination of the baleful and the sympathetic. 'I should have liked,' he said, 'to have taken you on at that. You would probably have beaten me—*at that*!' Personally I doubt it—and readers of *Little Wars* will easily understand why.

'How much better,' wrote Wells, 'is this amiable miniature than the Real Thing.' And how fantastically right he was! Right when he suggested that those people who cannot help but be fascinated, almost hypnotised, by the sensations of the business of war—its bravery, its suspense, its pageantry before the scientists got at it and spoiled it, its tactical and logistical problems—should be given one vast 'Temple of War, with cork carpets everywhere, plenty of little trees and little houses to knock down, and unlimited supplies of lead soldiers'. In such surroundings, and with such facilities, the great game of war could be played with none of its horrors: no hunger, no atrocities, no physical pain, no personal humiliation or degradation, no war correspondents. And among the players, I dare swear, would be found plenty of literary figures to follow in Wells's footsteps.

No person of sensitivity and imagination, certainly no artist, can think of war without revulsion; regard it as anything other than beastly, imbecile, and altogether vile. Nobody seriously denies that the pen is in fact mightier than the sword. At the same time can anyone seriously deny that the debt owed to the sword by the pen is a considerable one? Consider Homer's battle at the ships in the *Iliad*; Simonides' epitaph on the Spartan dead at Thermopylae; Thucydides' description of the naval fight in the Great Harbour of Syracuse; the marches and conquests of Alexander the Great from Asia Minor to the Indus. Consider Victor Hugo's account of Waterloo—fictional though it may be; the despatches of Drake in the Armada campaign; Masefield's *Gallipoli*; Sir Winston Churchill's tribute to the British armies that died on the Somme and at Passchendaele; the poems of Brooke and Wilfred Owen; *The Song of Roland*. That literature would be much the poorer without this offspring of war is certain. Whether the history of mankind would have also been the poorer must be at least arguable. Nor can everyone go all the way with Wells in believing that the great captains—Caesar, Hannibal, Marlborough, Frederick, and Napoleon—were no more, and no more important, than examples of permanently retarded adolescents.

The trouble of course lies in the huge gulf between theory and practice; between playing at the thing, or writing and reading about it, and actually participating in it. The former can be both fascinating and fun. The latter is hell. And this opinion can only be strengthened by the profound gratitude of one who was too young by a few weeks to be sent abroad in the First German War, and too old to be involved during the Second in anything more lethal than a number of air-raids. (I found such raids unpleasant, but endurable with the aid of a quantity of alcohol, largely because they did something towards salving my conscience with the experience of being 'under fire'.)

What I did learn during my training as an officer-cadet during 1918 was that day-to-day living in the Army—even when the trenches were artificial, the cartridges blank, and hot baths occasionally available—was uncomfortable and above everything else boring. After reading about Agincourt or watching Trooping the Colour one had doubts as to whether mediaeval armour and surcoats could have retained their picturesqueness in rain and mud; whether

43

good drill held much relation to the good life. Very brief experience of nights in an Army hut—the unpleasing personal habits of many of one's comrades, the interminable dirty stories, the monotony of the language of *Lady Chatterley*, now so curiously sanctified by liberal intellectuals—and of days spent in absorbing useless information and performing menial or largely futile tasks, was enough to knock the romantic tradition of soldiering firmly and for ever on the head.

None the less the temptation of the history—no longer, alas, of the game—persists. I find that my collection of books on military subjects tends almost imperceptibly to grow; that I find a volume such as Mr Michael Howard's brilliant history of the Franco-Prussian War infinitely more absorbing than the novels of Miss Spark or Sir Charles Snow. In my more objective moods this surprises me. During most of the First German War I was at Rugby School, supposedly being educated for the business of living. Instead of which I spent a disproportionate amount of time in becoming attuned to the likelihood of extinction at the age of eighteen. This did not embitter me, as it seems to have embittered the genuinely angry young men of my generation. (I have wished on occasion that admirers of *Look Back in Anger* had bothered to study the plays and novels of the early Twenties.) But I doubt if it did me any good in terms either of ethics or aesthetics, and it may well have permanently affected my sense of proportionate values. When the Second War broke out I think I can claim without unreasonable vainglory that I had reached the water-shed between professional achievement and failure. The next five years must have been crucial. Inevitably they were wasted, except in so far as a job of infinitesimal importance concerned with *morale* and propaganda on the Home Front seems to have been carried out reasonably well. The years were eaten by the locust. Opportunity and spirit decayed together. Compared with the sacrifice of others mine was trivial. In my own eyes and my own heart it loomed disagreeably large. In consequence I feel that any aspect of war, however remote, should be anathema to me. But the military books continue to demand more and more space on my shelves, and I still finger with a certain shame-faced nostalgia the ill-typed records of those little wars fought across the boards of the top room in Gledhow Gardens fifty years ago.

44

Can it be that somewhere buried in my subconscious lies the memory of a Gielgud who may have left his fortalice, which guarded one of the crossings of the Niemen, to help in the destruction of the Teutonic Knights at Tannenberg? Or—less romantically—of that Antony Gielgud, general of the Polish Insurrection, who was shot by one of his own men for making an unholy mess of his share in an altogether disastrous campaign? Or is it simply that for a plain and bespectacled small boy with strong histrionic instincts the part of the Soldier was irresistible? Or was it that my sister's nurse, who came to us from the household of the colonel commanding the Sixth Dragoon Guards (the Carabineers), impressed the traditions of that Canterbury headquarters so firmly upon an adolescent mind that the influence could never be expunged?

Intellectually I am convinced that I should have made a bad soldier. Emotionally I remain aggrieved that I never had the opportunity to prove it.

CHAPTER FOUR

That was the B.B.C. that was

1. Prefatory Note

IT *was*. On principle I dislike italics and underlinings, but in this instance emphasis is, I think, justified, for the British Broadcasting Corporation as I knew it during thirty-five years, considered in terms of policies and personalities, has largely ceased to exist. The organisation I knew was led to years of discretion by the hand of Lord Reith, and experienced confirmation at the hands of Sir William Haley. In Sir Hugh Carleton Greene's stable stamps and frets a horse of quite a different colour. I hope it may not be considered altogether unreasonable if one who is proud to have been 'one of John Reith's young men' regards certain of the animal's antics with a faintly jaundiced eye.

Prominent of course among such antics must be the history of that singular programme-item *That Was the Week That Was*, occasionally referred to unkindly as 'Frost's Follies'. Once granted that it was desirable to change, even to destroy, the image of 'Auntie B.B.C.', the basic idea behind the programme was unexceptionable. Sir Hugh Carleton Greene was thinking of 'a show on the lines of the pre-war Berlin cabarets'; Mr Kenneth Adam of 'a sophisticated revue'. And the immediate reaction of the viewing audience, tossed bewilderedly between the fatuities of *Compact* and the self-conscious intellectualism of *Monitor*, to youthful freedom of expression, sardonic commentary upon people and things, and especially to Miss Millicent Martin, was favourable and for the most part benevolent.

However there are, I would submit, better ways of putting an aunt in her place than by ridiculing the shape of her bonnet or taking off her drawers in public. What justly provoked criticism was the fact that the hopes of Mr Adam and Sir Hugh Carleton Greene were simply not fulfilled. Instead of 'sophisticated revue' the audience was given the type of humour appropriate to an undergraduate 'smoker'. Instead of the genuinely satirical commentary upon personalities and politics which distinguished 'the pre-war Berlin cabarets' Mr Bernard Levin was licensed, indeed encouraged, to be plain rude after the fashion of vulgar little boys.

It was hard, if not impossible, to imagine Lord Reith competing with one of his programme controllers through the medium of a B.B.C.-produced booklet for the credit of originating such a programme—or indeed any particular programme-item. Activities of directors-general and heads of programme services surely lie elsewhere.

The simplest of gambits was adopted to blunt the edge of criticism. Of course the presentation was amateurish—the amateurism was deliberate. Of course Mr Levin was rude—that was the object of his engagement. Of course there were errors both of judgement and taste. What else was to be expected from a team so youthful, so enthusiastic, so splendidly determined to be 'with it'?

If the general result was to make more difficult the preservation of standards of impartiality and good taste in other B.B.C. programmes, it was just too bad. That problem could be left for solution to old-fashioned and fuddy-duddy administrators, brought up in the tradition that broadcasting was a service rather than a medium designed to give the greatest possible opportunities to exhibitionists.

I doubt if that tradition was restored by Sir Hugh Carleton Greene's light-hearted assertion—after the decision to drop the programme had at last been taken—that he had put it on as a cryptocommunist and taken it off as a fascist hyena. The mischief had been done. And the worst of the mischief was the slur cast on the Corporation's professional integrity.

It would be a pity to push the issue too hard. The programme is dead, and unlikely to be resurrected in spite of the orgy of self-congratulation indulged in by the cast, claiming that its demise was the final proof of its devastating influence on contemporary society. I mention it as a prefatory note to my reminiscences of the B.B.C. because *That Was the Week ...* marked in a sense the end of an epoch in the history of the Corporation. The people and things that I remember belonged for the most part to a different world. Different

—'did I say better?' Like Cassius I can only ask the question with appropriate diffidence.

2. Savoy Hill

I suppose that the most significant day in my working life was May 28th, 1928, when I first sat down on the opposite side of Eric Maschwitz's desk to assist him in editing the *Radio Times*. (For those interested in superstition connected with numbers my birthday is April 28th.) I fear that there was a flavour both of undue influence and frivolity about my engagement. I was at the time an actor out of work, whose only virtue probably was the realisation of just how bad an actor he was, combined with the determination to try something else as quickly as might be. Apart from having given a couple of talks, I had no experience of broadcasting. I had never acted in a radio play. I had never heard a radio play. Eric Maschwitz offered me the job not because he needed an assistant—no man needed assistance less—but because I was a friend of his. And the then General Editor confirmed the offer through the open door of his office without seeing my face or asking me a question. Not for me the ordeal of an interview with Admiral Carpendale, the Deputy Director-General, with his formidable reputation of a quarter-deck manner and brusque questioning about one's public school and one's athletic achievements. Not for me the more alarming ordeal of one of those appointments boards on so many of which I was to sit later among the inquisitors. It was probably as well. My public school would have passed muster, but I have never been any sort of athlete. I have never sat on an appointments board without realising only too well that from the other side of the table I could not have hoped to satisfy it.

I confess that I can never pass the eastern end of the Strand without a side glance down the steep slope towards the Embankment, and a sensation of melancholy and nostalgia. I remember so vividly my first office, when I had taken over direction of the Drama Department: an office so like a corridor that it was almost impossible to heat; an office looking out upon the graveyard of the Chapel of the Savoy with its shrill autumn chorus of starlings; the office in which for the first time I met a film star in the elegant person of

Miss Gloria Swanson, and a veteran of Variety in Sir Harry Lauder, only—if the truth be told—to be disillusioned by both. (Sir Harry indeed produced something of a sensation by insisting on making his appearance at the microphone in full Highland evening dress, complete with lace *jabot* and ruffled sleeves, and then made vigorous use of one of the big copper receptacles, which served in the studios for ash-trays, as a spittoon.)

My first impression of Savoy Hill, which experience only tended to confirm, was of a rather slaphappy family party in which a good many people spent a good deal of time wondering what exactly they were doing in that particular galley. Not least among the handicaps to the service in the early days of broadcasting was the fact that a number of the staff had drifted into the business with little belief in its prospects and less awareness of its potentialities. With the definite exception of the first Director-General, and the probable exception of the members of the Engineering Division, of whom one saw far too little, the staff seemed largely composed of individuals who had abandoned other careers in which they had not exactly shone, or who had come straight to the B.B.C. from their universities or from the Services, and lacked worldly experience accordingly. Hence the creation of the 'uncles and aunties' of the first *Children's Hours*, and such embarrassing programme-items as *The Grand Goodnight* in which, during the last night of the old year, J. C. Stobart took it upon himself to address greetings not only to the habitable globe, but to the solar system and the universe. Hence, on the entertainment side, there was an almost complete lack of professional standards, implying inevitably an equal lack of acknowledged professional standing.

None the less there was much good fellowship in an organisation so small that everyone perforce knew everybody else, working, as we did, under one roof. There were the growing excitement and enthusiasm engendered by increasing knowledge of what the new medium could do, by the fact that everything about broadcasting was 'news', as is everything about television today. There was the emergence of personalities, for the most part in those days in the Talks Department: Hilda Matheson, who seemed to fear neither God, devil, nor the Director-General; Lionel Fielden, who concealed a formidable and cultivated intelligence behind a deceptive Etoniancum-Regency *façade*; Mary Somerville, who was to make a permanent contribution to the educational system of the country; Charles Siepmann, whom I found it impossible not to admire and almost impossible to like.

Above all, both literally and psychologically, was the figure of the then Sir John Reith, with his scarred face, his piercing eyes, his indomitable self-confidence, his infectious sense of purpose, and his possession of what in successful French generals has been called 'the sacred fire of leadership'. In 1928 the B.B.C. had not grown beyond the capacity of direct control by a single individual, and no doubt was left in anyone's mind who that individual was. It was like a breath of fresh air out of the past to hear that supreme and superb self-confidence re-affirmed by Lord Reith not so long ago during his famous *Face to Face* television interview with John Freeman.

I met the Director-General for the first time when I found, rather to my dismay, that he had included himself in the cast of Ian Hay's *Tilly of Bloomsbury*, which I had agreed to produce for the B.B.C.'s amateur dramatic society. Like other indifferent actors I had always been fascinated by the problems of production. My first essay in the field, at the age of sixteen, was to handle a shameless plagiarism of *Raffles*—with my brother John as the adventuress swathed in ropes of remarkable sham pearls—before no less an audience than G. K. Chesterton in his studio at Beaconsfield. By the end of my first year at Oxford I had dragooned my personal friends into forming an amateur group of play-readers and presenting not, as might have been expected, Ibsen or Chekhov, but *The Man Who Stayed at Home*. It was accordingly in a frame of mind reasonably light-hearted that I involved myself with Ian Hay's harmless little comedy. Had I been able to imagine the effects of that production on my own future I would have felt differently.

For I have been told more than once—and I have never heard it denied—that I owed my appointment as B.B.C. Productions Director to my conducting of those rehearsals of *Tilly of Bloomsbury* in which Sir John Reith appeared, improbably but most successfully, as the vaguely drunken broker's man. 'If he can tell *me* what to do,' the Director-General was reported as saying, 'I don't see why he shouldn't be able to tell a lot of actors how to square up to a microphone.' But I fancy the words were spoken with that twinkle of the eye which accompanied his moments of unexpected charm, and with that sense of humour which he was supposed, quite falsely, to lack. My own belief is that Sir John was influenced less by any startlingly sudden realisation of my talent as a producer than by the lack of any obvious alternative candidate for the job. The state of the Productions Department—as it was then termed—was neither happy nor particularly efficient. Its head was responsible not only for drama but also for variety productions: a combination which I was to discover quickly to be both clumsy and unworkable. The departmental staff—with the shining exception of Mr Howard Rose—was notable neither for talent nor for loyalty. In spite of the apparent attractions of the one job in broadcasting which I would have chosen for myself, given the opportunity, it was revealed at close quarters as anything but a bed of roses. Fortunately at the time I was too young, too excited, and too enthusiastic to realise what I was letting myself in for. It is easier to put a knife into a man's back if he continually hesitates and looks back over one shoulder as he walks down a corridor than if he goes swiftly straight ahead. And, given the necessary support from above, a degree of dislike and opposition from below acts as a positive stimulant.

I have on occasion been called a pioneer in the field of dramatic broadcasting. This distinction I cannot claim. Cecil Lewis did a good deal in the shape of initiation while he was Director of Programmes. R. E. Jeffrey, whom I succeeded, did a little. Howard Rose did most. It was as a result of their efforts that it was realised that any attempt to broadcast plays from the stages of theatres was futile; that the broadcast play *must be brought into the studio*; that in consequence new techniques both of production and acting had got to be developed. It was due mainly to Lance Sieveking and Tyrone Guthrie that it was learned that plays could be written which owed nothing in their writing or construction to conventional stage models. There is, I believe, a direct link between this first breaking-down of the conventions of ordinary play-writing and the contemporary New Wave in the Theatre and even—a more doubtful blessing—the Theatre of the Absurd: freedom, and looseness, of construction; emphasis upon atmosphere rather than plot; reliance upon words rather than action. Samuel Beckett and Harold Pinter, John Mortimer and N. F. Simpson, Robert Bolt and Giles Cooper, Adamov and Ionesco, have all proved as successful in microphone performance as on the stage, in many cases more successful. Incidentally, to no one is greater credit due in this connection than to Donald McWhinnie for the imagination which could envisage this success and for the enthusiasm with which he underwrote and furthered its possibility.

But all this is a long way from Savoy Hill and the days when Lance Sieveking, intoxicated by the potentialities of the Dramatic Control Panel and the technique of multiple studios, contributed to broadcasting history with his production of *The First Kaleidoscope*; when *Squirrel's Cage* was no more than a twinkle in Tyrone Guthrie's eye. These first steps in the craft of pure radio were of course important. They were also immense fun, albeit regarded under raised eyebrows by amused and indulgent elders and betters. Two jobs seemed to me then, and indeed seem to me now, more immediate and more vital: first to give the Drama Department prestige and standing within the Corporation; secondly to achieve —and deserve—equivalent standing and prestige for B.B.C. dramatic output *vis-à-vis* the world of professional entertainment.

Neither problem was easy of solution. To begin with, the B.B.C. hierarchy lacked knowledge of the entertainment world and any particular convictions concerning the part that entertainment should play in programmes. The value and importance of talks, religion, and music were acknowledged by their advisory committees, composed impartially of expert enthusiasts and watch-dogs in their various fields. The virtues of outside broadcasts were there for all to hear, whenever the Colour was Trooped, the hooves of Derby runners thundered past Tattenham Corner, most of all when the Sovereign spoke to all his peoples on Christmas Day. Drama was not regarded so seriously. No one, least of all myself, would have dreamed in 1929 that twenty years later the play broadcast on Saturday evenings would draw a regular listening audience of more than ten million people. The official attitude to dramatic broadcasting was that it was desirable as being vaguely cultural; that it was, and would remain, inevitably a minority interest; that

52

it could safely be left to the tender mercies of youthful enthusiasts —who tended to wear beards or unusually long overcoats and to talk a rather high-falutin jargon of their own—with no more chaperonage than was implied by the appointment as 'consultant' of the amiable but ineffective George Grossmith Junior.

With the advantage of hindsight I can confidently affirm that this state of affairs was extremely fortunate for me. I occasionally amused myself by composing in my imagination the sort of advisory committee with which I might so easily have been saddled (Mr Basil Dean, Mr St John Ervine, Sydney Carroll, James Agate, Mr Gordon Craig, Lilian Baylis, Sir James Barrie, M. Komisarjevsky, John Galsworthy and Marie Tempest would only have been a few of the likely runners) and thanking my stars that I was left in peace to make my own mistakes and learn the lessons of experience through trial and error.

The Director-General, having established the convention in his own mind that as a result of my stage contacts and family background I must necessarily be—from his point of view—profligate, irreligious, and ferociously opinionated, seemed content to let me 'gang my own gait', even to the extent of producing an uncut version of *Othello* on a Sunday afternoon. It overran its time considerably at the expense of the Children's Hour. This caused far more trouble than the fact that a coach and four had been driven through the ukase that plays should not be broadcast which dealt with problems of the Eternal Triangle!

It was in this *Othello* production that the most striking example that I can remember occurred of the difficulty experienced by the older school of actors in coping with a new and unfamiliar medium. Henry Ainley was playing the name part, and I was particularly proud to find myself working with an idol of my boyhood, the acknowledged possessor of the most beautiful voice in the English Theatre of the time.

I hope it may not be considered as any sort of slur on his memory to record that Ainley's mental processes were not of the swiftest; that, for instance, he considered punctuation to be no more than an eccentric idiosyncrasy of authors which it was desirable on principle to ignore. On the other hand his manners were exquisite, and he was entirely without conceit. He took pains to explain to

53

me that he felt more than a little awed by the prospect of playing to the listening audience.

'Is it really true,' he asked several times, 'that several hundred thousand people will be listening to this performance?'

I assured him that I should be extremely disappointed if our audience did not top the million mark.

'Drury Lane,' he went on meditatively, 'seats rather more than two thousand. Excellent acoustics. All the same, acting in Drury Lane demands the broad approach—sweep, pulling out all one's vocal stops—'

I murmured something about the listener and the domestic sitting-room: an audience that was simultaneously the largest and the most intimate conceivable. His mind and imagination were elsewhere.

'Five thousand times bigger than Drury Lane,' he said, 'It makes you think, doesn't it?'

I assured him that it did.

Unfortunately I failed to convince him of the basic properties of the microphone; that the fundamental difference between acting in a theatre and acting in a broadcasting studio is that while in the former the actor must project voice and personality *outwards*, keeping always in mind the occupants of the back row of the gallery, in the latter he must project *inwards* to an audience every member of which is closer to him than the front row of the stalls. In Henry Ainley's mind the studio remained obstinately equated with a super Drury Lane, and he pulled out every stop of that magnificent organ his voice to such effect that I had to station two 'effects' boys—one at each of his elbows—to withdraw him gently but firmly to a distance from the microphone at which he would not 'blow' the transmitter off the air. His performance was magnificent, but it was not broadcasting.

None the less we became excellent friends. I owed more than I could ever hope to repay to him and to such veterans of their business as Leon Quartermaine, Frederick Lloyd, and Godfrey Tearle, who accepted my youthfully enthusiastic direction with such courtesy and good-humour, almost making me believe that they were learning a little from me while I was learning so very much from them. It was curious, and to me rather touching, that established masters of their craft showed a great readiness to study the new medium and take it seriously when the majority of up-and-coming players were speaking scornfully of work at Savoy Hill as 'charades' and of fees paid by the B.B.C. as 'cigarette-money'. It was hard to destroy these prevalent and hardening misconceptions. Without the help and encouragement of the Theatre's Old Guard it would have been impossible.

I am unlikely to forget the first performance in the *World Theatre* series, for which I had chosen somewhat rashly the Gilbert Murray translation of the *Hippolytus* of Euripides. As the whole project of the series had met with a good deal of criticism beforehand (in terms of broadcasting in those days it was considered and damned as fantastically highbrow!), it was more than normally important that the production should be successful. With Tearle as Theseus, Miss Diana Wynyard as Phaedra and Miss Gladys Young as the Nurse I felt I could be reasonably confident, even with the play's placing between the News at one end and Parliamentary Report at the other, which meant that there could be no latitude possible in timing. Even a second's overrun would mean the dropping of the guillotine. The play had been timed at rehearsal for seventy-five minutes. My feelings can be imagined when after the first twenty-five minutes of the performance we were already ten minutes slow. Miss Wynyard was very nervous; Miss Young had a frightful cold; the pace and rhythm of the Chorus failed together. Everything seemed set for a humiliating disaster, and I had to admit as much to Godfrey Tearle, who was waiting for his entrance in the control cubicle.

It was one of that fine actor's most endearing mannerisms to say that he could not understand why a young, intelligent, and up-to-date producer—meaning me—bothered to engage a stupid dyed-in-the-wool old 'ham'—meaning himself. (I was able to tell him later in the evening that if he hadn't known before he should know now.) He heard my tale of woe with the suspicion of a smile and a consoling pat on my shoulder. He then walked in to the studio and proceeded without fuss, flurry, or any apparent change in his performance as rehearsed, to recover those lost ten minutes by sheer technical accomplishment. It was achieved not only by the imperceptible quickening of tempo of his own speech, but by his effortless control of the situation, which was infectious to the point of restoring the morale of the rest of the cast. I have never seen a professional job of work better done.

In terms of strict chronology *Hippolytus* belongs to the early Broadcasting House rather than the Savoy Hill period. On the other hand Eric Maschwitz's adaptation of Compton Mackenzie's *Carnival* was the most typical, as it was the liveliest and most notable, of Savoy Hill productions. It was begotten by vigorous personal enthusiasms, the adapter's and the author's; it was sponsored with equal enthusiasm by me—quite irregularly, as I had not yet been officially appointed to the Productions Department and had plenty of spare time on my hands in the *Radio Times* office. It destroyed—alas, by no means for ever—the theory that the proper length for a broadcast play was half an hour, and the notion that it was a pipe-dream to imagine that listeners could be found prepared to give a play attention for more than an hour. (*Carnival* ran for two hours and three-quarters, and produced a listener reaction almost unparalleled in those days.) With its birth, wedding-night, and seduction sequences it broke through or side-stepped most of contemporary B.B.C. internal censorship. It borrowed from and applied Sieveking's *First Kaleidoscope* technique of production with remarkable success. The whole thing was enormously exciting.

It remains memorable for me personally for two things: my meeting with Compton Mackenzie, one of the few of my literary idols who has not disappointed me in the flesh, and the invention of the famous B.B.C. seagulls.

Personally I rather regret that 'Monty' has now become Sir Compton, acknowledged and revered as a—if not *the*—Grand Old Man of English Letters, oracle and television personality. He retains my affection and my admiration. But there hangs no longer about him the fascination of the rebellious eccentric, who had had his *Sinister Street* banned by the libraries; who had stood in the dock at Bow Street for trial under the Official Secrets Act; who lived in splendid isolation on the isle of Jethou; and who had shared the legend of slightly sinister disreputability in Capri with D. H. Lawrence and Norman Douglas. He has mellowed smoothly and graciously, like the binding of a loved and valued book. He tells a

56

story as well as ever, just as he still relishes his oysters and champagne. But in the days of *Carnival* his wit was flavoured with acidity, his stories with occasional engaging malice, especially when he told them of Hugh Walpole. (He once read the whole of the last chapter of *Fortitude* aloud to me, giving full value to its profusion of dots, with a result devastating to someone who had greatly admired that novel.) And I rather doubt if he would still sing Victorian music-hall songs aloud in a public place, as he did frequently while we were discussing appropriate music for *Carnival*.

As for those seagulls, I wonder if George Inns, whose name is now a household word as producer of *The Black and White Minstrel Show*, ever thinks of the day when he saved the bacon of *Carnival*'s producer. As most people know, the story ends on a Cornish cliff with the crying of the seagulls through the mist when Jenny Pearl has been shot by her husband. That 'screaming dismay' was probably the most important sound-effect of the whole production, and a recording-van had gone accordingly to the Thames Embankment to secure the real thing. It returned with some excellent recordings of L.C.C. trams. Maschwitz, Peter Cresswell, and I gazed blankly at each other. At which point George Inns, then an 'effects' boy of, I imagine, about sixteen, took from his pocket some elastic and a piece of wood, and after some mysterious fashion of his own did the trick.

That too was very typical of Savoy Hill.

CHAPTER FIVE

Broadcasting House

WITH THE moving of the B.B.C. from Savoy Hill to Portland Place a new chapter was opened in the story of broadcasting in general and of the Drama Department in particular. It swiftly became apparent, in the shadow of those concrete battlements, that the days of the slap-happy amateurs were over; that *professionalismus* was coming to stay. Gear and studios had been designed—as opposed to 'lashed-up'—for the jobs they had to do. That the objects of our lives were both real and earnest was symbolised by the grandiloquent Latin text above the entrance hall, and underlined by the gradual proliferation of administrators who were not always as efficient or as necessary to programme output as they imagined. There were fewer games. There was less fun. On the other hand, the work itself became immensely more significant, and rewarding in proportion. In terms of experiment, progress, and recognition the radio-drama producer 'never had it so good' as during the years between 1932 and 1939.

This, however, is a personal record. I have written extensively elsewhere of the development and history of the broadcast play. And for me personally the main result of the move to Broadcasting House was the realisation that I had found my professional feet; that a good many childish things had, albeit regretfully, to be put away; that, after all, my father had been right in believing that what my temperament chiefly needed was the ballast of a steady job and the keeping of office hours. I found it possible to become surprisingly industrious, reasonably business-like, and almost morbidly punctual. I achieved a masochistic satisfaction in sacrificing my private life to the demands of broadcasting. This, I fear, hurt certain other people more than it did me.

Another result was to find oneself for the first time something of a public figure. In this television era it is difficult to remember, almost impossible to believe, that there was a period when every detail of radio drama was news; when a producer's personal idiosyncrasies were good for innumerable gossip paragraphs; when an ill-considered phrase made a Fleet Street holiday, and an ill-chosen or controversial play broadcast made headlines. Yet so it was. The first months in our new headquarters were enlivened by a ferocious attack by the *Daily Herald*—rather curiously abetted by the British Empire Union—on a broadcast of Patrick Hamilton's *Rope*, in which Mr Ernest Milton repeated his stage *tour de force*. In this instance amusing compensation was provided by the appearance of Hannen Swaffer for the defence, and by the fact that the author was so intrigued that he began to write specially for the microphone. His *To the Public Danger* remains one of the very best of radio plays.

I have wondered occasionally why I seem to have fallen foul so often of the *Daily Herald*. Many years were to pass before the paper's volcanic eruption over *Party Manners*—of which more later. But its damp squib over *Rope* had hardly fizzled out before I found myself in more trouble. I wrote and produced a forty-minute piece called *Friday Morning*, based upon an extremely alarming personal experience, which dealt with the reactions of the passengers in an aeroplane to a forced landing. Even in the early Thirties I should have thought this was commonplace and harmless enough as a subject. Not so the *Herald*, which discovered in the play some sinister propaganda design against air travel. The company in whose machine I had so nearly broken my neck promptly demanded an apology from the B.B.C.—an apology which I am delighted to remember that it did not get.

Such publicity episodes—and there were to be plenty more—were sometimes acutely disagreeable and always wearing to the nerves. Their effect upon the broadcasting hierarchy was never predictable—though the Director-General was never slow to make it clear that if members of his staff deserved 'carpeting' he proposed to do that 'carpeting' himself without assistance from outsiders. But, to be entirely honest, there was another side to the picture. To a large extent both Eric Maschwitz and I asked for what we got.

By this time Eric had exchanged the *Radio Times* for the Variety Department, relieving me of a field of operation in which I knew myself to be both ignorant and inept. His terrific vitality, endearing bonhomie, and vigorous sympathy with everything implied by the phrase 'show business' blew a veritable wind of change through the slightly stuffy corridors of the Programme Division: a process in which I did my best to aid and abet him. Life in Broadcasting House might be real and earnest, but were there to be no more cakes and ale? Not if he knew it and could help it. He believed—and I came enthusiastically to agree with him—that any publicity was better than none. He believed in the value of publicity to broadcasting, and, as a corollary, in the value of publicising personalities in broadcasting, including any members of the staff who could get it— Maschwitz and Gielgud in particular. Radio critics referred to us sneeringly as 'the Turn of the Variety Twins'. Mr Herbert Farjeon had us impersonated, none too lovingly, in one of his revues. Some of our colleagues felt that our lively duologues at programme boards —in which we freely criticised matters not strictly our business in addition to cheerfully slanging each other's work—were too frequent and too frivolous. It was suggested that we were too big for our boots, and too evidently 'on the make'; even that it was peculiar, to say the least of it, that the heads of two of the producing departments of the *British* Broadcasting Corporation should be so vocally proud of their *Polish* origin. We were, in short, made the targets of much the same sort of criticism and denigration which is borne so cheerfully today by Cliff Michelmore, Richard Dimbleby, and Huw Wheldon.

The Corporation's attitude towards this whole business of personal publicity for, and outside activities indulged in by, members of its staff seemed and seems to me typically British in its incon-sistency and its common sense. In principle it disapproved. In practice it tolerated, for the most part tacitly. The Variety Twins might be opinionated, exhibitionist, even vulgar. To an extent they came to win the affection accorded to licensed jesters, and the indulgence permitted to uninhibited enthusiasts. In our specialised spheres we seemed to know our business. Our working records were satisfactorily vigorous, and sensible; occasionally even artistically and culturally stimulating. That our names and our work made news certainly did us no harm in the eyes of the general world of entertainment. And when welfare-conscious colleagues enquired whether our holidays would not do us more good if we took exercise on mountains or golf-courses instead of writing plays and novels and dabbling in films it was sufficient retort to emphasise our continuing and almost blatant physical fitness. Incidentally, when we collaborated in the writing of *Death at Broadcasting House*—a project we undertook with misgivings for obvious reasons, and because we could persuade no one we knew to implement a basic notion which we believed, rightly as it proved, to be sure-fire for a detective story—the Engineering Division lent us the blue-prints of the Broadcasting House studio plans to ensure accuracy. It was one of these plans which gave me the opportunity to prove Dorothy Sayers in the wrong when she criticised the book: an experience never, as far as I remember, to be repeated when I came to know her well and work with her on the famous series *The Man Born to be King*.

There was another aspect of public relations over which I found myself something of a stormy petrel or lonely unicorn. In general it was, and remains, the practice of the B.B.C. to ignore criticism, even if that criticism is ill-founded, plain ignorant, or obviously malicious. I confess that I always found this attitude exasperating, and that I resented it profoundly. It may be true that rebuttal can never overtake criticism. It is certainly true that the critic can be certain of the last word. And there is much in the argument that a caravan of the size and importance of the B.B.C. can afford to move on, leaving the dogs to bark unregarded. However, in my own case the comments and attacks were—for one reason or another—so frequently personal in the highest degree that the temptation to shoot back was irresistible. And here also officialdom for the most part turned a blind eye.

Leaving aside the offensive innuendos of gossip-writers, I find from my records that over the years three criticisms appeared and re-appeared with monotonous regularity. First, that I chose plays on a basis of personal liking or disliking. Secondly, that I chose too many plays that were sordid in subject and depressing in atmosphere. Thirdly, that I chose plays that were far too long—or alternatively were not long enough. There was also the perennially debated argument for or against a permanent company of B.B.C. actors. It was principally over these points that I corresponded: viciously with Jonah Barrington and Garry Allighan; urbanely with Mr

Collie Knox; pleasantly with Miss Mary Crozier; lengthily and entertainingly with Mrs Grace Wyndham Goldie. And I will cheerfully admit that my intentions were to be readable, to keep to the point, and to be positive even unto arrogance.

Summed up, my reactions were as follows. I chose plays on a basis of personal like and dislike, because I knew of no other way of choosing plays with any sense of personal responsibility. I considered that I was paid to do the job I did, because my opinion on the choosing of plays for broadcasting was considered the best available. If that opinion was bad, I should have been replaced. If it was not, and if I chose plays on the advice of a panel of listeners or from the findings of an opinion poll, I was shirking my proper business. Obviously I included plays in my schedules which I personally liked and admired. Perhaps less obviously I also included plays which personally I very much disliked, as I believed that such plays would find a vast number of admirers. The plays I was always unwilling to include were plays concerning which opinion was tepid, and which accordingly I believed would provoke tepid reactions among listeners.

That I was too prone to the broadcasting of sordid and depressing pieces can be more briefly answered. From the date of my first appointment to the Drama Department I announced that I intended to include the plays of Chekhov, of Ibsen, and of Strindberg in programmes as part of our regular repertory of classic productions. I said also that I believed that the works of these authors—and particularly of Ibsen—were outstandingly adaptable to the radio medium and would prove outstandingly acceptable to the radio audience. I doubt if there is anyone today who would seriously oppose these assumptions.

As to the question of the right length for broadcast plays it is a matter of fact and sense, not of argument. If a listener is interested enough to continue to listen to a play after its opening three minutes he will listen until the end, no matter how long or how short it may be. To say that the ideal length for a play broadcast is half an hour is as foolish as was Mr Herbert Farjeon, when he rebuked me for my cutting of Henry V, and proved justification of his rebuke to his own satisfaction by listing the number of lines cut and adding that he had listened with a copy of the play open on his knee for that purpose. The picture called up in one's imagination by this labour of hate was certainly a sombre one.

With the transfer of the B.B.C. to what I have heard called 'that damned monolithic concrete imitation of a battleship in Portland Place' I fancy that the Corporation lost a good deal of its former popularity. There had been something essentially cosy, something safely middle-class, about the Happy Families atmosphere of Savoy Hill, most pleasantly symbolised perhaps by the intimate and individual voices of Sir Walford Davies and A. J. Alan. There was nothing formidable or withdrawn about the Savoy Hill building. You could stroll down to the Embankment and peer through the windows. In its reception room the white-moustached and genial Colonel Brand played host.

Broadcasting House was functional and efficient—except that it proved too small even before its building was completed. But its general impression, inevitably, was of bulk, chill, and a busy officialdom, and for the most part its decoration was an aesthetic disaster. (This is true of most broadcasting buildings. Nothing in Broadcasting House was quite so hideous as the purple tiling which adorned the vast *Rundfunk* building in the *Masurenallee* in Berlin. Nothing was so unpractical as the echoing parquet flooring of the control-room of Budapest Radio. The finest broadcasting studios I have seen are those in Copenhagen and in Oslo, the latter constructed by the Germans for their own purposes during Hitler's War.) In Portland Place the trouble was simply that of too many cooks, and in consequence of too many styles. Pure functionalism, the wish to encourage contemporary fashion in art, a yearning towards dignified grandeur, seemed to have provided too mixed motivations. And then there were trimmings of unconscious comedy: the Talks Studio lined with bogus book-backs, like the studies of innumerable detective plays; the Religious Studio, which could not be consecrated because apparently consecration cannot be confined to one floor of a building and some floors immediately below was a studio devoted to the production of Variety programmes.

On one occasion I had the pleasure and privilege of conducting the famous French film-director, René Clair, over Broadcasting House. He expressed the most polite interest, but his comments grew more and more brief—whether owing to the indifference of

63

my French or the slightly stunning effect of our décor I could not tell. At last we reached the Council Chamber, whose lighting in those days was cunningly concealed within what looked like rather pot-bellied vases of carved wood. I explained their function, and M. Clair allowed himself to smile.

'I see,' he said gently. 'I wondered. At first glance I had imagined they were designed for the reception of the ashes of dead Directors-General.'

As a conceit it was typically imaginative. Personally I am glad to know that it is Lord Reith's portrait which presides over that rather gloomy chamber, whose acoustics were so abominable, and in which the Variety Twins—so they fondly believed—brightened the proceedings of so many programme boards.

But there was little time and less leisure for the niceties of aesthetic criticism during the years between 1932 and 1939: years which I like to recall as being truly vintage in the story of radio drama.

There was my production of *The Ringer*, in which I had acted at Wyndham's as an unconsidered understudy. Miss Dorothy Dickson came to play her original part, and proved just how helpful, friendly, and unassuming an acknowledged leading lady can be. There was the full-length production of *Hassan*, with Henry Ainley, Leon Quartermaine and Malcolm Keen, which I still believe to be more effective on the air than it can ever be in the theatre. On the stage the vital scene of the ghosts of Pervaneh and Rafi which should follow the Procession of Protracted Death is unplayable. Over the air the gradual dissolution of their voices into the icy wind of eternal oblivion could register unforgettably. There was Clemence Dane's *Will Shakespeare*, with Emlyn Williams and Haidée Wright, to prove just how mistaken critics and public had been when they allowed one of the finest modern verse plays to fail at the Shaftesbury. There was *The Seagull*, with Jeanne de Casalis and Harcourt Williams.

Following upon that production I was so rash as to go to the microphone and to make a direct appeal to the listening audience for comment on my predilection for Chekhov. The Corporation's programme correspondence section very reasonably took a poor view when more than twelve thousand letters came in during the next three days, and equally reasonably sent the sacks containing them to my office for acknowledgment. It is fair to add that they included two postcards vigorously critical, and one quite remarkably obscene.

It was in August of the same year that the radio play received its official accolade. It was made the subject of a Special Supplement in *The Times*.

I would not pretend, however, that everything was 'gas and gaiters'. There was the episode of the first radio presentation of *Ghosts*. Having regard to its subject, I felt that I had better get the sanction of higher authority, who turned out in this case to be the Deputy Director-General, Admiral Carpendale. He had not read or seen the play, but he knew of it by reputation—a reputation unfortunately based on Clement Scott's famous notice which stigmatised it as 'an open drain . . . a dirty act done publicly', amongst other things. In some way *Ghosts* had become associated in the Admiral's mind with the friskier type of Paris *boulevard* comedy of sexual entanglements and marital infidelity. I failed to disabuse him of this notion, and he left for Cardiff taking with him a copy of the play to read in the train. He made it clear that he rather expected it to enliven a dull journey, and equally clear that I had better give up any idea of the production. On his return he sent for me, and received me with an expression so gloomy that my last hopes faded.

'I don't see why you should want to do the thing,' he said. 'It's very long—and very dull.'

But *Ghosts* reached the microphone after all. It may have been long, but with Leontine Sagan as Mrs Alving it was certainly not dull, and it has turned out a 'natural' both for broadcasting and television ever since.

There was the occasion when Tyrone Guthrie brought his Old Vic production of *Macbeth*, with Charles Laughton, directly to the studio as it stood. As always imaginative and eager to experiment, Guthrie decided that his cast could and should play without scripts, and that to do so would relax and vitalise their performances. The result was not happy. In unfamiliar surroundings the actors' memories proved all too fallible, and I had to force open the door of a locked library to secure a printed copy of the play for a hastily recruited prompter.

65

E

And there was the time when Eric Maschwitz allowed himself to be persuaded by a film-producer to include Miss Sylvia Sidney in two scenes from *Romeo and Juliet* in one of his *In Town Tonight* programmes, and I was foolhardy enough to allow him to persuade me to handle them. Miss Sidney is a capital actress and a most delightful person, but I fancy that this was her first essay in Shakespeare, and she was not helped by the film-producer who insisted on being present at the rehearsal, sat glowering at her through a haze of cigar-smoke, frequently lifted up an unpleasant voice, and was hardly to be restrained at one point from laying violent hands upon her. Even with the professional support of Ion Swinley—an actor insufficiently appreciated, with one of the loveliest voices ever to be heard on the air—the result was disastrous. I am glad to remember meeting Miss Sidney some years later in New York, when I learnt from her that I had been forgiven for my share in what must have been for her an extremely disagreeable experience.

By contrast the record of my meeting with another fine film actress, Miss Elisabeth Bergner, holds nothing but the most pleasant of memories. I had always admired her on the screen. I had heard my father speak of her stage performance of St Joan in terms which, coming from his lips, were fantastically flattering. When I heard that she was in England I was most anxious to meet her, and a mutual friend arranged the introduction. To my surprise she proved not only personally approachable, but professionally interested in the technique of acting at the microphone, so that I was emboldened to invite her to play Hedwig for me in Ibsen's *Wild Duck*. It was only at this stage, I think, that we both realised that, while she understood English perfectly, her command of the language was anything but fluent. It was therefore necessary to combine rehearsals with what amounted to language lessons, conducted in her rooms in her hotel late into the night: a proceeding which Miss Bergner's husband, Doctor Czinner, suffered with amiable and hospitable tolerance. I have seldom been prouder of anything than I was of the resulting performance. I will even risk saying that Miss Bergner never did anything better. As I had found previously in the case of Miss Sagan, the actress was content, as far as microphone technique was concerned, to place herself without reservation in the producer's hands, confident that by so doing she could most freely exploit her gifts of personality, sensitivity, and charm.

With the programme records contained in a shelf full of scrapbooks at hand, it is difficult to avoid the danger of this chapter becoming no more than a catalogue of productions successful—and not so successful: a list of names of distinguished silhouettes. I have to remind myself that during these years, although I was most interested in the business of consolidating a reputation as an individual producer—one with the supreme advantage that he never had to handle a play which he had not chosen himself!—I could not afford to let myself neglect the routine business of running a department with an output rising to nearly three hundred plays a year. I believed, I still believe, that the head of a producing department can only do his work properly with the regular experience of studio production behind him. And I would not for a moment deny that I found the handling of plays and players the most fascinating and immediately rewarding aspect of my job. At the same time, considered in longer terms, other matters were of equal and even greater importance. One was certainly the development of the section which was ultimately to become Laurence Gilliam's Features Department. Another was occasional representation of the Corporation *vis-à-vis* my opposite numbers abroad.

For the embryo of Features, as for many other significant movements in broadcasting, Lance Sieveking was responsible. Towards the end of the Savoy Hill period he persuaded the powers that were that it would be valuable to establish a small section of individuals in the Programme Division, responsible to no single department, with a roving commission over the whole programme field. This Research Section, as it was called, was made up of four people: Sieveking himself; Archie Harding, who later made a name for himself as Programme Director of the Northern Region and first head of B.B.C. Staff Training; E. J. King-Bull, who had been a naval officer and colonial administrator; and Mary Hope Allen, who had been secretary to Naomi Royde-Smith, the novelist. All in their separate ways had won and deserved attention for gifts of imagination and intelligence which hardly fitted in with or conformed to the routine activities of the conventionally categoried departments. All of them believed, although working along indi-

67

vidually different lines, in a theory of 'pure' radio, in programme-items that owed little or nothing to stage, concert-hall, or lecture platform: items conceived in terms of radio, and only capable of production in terms of radio's specialised technique.

Unfortunately—and it is as true today in the field of television as it was in the early days of radio—while the theory was absolutely sound, the putting of it into practice was almost impossible. The gear, studios, and facilities required for what amounted to an experimental laboratory did not exist. Such facilities as there were—studios in particular—were already used to capacity as the result of the increasing demands of an insatiable public. This demand always exceeded supply. As a result the individuals in Research, lacking the support of any regular departmental organisation, vulnerable to allegations that they were consciously 'highbrow' or 'dodging the column', hardly beloved of colleagues who were tied strictly to office hours and the daily round, found themselves in the position of very lonely unicorns. Their ideas blushed unheard. Their pro-grammes remained on desks or in files. The tidier minds of the Corporation were offended by their irregular situation, and seriously questioned any virtue in their continuing activities. For a time they were grouped, not very convincingly, under the nominal headship of my predecessor in the Drama Department. When finally R. E. Jeffrey left the service of the B.B.C. to become 'the Golden Voice of the Silver Screen', I was told in confidence that either I must take the Research Section under my wing, or it must be disbanded.

The alternatives were painful for me to face. Sieveking was an old friend of mine. Indeed it had been partly due to him that I had joined the B.B.C. in the first place, and in slightly different circum-stances I might easily have been working under him. I knew that both he and the other members of Research prized nothing so much as their freedom from departmental supervision, and would resent nothing more than returning to it. I knew also that they had no idea of the precariousness of their situation, and that there was no inten-tion of explaining it to them.

In the event I accepted the assignment, fully realising—what of course actually occurred—that I should be supposed to have plotted the whole thing with a view to the expansion of my staff and my responsibilities. It was further suggested that my principal motive

68

was a shameful jealousy of individuals more brilliant than myself. The resulting atmosphere was not pleasant. In one quarter it was never wholly dispelled. But with the advantage of hindsight I regret nothing less than that particular decision. The Section, working along its own lines, became a more and more valued part of the Drama Department. It discovered the dramatised documentary. It furthered the original radio play. It experimented with combinations of music and poetry. It found recruits in D. G. Bridson, in Jack Dillon, in Maurice Browne, Stephen Potter, and Louis MacNeice. Under Laurence Gilliam during the Second German War it achieved its finest flowering and complete justification. And when Features became a department in its own right I dare swear that no one remembered, or would have believed, that in 1931 the very existence of the Research Section was at stake. I very much regretted, though I did not in the least resent, the divorce of Features from Drama when it was made absolute.

One, though not the main, reason for this regret was that at intervals I had made personal contributions to the output of Features: programme-items which had certainly given me a great deal of pleasure to handle, dealing, as they did, with historical or military subjects. Of these I recall most vividly *Lepanto*, *Waterloo*, *Gallipoli*, and the first of *The Thin Red Line* series, *The Grenadier Guards*.

Lepanto was simply Chesterton's great ballad, read by four carefully contrasted narrative voices, and illustrated musically by the Fourth Symphony of Tchaikovsky. It horrified musical purists, and irritated a number of the critics, who objected on principle to one narrator—let alone four! On the other hand it proved popular with listeners, and achieved considerable acclaim in New York when I produced it there in 1938 for the National Broadcasting Company with its superb symphony orchestra under Frank Black. Was it altogether absurd of me to be as irritated as I was when the suggestion that the programme should be repeated in 1941 was turned down on the grounds that it would inevitably give offence to the Turkish Government, and even influence their attitude towards the war?

Waterloo—a dramatised documentary of the Hundred Days— remains in my mind chiefly as being responsible for one of the most

69

valued of my friendships. Gladstone Murray, the genial and pleasantly cynical head of B.B.C. Public Relations, introduced me one day at luncheon to a Mr Norman Edwards, who at the time was editing *Popular Wireless*, a successful weekly published by the Amalgamated Press. In the course of the meal Mr Edwards and I discovered a mutual interest in Napoleon, and he gave me the freedom of his Napoleonic library, which included an exhaustive collection of books concerning the St Helena exile. The *Waterloo* programme was the direct result of that meeting. An indirect result was that Norman Edwards became a well-known name among original writers of radio thrillers, as well as an intimate friend. I fancy that nowadays he would agree with me that *Waterloo* itself was on the crude side. It was carefully documented for accuracy, and we succeeded with the help of the then Duke of Richmond in getting hold of nearly all the actual music played at the famous ball in the Brussels Wash-house. But on one point we came to grief. We allowed General Lord Hill to swear under the stress of battle-field emotion, and an erudite listener wrote to us to point out that Lord Hill was never known to use bad language! It ultimately emerged that there had been two Generals Hill, and that the one who swore had commanded a detached force at Hal, which took no part in the battle!

Gallipoli was my own favourite among these features, a script and production of which I remain impenitently proud to this day. Its original conception belonged to Lionel Fielden, who had served on the Peninsula at the time of the evacuation. But a few weeks before the programme's scheduled date—April 25th, the anniversary of the landings—Fielden arrived in my office with a formidable pile of books, which he planted determinedly on my desk. It appeared that he was so oppressed by his work in Talks that *Gallipoli* was going by default. Would I take over the assignment? I leaped at the chance. The classic background, the unparalleled grandeurs and miseries of a great feat of arms, the material ready to hand in the writings of Rupert Brooke, Masefield, Compton Mackenzie, Winston Churchill, and Sir Ian Hamilton himself; all combined to stimulate imagination and offer outstanding opportunity. To sit in the control cubicle with the man who had actually commanded the campaign was to experience, however humbly, the sensation of being part of a footnote to history—even though Sir Ian might murmur gently that the noise of my broadcast bombardments was louder than any that he himself could remember! And among my books there are few that I value more than one sent to me after the broadcast by its author, John Still, one of the handful of British soldiers who looked down upon the Narrows from the top of Sari Bair, and a copy of Mr John North's *Gallipoli, the Fading Vision*, which he inscribed 'to Val Gielgud, who so magnificently gave Gallipoli a voice'.

Last year I achieved an ambition long cherished, and sailed through the Dardanelles for the first time. The hills seemed very bare and curiously low. The sea was grey. Everything was very quiet. But for the stark outline of the Turkish war memorial there was nothing to recall the blood, the agonies, the ultimate heart-shaking failure of 'the men who died before Byzantium to save the fishy straits of the sea'. On board our boat was one who had served at the landings with the Royal Naval Division, and had come to revisit his past. I asked him what he had felt like during the early hours of that famous morning.

He borrowed my field-glasses and looked towards V Beach, which seemed too small to have accepted that great cargo of heroism carried in the *River Clyde*. 'It was a bit chilly for April in the Mediter-ranean,' he said.

The script of the documentary telling the story of *The First or Grenadier Guards* was written by Sir Arthur Bryant. His detailed knowledge was as confounding as his enthusiasm was infectious, but my principal recollection of the programme is not of this agreeable association, but of a meeting with the then lieutenant-colonel and adjutant of the Grenadiers in the headquarters in Buckingham Gate whose walls are hung with those colours of the King's Company of the Regiment which have lain on the coffin of the Sovereign at royal funerals. It was the time of Munich. In the general atmosphere of depression, apprehension, and confusion, it was not surprising that there should have been rumours that troops were to be called out 'in aid of the civil power'; but it was distinctly surprising that two busy and responsible soldiers should have found time to discuss the contents of a historical programme with a broadcasting executive.

71

However, my appointment was kept to the minute, and I found myself facing a desk covered with books and papers, behind which stood two cordial but apparently worried men. I apologised for taking up valuable time, but was immediately reassured.

'There's just one thing that is really bothering us,' said the lieutenant-colonel.

He looked at his adjutant, who nodded gloomily. I shifted my feet, wondering what would follow: desirability of postponement of the programme, a confidential whisper of a Hitler ultimatum, wars and the rumours of wars . . . ?

'We've looked up every record we can lay hands on, Mr Gielgud. I'm extremely sorry to disappoint Mr Bryant [as he then was], but we can't find out just how many paces to the minute the Regiment marched at Fontenoy.'

I went out into Birdcage Walk more than ever firmly convinced that there would always be an England.

Travelling abroad on the Corporation's business was of course one of the most pleasant and rewarding of perquisites. It gave one the chance of seeing new places, eating strange food, and conversing with perfect strangers, but the main object was to make and maintain personal contacts between radio practitioners. The B.B.C. was always in the van of those who believed in and encouraged what might be called international craft-union. Between 1932 and the beginning of the war I was lucky enough to visit Germany, the Scandinavian countries, Belgium and Hungary under official auspices; to study their programmes and their production methods; and to be astonished to discover how well British radio was thought of abroad, how much higher British radio drama was esteemed in Europe than at home.

Certain critics, as ever on the look-out for any stick with which to beat the B.B.C. dog, 'had themselves a ball'. When my German visit was announced I was roundly informed that I would do better to improve my productions in London instead of going to school in Cologne, Berlin and Breslau. It was apparently immaterial that—until Doctor Goebbels debauched German radio—German plays and production were the best and most advanced in Europe. When I expressed the hope that I might bring back some representative pieces from Scandinavia it was obvious that I was plotting to swamp the British air with an even larger dose of Nordic gloom. And when Eric Maschwitz and I went to Hungary together to present a fortnight of programmes direct from the capital titled *Night Falls in Budapest* one gentleman, who had formerly been employed by the B.B.C. and had left under something of a cloud, almost had an attack of literary apoplexy. The Corporation's playboys were at it again. The Corporation's money was being squandered in the nightclubs of Eastern Europe. Was it really necessary for us to have been accompanied by a notably good-looking actress? What, in fact, was the whole thing in aid of, unless the Variety Twins were getting away with a more than usually shameless self-advertising racket?

Fortunately by this time our skins had thickened. A few bad-tempered and worse-mannered newspaper paragraphs were a small price to pay for the experiences and the hospitality we met with everywhere. It is pleasant to remember Doctor Carl Dymling, my genial and rubicund host in Stockholm, and his individual cigars which were kinked like the tail of a Siamese cat. He roused envy in my breast with his emphatic assertions of the established popularity in Sweden of radio plays, conducted me in person to the top of the Stockholm Town Hall, that modern Wonder of the World, and horrified me at the end of an official luncheon, which had begun at midday and ended at half past four in the afternoon, by demanding that I should reply to the toast of the British Broadcasting Corporation in French! At that moment I would have been hard put to it to do justice to the theme in my native tongue.

It is less pleasant—though the experience was both fascinating and educational—to remember the atmosphere prevailing in Germany when Archie Harding and I arrived there in the summer of 1932. The *Credit-Anstalt* closed its doors on the day we arrived in Berlin. The Nazis could see power almost within their grasp. And the many brilliant Jews who occupied important programme posts in German radio at the time were only too conscious of the wrath to come. Within the next few years I was to hear that several producers, and at least two programme-controllers with whom I had talked, had disappeared into concentration camps. It might be true that the B.B.C. felt it necessary to give its programme people administrative assistants, who should watch their steps, put a brake on their notorious tendencies towards extravagance and lack of business

73

sense, and to some extent diminish their responsibilities. But I felt it was time to count my blessings when in Berlin I found myself bear-led by an avowed Nazi Party Member—he was incidentally a skiing champion and a magnificent physical specimen—with the evident duty of keeping my conversations within safe technical bounds, and firmly steering them away from the dangerous sphere of political controversy; and when in Breslau I saw the most talented of the advanced school of young producers brow-beaten and threatened by a recently-appointed *Intendant*, who had clearly modelled himself in appearance and manner upon Julius Streicher.

If there was something Kafkaesque about that visit to Germany, my expedition to Budapest with Eric Maschwitz and Frances Clare was remarkably reminiscent of Anthony Hope. Under the presidency of an admiral who had no fleet, with flags permanently at half-mast in melancholy memory of the Treaty of Trianon, with its background of *Zigeuner* music and flood-lit mediaeval buildings, with its notables attending the opening of the Diet wearing hussar pelisses and fur-topped boots, and jewelled sabres at their sides, Hungary seemed remarkably and delightfully akin to Ruritania or Kravonia. It was necessary to get away from the capital to escape the influence of a brittle unreality, of a picturesque but decadent charm. On a small estate in the country at the Festival of Harvest when the peasants sang their lament for the lost Hungarian lands with tears streaking their dusty cheeks in the sunshine, and the great spaces of the *hortobagy* dissolved eastwards into haze, it became possible to think of the Magyars as the old wardens of the eastern marches of Europe, of the battlements of Buda as other than the back-cloth of a musical comedy.

It was Eric who was the hero of *Night Falls in Budapest*, and I played second fiddle to him very willingly. To begin with, the trip was of his initiation. To go on with, it was he who blarneyed an archbishop into allowing us the use of his choir; refused to take 'no' for an answer on the many occasions when the Hungarian chief engineer, oyster-like, shook a heavy head over our requests for the planting of microphones in peculiar places; who kept his temper at eight o'clock in the morning when, having worked all night on a script, we were blandly invited by an actress to admire a new hat; who absorbed unlimited apricot brandy without getting drunk, and

74

danced the *czardas* into the smallest hours without falter or flagging; who was undismayed when he found an audience predominantly feminine assembled to watch him broadcast from a mud-bath where he arrived in the nude.

I did what I hope was my best, and for the most part enjoyed myself immensely. But I could not really compete. I could not easily reconcile myself to being whirled about the city in a huge car, flanked by motor-cyclist outriders with screaming sirens. I was frankly furious when I heard from London after our second broadcast that the Czechs, for some obscure political motive of their own, had interfered with the land lines and ruined the performance. I longed for a little quiet, some surcease from strain, and a lot more sleep, and wondered at intervals whether the programmes were not a good deal more trouble than they were worth. Still, there were consolations: in being caricatured—favourably—in the newspapers, when a Jewish band-leader refused flatly to play for us without an exorbitant fee; in Frances Clare's *cortège* of admiring barons; in the swimming bath of the Gellert Hotel with its artificially created waves; in sampling *fogas*, most delicious of white fish, from Lake Balaton; in the wonderful panorama of the city and the great sweep of the Danube seen from a little kiosk above Buda—the twinkling lights along the Corso, the floodlit Palace with its statue of Prince Eugen, the Fisherman's Bastion—with the soft, melancholy notes of the *tarogatu* rising out of the darkness behind us. In those moments London seemed impossibly distant, and the business of broadcasting no more than an exasperating intrusion.

I have said that with regard to these foreign excursions the B.B.C. gave evidence of a broad-mindedness and sophisticated sense with which it has been seldom credited. In another direction, too, it showed me an indulgence for which I shall always be grateful.

I imagine that Sydney Carroll will be remembered in theatrical annals principally for his discovery of Miss Vivien Leigh, and for his gallant attempts, supported by Robert Atkins, to defeat the English weather and establish the Open Air Theatre in Regent's Park. But at times he made courageous forays into the jungle of West End theatrical management, one of the first and most optimistic of which was the production of a play about Napoleon which purported to have been written in collaboration by Mussolini and a

Signor Giovacchino Forzano and had been adapted for the English stage by John Drinkwater. As Mr Atkins, who was producing, was also playing the considerable part of the Emperor, Mr Carroll took upon himself much of the responsibility of direction. As luck—from my point of view—would have it he had come across a recently published novel of mine, *Gathering of Eagles*. (It dealt with the retreat from Moscow, and had a depressingly exiguous sale.) On this flimsy foundation Mr Carroll built me up in his imagination as an expert on the period, and invited me to attend rehearsals as an unofficial adviser: an invitation which the B.B.C. made no objection to my accepting.

The play was elaborate, wordy, pretentious, and quite unworthy of its theme. The cast was enormous. Arthur Wontner as Fouché gave the sort of performance invariably called 'polished' by the critics, and Frederick Lloyd, as always, never put a foot wrong. But Mr Atkins's conception of Napoleon seemed limited to belief in the legend that he always threw snuff-boxes about in moments of irritation, and most of the actors appeared as uncomfortable in their parts as they were in their clothes.

My own contribution to an almost unrelieved failure was insignificant. I found myself with a pair of scissors cutting the Bourbon *fleurs-de-lis* from a number of supposedly Bonapartist uniforms, and I was able to make a number of suggestions regarding appropriate noises off to accompany the final stages of the Battle of Waterloo. I spent most of my time admiring the *sang-froid* and continuing optimism of Sydney Carroll while rehearsals dragged out their interminable length, his actors grew progressively more temperamental, and any hopes of success progressively fewer. The most dramatic moment provided by the piece occurred, unfortunately, at the dress rehearsal, when after spending some hours in the dark seclusion of the dress-circle Signor Forzano made a sudden appearance in the stalls and addressed Sydney Carroll in ringing tones.

'If things are to continue in this fashion,' he cried, with a sweeping gesture towards the roof of the New Theatre, 'I will without question hang myself from that chandelier!'

Sydney Carroll remained unmoved, sustained, I imagine, at that point in the proceedings by the courage of despair. In place of

76

fulfilling his threat Signor Forzano departed abruptly for Italy, in order presumably to explain to the Duce how a mixture of English phlegm and ineptitude had ruined his masterpiece.

To have witnessed at close quarters, and to have shared however slightly in, a catastrophe so expensive and so over-publicised did not strike me as a hopeful beginning to what was to become a very pleasant association. During the rehearsals of *The Mask of Virtue* I was so fortunate as to be among the first few people who saw the public flowering of Miss Vivien Leigh's beauty: beauty which was to bring *blasé* critics hurrying from the bars so as not to miss one minute of that first night's final act; beauty which, it was reported, sent Sir Alexander Korda hot-foot to Miss Leigh's dressing-room, film contract in hand, before the end of the play.

Another cherished recollection I owe to Sydney Carroll is that of watching George Robey rehearsing Falstaff in *King Henry IV* at His Majesty's. This adaptation of supreme music-hall technique to the demands and opportunities of a great classic part impressed me enormously, and threw a fresh light on the problems of Shakespearean production. It resulted, years later, in my attempt—alas, unavailing—to persuade the Crazy Gang to play the 'rude mechanicals' in a broadcast of *A Midsummer Night's Dream*. (Bud Flanagan explained with much charm over a large glass of whisky that it was a nice idea, but that after due consideration the Gang didn't think the script was so hot!) The same idea was at the back of my head when Professor Jimmy Edwards and Miss Beryl Reid were induced to play Sir Toby and Maria respectively in a broadcast *Twelfth Night*. Their success, in spite of astonishing incipient nervousness, was immediate and unqualified. I would not suggest that Mr Tommy Steele should be cast as Hamlet, or Miss Shapiro as Desdemona, but I believe firmly that the talent, vitality, and supreme technical know-how of great contemporary comedians should be harnessed to the playing of great classic comedy parts.

It would be a pity, though it might be kind, to make no mention of *Royal Cavalcade*, that remarkable British film production designed to celebrate the Jubilee of King George V. Several producers and no fewer than five individual directors were involved. Eric Maschwitz provided the original idea for a story-line, and—presumably, owing to my experience with historical features—I was engaged to

77

write the linking narrative. The result, particularly as everyone concerned was working desperately against time, was unhappy. Indeed at the Trade Show at the Marble Arch Odeon two reels of the film failed to put in an appearance, which considerably disrupted such continuity as there was. However, opportunities for taking part in the tribute were seized avidly by an unparalleled all-star cast, and from that point of view a good time seemed to be had by all. I have to admit to a certain prejudice. Rather more than half-way through the production I found the responsibility for narrative transferred to an aristocratic lady of great intelligence and charm who had in fact been engaged to advise on dress, manners, and social behaviour. The change may have been for the better, though the lady seemed as puzzled by it as I was.

It was my first, though by no means my last, experience of the curious goings-on of film-producers, who surely qualify in the history of our times to come under the label of Fabulous Monsters. In the film *Goodnight Vienna* the producer was so good-natured as to hire me as an actor for no better reason than that I had originally produced the piece on the air; and I found myself writing in a scene for which a vast set had been built but neither incident nor dialogue existed. The producer had been unable to resist the temptation to reproduce a ballroom in Schönbrunn Palace which had taken his fancy while he was in Vienna. I have mentioned earlier (pages 18-19) some of the peculiar happenings incidental to the making of the film *Men Are Not Gods*, and in Hollywood I was witness to a state of affairs in which the director of a picture was at the mercy of eight or nine technicians, each of whom had to be satisfied individually before a 'take' could be passed for printing. I was credibly assured that any attempt to break this fantastic tyranny—a tyranny which inevitably lengthened the period of work for the technicians concerned, and sky-rocketed the costs of making the picture—would not only have led to a walk-out of the entire production unit concerned, but also to a sympathetic strike by all the technicians employed by the Metro-Goldwyn-Mayer organisation. I confess that such examples have raised occasional doubts in my mind regarding the methods, sophistication, and even the common sense of both sides of what is commonly called 'big business'.

In spite of—perhaps to some extent as the result of—such diversions I think I can fairly claim that the stock of radio drama climbed steadily higher during that last pre-war decade. More and more artists of reputation were found to accept the point of view that there might be more in broadcasting than appearances for the sake of publicity. Malcolm Keen repeated his unforgettable stage performance in *A Bill of Divorcement*, playing opposite Edna Best, who proved equally unforgettable in *The Silver Cord*. And at long last, and after frequently expressed misgivings, Marie Tempest faced the microphone—very suitably in *Theatre Royal*.

This appearance of the Dame—and with all respect to Dame Edith and to Dame Peggy, the words 'theatrical Dame' must always mean Marie Tempest for me—was a portent not to be ignored. When Tempest played could anyone refuse? I had needed all the powers of persistence and persuasion that I had, and fortunately Dame Marie had proved susceptible, if not to me personally, then to the professional claims of my Terry background. Not that in the studio was one jot or tittle abrogated of the personal dignity and self-assurance which were her acknowledged attributes as Queen of the English Stage. On a later occasion, proving that she was a far finer actress than most of the parts she chose to play allowed, Dame Marie gave a superb performance as Mrs Alving in *Ghosts*. The producer was a young man with less tact than talent. The Dame considered herself affronted, remarked that he had no business to try to teach the equivalent of his grandmother to suck eggs, and called upon me in my office in dudgeon to tell me that she must regretfully but firmly withdraw. I only managed to change her mind when I told her that the producer's mother had been an actress, one whom Dame Marie had known in younger days.

'Ah, that explains everything,' she said. 'Poor boy! Both her acting and manners left much to be desired.'

After which she returned to the studio, and a co-operation that was not only enthusiastic but affectionate.

1936 began well for me when I succeeded, with the help of R. Ellis Roberts, in bringing Kipling to the microphone for the first time with readings of *Just So Stories*. This fulfilled a long-cherished and admittedly sentimental desire. When from time to time I have suffered praise or blame for authors or books or plays that I have sponsored, I have often thought of the sardonically amused expression my father's face would have worn had he realised just how much his tastes, reflected in my personality, had influenced the choice of material for broadcasting, a medium which he never bothered to understand, one indeed of which he tended to be contemptuous. It is none the less true that without his praise of *The Man of Property* there would probably have been no broadcast of *The Forsyte Saga*. It was on direct prompting from him that I first read Granville Barker's *Waste* and *The Voysey Inheritance*, the novels of Joseph Conrad, whom he had known personally, Dumas, Victor Hugo, Hilaire Belloc, Kipling, and Thomas Hardy. I am not pretending that such inspiration was particularly original, nor that it might not have been provided elsewhere. But I still look back to that library in Gledhow Gardens with nostalgic affection, to the rows of book-cases, regrettably glass-fronted, to the smell of my father's cigar and the lift of one eyebrow as he sat reading. That library and its contents were continually in my thoughts during hours in Broadcasting House when I was puzzling over my quarterly schedules and cudgelling my brains to find a sufficiency of material to satisfy a Moloch already devouring an average of a play a day all the year round.

It may have been due to over-confidence engendered by success in the case of Marie Tempest that I found myself in trouble over another distinguished actress, Miss Mary Clare. Felix Felton and I were to produce Mr Coward's *Cavalcade*, and naturally hoped that she would repeat her Drury Lane triumph in the studio. Unfortunately at the time Miss Clare was playing for Sir Bronson Albery. Our production—it was before the days when programmes were recorded almost as a matter of course—was to go out 'live'. This meant that Sir Bronson must put on an understudy for one night, if Miss Clare was to work for us. This, very courteously, he declined to do. It would be as reasonable to ask him to close his theatre for the occasion. I promptly suggested that he might do just that thing. Resulting publicity would be enormous. The consequent good will generated between broadcasting and the theatre would be great and lasting. Sir Bronson was not to be persuaded. So Miss Mary O'Farrell played the part, proving not for the first or the last time that she is in the front rank of radio actresses.

The incident is only worth recalling as an outstanding example of an attitude common among West End managements which I could never quite understand. Whenever they failed to secure public support for one of their enterprises they moved heaven and earth to have a scene, a part, an act, or the whole of the play broadcast. This was supposed to be an infallible nostrum to cure failure. Simultaneously they blankly refused to allow any production of theirs to be broadcast if it had succeeded. I found it an odd theory to assume that to broadcast something which had proved demonstrably bad would bring audiences in to see it, while to broadcast something equally demonstrably good would infallibly empty the theatre. Yet so it was, and so it remained.

There was, however, something of a jinx upon that *Cavalcade* production. I have told elsewhere the story of how one of the many studios involved 'packed up' in the course of actual transmission, and how disaster was only averted by Felix Felton's ingenuity and the unruffled certainty and sense of the studio manager, Fred Bell, who switched actors from studio to studio with a dexterity any conjuror might have envied. We thought that all had ended well. As far as the general listening audience was concerned we were right. To our amazement the following week's edition of the *Era* pilloried our work roundly as 'Bolshie'! The miasma of anti-patriotism, it seemed, had pervaded every aspect of the production. We felt considerably affronted until we realised that the writer was the paper's *musical* critic, and that outside his own field he was patently ignorant of what he was writing about. I wonder what his verdict would have been on *Oh What a Lovely War*!

In spite of another minor 'scoop', when Noah Beery, of *Beau Geste* fame, on holiday from Hollywood, suggested playfully that a vehicle for him should be written and produced within a single week and was taken at his word, 1936, which had opened so encouragingly, ran into more than its fair share of storms and troubles. When Moray McLaren left the Talks Department to join Drama Mr Collie Knox discovered evidence of a growing conspiracy to down-grade talks and substitute in their place more and more dramatised features. Further and yet more sinister evidence of my spreading influence and insatiable ambitions appeared when for a time the supervision of a reorganised *Children's Hour* was added to my responsibilities.

81

In practice all that this amounted to was that the general policy of the *Children's Hour* throughout the Corporation was rationalised, and its aims and objectives were more precisely defined. It had been realised—and I must admit that from time to time I had urged it— that even a *Children's Hour* must grow up and become adult in the best sense of the word; that the children who were listening to broadcasting in the Thirties were no longer quite the same as the comparative handful who had been fans of the 'aunts' and 'uncles' of Savoy Hill; that in this field also the time for a cosy middle-class amateur approach to the problem was over. I did not pretend that I was better equipped professionally than such an expert as Derek McCulloch, who together with the rest of his staff in London accepted the change with good grace. And I saw, and see, no reason to apologise for having suggested that perhaps the works of E. Nesbit, Kenneth Grahame, Kipling, and even Rider Haggard and Conan Doyle, might be made use of to a greater extent than they had been.

Unfortunately the usual press conference was held at which the usual fatuous questions were asked, and my answers were both forthright and indiscreet. I spoke of the 'uncles and aunts' convention as childish. I said that I did not believe that most children wished to be talked down to, and that such children as I knew were happiest when treated as adults by adults. I was widely reported either inaccurately, or accurately out of context, and newspaper readers could have been forgiven if they thought of me afterwards as a second Herod. Comprehensibly enough certain retired 'uncles' and 'aunts' rushed into print to say how dearly they had been loved personally by their little listening friends, and to complain that a tyrannous bureaucrat was crushing out all humanity from the programme. Finally the B.B.C. regions exploded in a unanimous howl of protest against such a monstrous example of increased centralisation of authority: a howl which was all the louder because it was the Regional *Children's Hours* which were the worst offenders in refusing to move with the times.

I must have been a glutton for punishment in those days. I was still in process of being buffeted between critics and colleagues on account of *Children's Hour* when I became involved in a lively con- troversy with Miss C. A. Lejeune, the well-known film critic of the

Observer. I fear that I let myself in for this deliberately. The occasion was the showing of the M-G-M film of *Romeo and Juliet*, which Miss Lejeune, a critic whom in general I both respected and admired, chose to extol in the warmest terms. I had already been outraged at the Trade Show of the film, where a programme of astonishing elaboration and vulgarity seemed to me to have gone beyond any joke in subtitling *Romeo and Juliet* as 'Boy Meets Girl—1436', detailing the vast numbers of extras dressed up as Montagues and Capulets and the quantities of bricks used to build the sets, and emphasising everything about the film except the play which it pretended to reproduce.

None of this would have mattered, had it not been for the casting of the two principals, Miss Norma Shearer and Mr Leslie Howard. They were hardly to be blamed for the fact that, admirable players in sentimental or romantic comedy though they were, they simply did not carry the necessary guns. Tragedy was outside their scope, as verse-speaking was apparently outside their experience. For Miss Lejeune it was enough that as established stars they would ensure the film's success and popularity, and she committed herself to the opinion that this was the way to bring Shakespeare to the masses. She added, apparently as an afterthought, that she had never seen the play acted on the stage of a theatre. There ensued a vigorous correspondence between us, in the course of which tempers on both sides became frayed. It is an incident of which I am not particularly proud, for I have never enjoyed a quarrel with a lady. But I still think I was justified in making my point. When a film is a reproduction of a classic piece it cannot be regarded *pur sang*. And a critic who has never seen such a piece in the theatre should walk warily before commending its film version to people who have had that experience; still more warily before suggesting that the film version is superior to its original. Audiences which were persuaded that Miss Shearer's Juliet was of higher calibre than the painstaking efforts of a high-school girl were not being introduced to Shakespeare. They were witnessing a travesty. It may be arguable whether there is genuine value in pressing Culture with a capital C upon the masses at all. If there is, then I suggest that the Culture should be the genuine article, and not an expensive box of chocolate-creams wrapped up with pretty ribbons.

One of the effects of Hitler's War was to make much of what happened before it blurred, unreal, or simply forgotten. I am surprised, looking back at the records, to find that so much which was hailed as original in post-war broadcasting had already appeared in slightly different forms between 1932 and 1939. How many people remember that Mabel Constanduros was lineal predecessor to Mrs Dale when she appeared as the main character in *The English Family Robinson* in 1937? For the introduction of this first of the soap-opera-style serials into British broadcasting I must accept full responsibility, and I confess that it weighs upon my conscience to do so. It was a time when we were perhaps more influenced than we should have been at Broadcasting House by trends and fashions in American radio. We adopted the idea of the Columbia Workshop in our *Experimental Hour*, before we had developed practitioners of the calibre of Norman Corwin or Irving Reis. (The same idea was revived later by Features in their series *Writing for Radio*, and again technical experiment was allowed to outweigh content.) We imported a number of American horror-plays for late-night transmission, which apparently horrified no one very much except Jonah Barrington of the *Daily Express*. (I can only wish better luck to the series *Just Before Midnight*, which has been started in the Light Programme as I write.)

In spite of their shortcomings there was much to be said for the *Experimental Hour* and a certain amount for the horror-plays. Both implied branching off from the beaten track of broadcasting. Both encouraged curiosity and liveliness of mind. For the soap-opera in general, and for *The Dales* in particular, I can only blush and bow my head. I made no secret of my opinion that such programmes were aesthetically contemptible and sociologically corrupting. They tied up actors, producers, and writers alike in the equivalent of a chain-gang, offering the bait of security and regular employment, while simultaneously squeezing all virtue out of them by the process of a remorseless routine, demanding neither talent nor personality, merely application. In particular, certain actors became so identified with the characters they played that they became almost useless in any other capacity. From the point of view of the listener, the persisting drip-drip-drip of such programmes destroyed all possibility of criticism. The audience was gradually drugged into belief in the reality of a dream-world ruled by bogus values, entirely occupied with trivialities. Self-identification with this world was automatically encouraged. I wonder how many pleasant *bourgeois* families up and down the country endure today the gossiping, nagging, self-righteous attitude of its own Mrs Dale. I wonder—and I shudder.

For years this particular dilemma would come between me and my sleep in those small hours when everything tends to seem out of proportion miserable. Because *The Dales* needed actors, what passed for production, and an administrative machinery, their programme was categoried under the Drama label. Certain programme planners swore by it—its listening figures were always to be relied on. Various other executives persuaded themselves that it was redolent of democracy; that it might be silly but was certainly harmless; that it was greatly appreciated overseas. My objections were amiably noted, ultimately smiled at, gently put aside. In the long run I had to ask myself the question: was it worth while to make the continuation of *The Dales* a resignation matter?

There is little doubt in my innermost and most honest mind that I ought to have put it to the test. I didn't. I enjoyed my job too much. There were still too many things in broadcasting which I wanted to do. I tried to remember what I had read of Machiavelli and the theory of expediency. I told myself that it would be too stupid, too humiliating, to lose so much for so dingy, so second-rate a reason. I salved my conscience with perfectly genuine efforts to improve the programme, to put some 'guts' into the scripts, to relate the whole business at least to the amount of reality which made of *The Archers* at least acceptable hokum. It was no good. It was too late. The disease had become too widespread. A new head of the Light Programme backed me with courage and imagination. For our pains we got neither thanks nor results. Listeners had decided that Miss Powell might go and Miss Matthews might come, but Mrs Dale should go on for ever, or they—and those in Broadcasting House who thought they knew them best—would know the reason why. This is a confession of an ignominious failure which I am glad at last to make. It called for, it deserved, all the attacks which were made on me for other reasons, and which I learned to take almost in my stride.

Such an attack, which at the time caused some stir, resulted from my handling of a historical feature on the subject of the Russian Revolution. The script, written by the distinguished Cambridge historian, Professor Temperley was, as might have been expected, scholarly, carefully documented, and eminently impartial politically to any but the most jaundiced eye. As far as the production was concerned I admit I did not use the soft pedal. 'Revolutions', Napoleon is reported as once saying, 'are not made with rose-water', and I did my best to ensure that my revolutionary scenes were noisy, violent, and vigorous. It was also the case that the climax and close of the programme was the triumph of Lenin, which was demanded as much by the claims of dramatic construction as by those of historical truth.

My old friends of the British Empire Union made loud noises in their turn. With the support, this time, of the *Daily Mail* they screamed, 'Blatant Bolshevik propaganda!' It seemed that under-cover Reds were in occupation of Broadcasting House, and that if I was not actually in receipt of Russian gold, it was obvious where my political spiritual home was to be found. As my colleagues knew only too well that in so far as I have political views they tend to be of the extreme Right, to say nothing of including a prejudice against Russia common to most Poles, the outcry caused little beyond mild amusement. In the long run it boomeranged, for Professor Temperley wrote a letter to *The Times*, in which he not only justified unanswerably the accuracy of the facts in his script, but also was kind enough to refer to the production in most handsome terms.

I would not wish to leave the impression that my life in the B.B.C. was an unbroken succession of hair-raising emergencies and internecine disputes and intrigues. Happiness has little history worth recording; the daily task lacks interest and the common round drama. But I was often asked whether the Corporation was a good employer, and it is now possible and may be desirable to answer the question.

By and large the reply is an emphatic affirmative. As far as my own experience goes, the B.B.C. was not only fair, sensible, and infinitely painstaking in its staff relations, but also outstandingly humane in cases of illness and misfortune, and often, if not invariably, imaginative into the bargain. Much was made of its Calvinistic code of morality in the early days. Little was ever said of quite deplorable circumstances which provoked the attitude. And no one has better reason than I to know that morals apparently dubious could be regarded with indulgence and sympathy if combined with reasonably good manners. As the organisation expanded and the administrative machinery inevitably did likewise, there was a growing tendency towards bureaucratisation, a proliferation of regulations, an irritating increase in delay between decision and action. But although the 'usual channels' came to need dredging it was usually possible with ingenuity on one side and good will on the other to find a way by, through, or over. It is, I think, possible to make the criticism that salary scales tended to be low—especially in the case of producers in the entertainment departments. (I must add that personally I never considered myself underpaid, though I doubt that any theatrical manager would have thought of my salary as other than 'chicken-feed'.) But particularly for junior Variety producers the discrepancy between the standard of living they could afford and that of most of the people with whom they had to work and deal was too great. It was certainly responsible for the many charges and the very few proven instances of corruption. In such circumstances temptation must have been irresistible.

It might also be mentioned—though at the moment it is unfashionable to say so—that the Corporation drew and draws its revenues from public money, and has therefore a peculiar responsibility for economy and against extravagance. It was impossible for the B.B.C. to emulate the glorious extravagances of a C. B. Cochran, or to indulge in the frantic squandermania of the film industry, if it was to preserve its reputation as a worthily representative organisation. It is true that in the days of Savoy Hill the fees offered both to actors and authors were too low, partly owing to ignorance, partly to lack of precedents. As a result it became established as an axiom that the B.B.C. was mean. The fact remains that it was never possible for the Corporation to compete on level economic terms in the world of entertainment, though it was always difficult to persuade actors used to star salaries and authors flushed with Hollywood contracts of this unfortunate truth.

Perhaps the most singular—and to the outsider incomprehensible —aspect of the whole B.B.C. set-up was the relationship in the Programme Division between the programme planners and the departments. It was the business of the planners to balance the programmes and to allot the times which the programmes occupied. It was the business of the producing departments—Talks, Music, Features and Drama, Religion—to provide the programmes and to be responsible for their professional quality. Obviously these spheres of activity overlapped. Planners found themselves interested in the content and quality of programmes, while producing departments were concerned with the lengths of time given to programmes and the places in which such programmes were placed in overall schedules. In terms of strict protocol a planner could order a play of a particular length for a particular scheduled time, and he could stipulate in vague terms the type and weight of play he wanted. But he could not commission a play. He could not produce a play. Commissioning and production were the jobs of the Drama Department, which had no power to bring any play to the microphone without the consent of the planner. When it is realised into the bargain that programme budgets were largely in the hands of the programme planners, who inevitably and properly worked in the closest contact with the Controller of the Programme Division, it is easy to see what opportunities were present for confusion, argument, disputes and bad feeling.

It is, I think, a remarkable tribute to all concerned that no deadlock ever arose in my experience. The plays produced by my department did reach the microphone. The balance of dramatic output demanded by the planners was achieved. It only needed a few people to be a little worse than normally pig-headed, or to stand on their hierarchical rights, to produce a sequence of spaces without programmes to fill them, and a mass of material denied access to the air. With one single exception, during my service with the B.B.C. I found the planners accommodating, reasonable, friendly and, above all, helpful. I only hope they can say the same of me. It was a working tradition established firmly by Sir Lindsay Wellington over many years. To him and successors like Ronald Lewin I owe an incalculable debt for co-operation, sympathy and forbearance. Planners get no credits in the *Radio Times*. They are born to blush unseen, and frequently to be anathematised by producers in the heat of the moment. Their contribution to broadcasting deserves to be remembered.

If 1937 must wear a black spot for the introduction of the soap opera into B.B.C. programmes, it is to be marked also with certain white stones, two in particular: the first for Humbert Wolfe's translation of *Cyrano de Bergerac*; the second for a curious Russian play called *Autumn Violins*.

I had been an unashamed devotee of Rostand's play ever since one of my aunts introduced it to me at the age of sixteen. She would read it aloud to me in the original French *con brio*, moving both herself and me to tears. I never understood how Fred Terry, that prince of romantic actors, could have left the playing of the part to Robert Loraine, nor why in the famous Olivier-Richardson season, when the Old Vic was housed in the New Theatre, it was Sir Ralph and not Sir Laurence who wore the celebrated nose. I had frequently considered the possibility of bringing the play to the microphone, and as frequently had given it up as a hopeless proposition. The difficulty of length alone was formidable. The problem of making the switching of identities in the balcony scene without the aid of vision seemed insoluble. Add the fact that the only translation into English of which I was aware was inadequate, and any production project seemed doomed.

I then had the good fortune to become acquainted with Humbert Wolfe. I learned from him that he had been commissioned by Sir Alexander Korda to make a new translation of *Cyrano* for a film which was to star Charles Laughton in the name part. Being a sworn admirer of Humbert Wolfe as a poet of elegance and wit, I asked excitedly if I might read his translation. In agreeing he mentioned casually that for a variety of reasons the film was not going to be made. Would I be interested in discussing with him and Laughton the possibilities of a radio version? Naturally I was.

When I had read the translation I was not only interested, I was passionately enthusiastic. Felicity of phrasing, fire, sweep, sensitivity, above all the coloured elegance and sense of period of the original had all been achieved. And when I had heard Charles Laughton declaim some of the great speeches against the unpromising background of my office I knew that I had been present at the walking of the ghost of what must surely have been a classic among films. But would enthusiasm, however passionate, be enough to overcome the practical problems that still loomed up against a successful radio production of *Cyrano*? With the deceptively quiet diffidence so typical of his personality Humbert Wolfe suggested that he would like to make a script for broadcasting himself, and that he was prepared to write linking and explanatory verse-narrative which would make the piece manageable in terms of length and remove any confusion that might be caused by lack of vision.

This was the sort of co-operation from an author that I always dreamed of and seldom got. All went swimmingly—except that Charles Laughton had to fall out owing to an American commitment. Frank Cellier—and in a later revival Malcolm Keen—gave admirable performances.

Autumn Violins came to me out of the blue as the result of correspondence with an elderly lady who wrote to me expressing her satisfaction with one or two of my productions of Chekhov. It appeared that she had spent some of the early years of her life in the Moscow of Imperial Russia, and had become a devoted admirer of Chekhov's widow as an actress. She had seen the latter in a play whose title she remembered, but she could not be sure about the author. She had an idea that it was an early piece of Chekhov's, unknown in this country.

I was immensely intrigued, though it seemed too good to be true that I might have the opportunity of putting an unknown Chekhov play on the air and introducing it in England for the first time. And so it proved. Complicated enquiries revealed that *Autumn Violins* had certainly been acted by Chekhov's widow, and that a script of the play in French was obtainable. The author was not Chekhov but a certain M. Sourgutcher, of whom nothing seemed to be known except that he was a Chekhov disciple; a fact which became self-evident when I read the play. Its exquisite sensitivity, its atmosphere of melancholy and philosophic charm, its 'dying fall' were almost worthy of the master himself. It was beautifully interpreted in production by Jeanne de Casalis and Robert Farquharson.

However, M. Sourgutcher, like a good many other continental authors, had been ill-advised in disposing of his foreign rights. On the very eve of our production I was threatened with an injunction by a West End management which claimed to have acquired the British rights in the play and had had an adaptation made of it in English which represented the characters as members of the English upper-middle class and set the play in the environs of Sloane Square! I could not feel that our version could be considered as competing seriously with such a travesty of the original, and refused to be bullied. The threat did not materialise, and the stage production was, as I remember it, rather more successful than it deserved to be.

A celebrated headmaster was once reported as saying that boys were always reasonable, masters occasionally, and parents never. There were a good many occasions when I felt his verdict might have been applied with equal truth to actors, producers, and authors in equivalent order. Even the most amiable of the latter tended to prove temperamental when working in a medium largely unfamiliar and with a monolithic organisation whose machinery they could hardly be expected to understand. Peter Cheyney was an outstanding case in point.

When I was first introduced to him by Norman Edwards he was already a best-seller: a singular combination of Ian Fleming and John Creasey. Our early relations were cordial in the extreme, and even after they had ceased to be so I always found something endearing about his ebullient and permanently schoolboyish personality. I fancy that his interest in broadcasting lay in the medium's advertising rather than its literary or dramatic attractions. But then Cheyney, though he could tell a story with ingenuity and enormous gusto, could hardly put pen to paper and prided himself on dictating his work over a private telephone line from his flat in the West End to a secretary somewhere in South London. He would talk about himself—frequently in the third person—more continuously and more loudly than any actor I ever met; and, until repetition made it boring, his habit of greeting one with figures of his circulation in Iceland or Peru was disarming in the naïvety of its satisfied conceit.

In appearance and manner he did his best to live up to his tougher fictional creations, helped by a round bullet head, a pencil-thin moustache, and a picturesquely split ear. Of the latter he would tell you alternatively that it had been caused by a bullet, and by an accident that had occurred during a championship fencing bout. He also prided himself on having been a Black and Tan. He attributed much of his success with women readers to the care and detail with which he described his heroines' clothes, and I believe it to have been true that one of his youthful jobs had been with a fashionable *couturier*. With the raising of the Home Guard he came into his element. He would stride into the Ivy, or into my office, wearing the battle-dress of a captain, bristling with revolvers. Envious fellow-authors of his publisher averred that he secured the paper for reprints of his books, when its supply was strictly limited, by sheer physical intimidation of the firm's managing director. (Knowing the latter personally, I doubt if this was true.)

To a schoolboy's passion for a parade of masculinity and aggressiveness he added an adolescent's romantic view of and passion for the Theatre. Nothing gave him greater satisfaction than to mix with and entertain actors and actresses, particularly if the latter were good-looking. I believe he would cheerfully have sacrificed much of his boasted circulations to have written a successful play. And it was ironic that adaptations of his books should only have reached the stage after his death. I am inclined to think that in his radio plays he found a substitute for this wish-fulfilment, and over his first efforts, a series called *The Adventures of Alonzo McTavish*, he took both endless trouble and expert advice. Helped by a typically charming and distinguished performance in the name part by Nicholas Hannen, these plays found considerable favour. And from that moment our troubles began.

If B.B.C. files are destroyed with the death of their subject, a remarkable literary curiosity disappeared with the Peter Cheyney file. In the later stages of our association the slightest criticism of one of his submitted scripts provoked interminable arguments. Rejection produced a storm of invective. Typed by the devoted South London secretary on a special yellow paper, these reactions would usually amount to several thousand words, in which I was excoriated as an incompetent, an ignoramus, a hide-bound bureaucrat, and a false friend. One tenth of the time and effort wasted on these astonishing letters, if it had been applied to reconsideration and revision of the scripts in question, would have made them acceptable. He preferred to hug to his breast the daggers of grievance and injured vanity. And it distresses me to think that a man who was fundamentally generous (he was an excellent host) and good-hearted (he did me and other people many unostentatious good turns) should have driven me ultimately to the retort discourteous and the counter-check quarrelsome.

To pass from recollections of Peter Cheyney to those of Dorothy L. Sayers—she was always insistent upon that L.—may seem too sudden a shift from the mildly ridiculous to the almost sublime. What prompts my doing so was their mutual determination to view the theatre and actors through rose-coloured glasses. Cheyney revelled in the elaborate entertainment of his casts at the Ivy. Dorothy Sayers would no more have missed one of her rehearsals than she would have passed a false quantity. Unlike Cheyney, however, she was usually helpful in the studio, almost always reasonable, and invariably well-mannered. In her own preface to the published version of *The Man Born to be King*, she has told the story of how that remarkable series of plays was broadcast in the teeth of the objections of the Lord's Day Observance Society and the statement headlined in the *Daily Sketch* that Broadcasting House was 'a Temple of Blasphemy'! It was a triumph achieved almost entirely by the combination of her own common sense with the courage, persistence, and diplomatic abilities of James Welch, who was at the time head of Religious Broadcasting: a triumph with which I was privileged to be associated as producer. I owed that privilege to my meeting Dorothy at Christmas 1938, when I accepted and handled a Nativity play, *He That Should Come*, which both in form and content was a prologue to the later famous series.

He That Should Come initiated a friendship that I came to value highly. It began unpromisingly, for, as a sworn admirer of her detective novels, I had expected to meet a feminine version of Lord Peter Wimsey; something of an intellectual and academic snob, with an exotic taste in wine and cigarettes. I confess to having felt a mingling of shock and disappointment when I came face to face with a square-shouldered, tweed-clad, evidently practical woman in pince-nez with something of the air of an amiable bull-terrier. On her side, as she told me later, she had anticipated the worst between the beard that I then wore and my gossip-paragraph reputation. Fortunately we lost no time in finding tastes in common which developed into a mutually appreciative affection. We both loved Oxford. We were both extremely positive in the expression of our opinions. We both hated humbug, waste of time, and bad cooking. We were both friends of John Dickson Carr.

Among the authors whom I have known and with whom I have

93

worked, she was exemplary in her realisation of where the line should be drawn between the spheres of action of author and producer. She had ideas about acting. She had ideas about production. But they were always expressed to the producer, never to the actors. On the other hand she demanded to be convinced with good reason before she would alter a line, and she was resolutely opposed to the changing of lines by actors just because words or phrases were unfamiliar, or because they seemed difficult to speak. She was always patient. She appeared continuously interested. She was lavish of praise to the cast. Criticism she confined to the producer. This made an ideal working arrangement. Both of us minded our own business. When disputes arose, as of course on occasion they did, they were settled privately between us. The actors were never in a position to play us off against each other, or bewildered by mutually contradictory direction.

Few rehearsals in my experience were as complex, as difficult, or as liable to disaster as those of *The Man Born to be King*. They were carried out in a temporary studio—what was once the Monseigneur Cinema at Marble Arch—under wartime conditions with quite inadequate technical gear. All twelve plays went from first read-through to 'live' production within forty-eight hours. All twelve plays contained scenes that included large crowds. In its earlier stages the series was liable to interruption by visits of inspection by various ecclesiastical dignitaries, who had to be assured that we were not indulging in an approximation to the Black Mass. Dorothy neither faltered over her crowds, nor flinched before the dignitaries. And I have seldom been so proud as I was when I read my name on the dedication page of the published *Man Born to be King*. I doubt if I have ever been what is conventionally called a good Christian, but I think I came near to being something of the sort during those rehearsals.

Proverbially pride goes before a fall. It is therefore perhaps appropriate that at this point of the story of my career in broadcasting I should leave the scene of what was generally acknowledged to have been success for the surroundings of what was failure in no uncertain terms. Shortly after Easter 1939, and at my own suggestion, I was seconded as an individual television producer to Alexandra Palace.

CHAPTER SIX

Leaves from a Wartime Diary

IF MISS JOAN LITTLEWOOD is to be believed the Kaiser's War is nowadays nothing more than a subject for 'sick' humour. Hitler's War, particularly in the eyes of a generation too young to have had actual experience of it, seems little more than a tedious excuse for generals to re-fight it—and each other. Anecdotes of the Blitz had become 'old hat' or a form of 'line-shooting' even before the last doodle-bug and the first V2 had fallen on London. I do not propose to tell all over again the story of the B.B.C. Drama Department's exile to Evesham, and later to Manchester, nor to detail the effects of wartime conditions on the development of radio drama. Enough to say here that the combination of air-raids and black-out provided broadcast plays for the first time with a vast ready-made audience, kept at home and attentive by circumstances, whether they liked it or not; that exile from London compelled a radical simplification of our production methods and techniques; and that by the end of 1945 the accepted figure for listeners to *Saturday Night Theatre* was not less than twelve million.

At the same time six years of one's life—and particularly six years of one's forties—cannot be entirely ignored in any personal record. Yet there are no years which I find more difficult to recollect in tranquillity and with hindsight. One lived so strenuously, so much from one day to the next, that memories tend to be both blurred and formless. I have come to the conclusion that a few extracts from the diary that I kept at the time—unedited save for the occasional excision of a name—are more likely to give a true impression than any considered writing. They are offered accordingly with all their imperfections only too evident. If opinions seem jejune, prophecies absurd, and the picture of one's existence neurotic and over-coloured, I can only plead that this is how things appeared at the time. Perhaps I should add that this diary was written up at very irregular intervals. And I am well aware that to the affluent Society of the Welfare State the repeated mention of food and personal discomfort must seem puerile. At the moments of writing they had their significance.

1939. EVESHAM. SEPTEMBER 7TH.

At last I have a moment to write up this record, being in the office on night duty as Senior Programme Official with censoring and planning responsibilities added temporarily to my normal job. Wood Norton is the appropriate setting for nightmare. Once the home of an exiled Duc d'Orléans, it sprouts *fleurs-de-lis* on everything from weather-vane to bath-plugs, and has a bear-pit in the garden. To my horror one may not smoke in it. I work in one room with Moray McLaren, Laurence Gilliam, Howard Rose, and three secretaries. Parquet floors are not a |good base for typewriters. I have had to take to a bicycle again—after fifteen years. My billet is vile. Its owners seem to regard one rather as if one was a mediaeval *condottiere*, likely to steal the silver and ravish the daughter as opposed to hoping for bed and breakfast! I fancy, too, that one's inevitably irregular hours of going and coming have raised doubts in their minds about one's morals. The weather is superb, and there is a grim irony in finding oneself strutting a well-kept lawn, as the Orléans peacocks must have strutted, while Warsaw endures the fate of the Cities of the Plain.

SEPTEMBER 11TH

Still pretty fine. I spoke on the telephone with Francis Czarnowski at the Polish Embassy, who ended gloomy tales of the fighting with: 'We must pray for rain.' J., back from a day-trip to London, tells me that the morale there is as dim as the streets. I feel sure that this black-out business is being grotesquely overdone. Managed to get moved over into a furnished house which I have taken with Laurence: not bad in a rather North Oxfordish manner, and it was good to be able to release Hugo* from his captivity. Long talks with Laurence and Frank Phillips about air-raid precautions and programme plans until three in the morning. We felt pretty gloomy, as we cannot begin to justify our security hide-out and size of staff

* My Siamese cat. See chapter 11.

96

unless we do really active work. Not exactly encouraging to get a memorandum from Head Office saying that plays of greater length than half an hour are not for the present envisaged, and it is suggested they should be 'of *Children's Hour* type'! Heard from S. and N. America might be in another world. For the moment I sleep on a camp-bed in Lochhead's office. As Philip Wade said to me this evening, 'What a gigantic bore everything is!' Stephen Potter finds himself, rather typically, billeted at a fantastic farm with the biggest collection of caged birds in the country, and wallabies running loose.

SEPTEMBER 15TH

Returned by midday after spending a hectic yesterday in London. My flat, boarded up and garnished, looked depressing in the extreme. Collected a case of wine, a bottle of kümmel, a thick overcoat, gloves, a coffee-pot, a huge electric torch which, set in solid rubber, can be used as a truncheon (!), and got my hair cut. Met my mother for lunch at the Ivy, she looking old but astonishingly cheerful. Nice to see Humbert Wolfe lunching with Peggy Scott and Pamela Frankau. Not so nice to see a lady journalist flaunting a gas-mask container to match her frock. Czarnowski came in with two other Poles, whom it was hard to face without a feeling of shame. Followed at Broadcasting House a rather stormy interview with Charles Siepmann. His very vocal satisfaction with the way in which, he having 'pulled the levers', all the arrangements for the change from peace to war conditions had gone so smoothly. I remarked coldly that I thought the attitude of Casabianca was a little absurd when there was no sign of any burning deck. He was not amused. Did my best to make the point that it is not much use to fight for civilisation if simultaneously you throw away every symptom of that civilisation—in our case the standard of broadcast programmes. Cecil Graves sympathetic, and, as always, friendly and sensible. Spent the night on the sofa in Norman's flat, managing to read myself to sleep with a volume of Gibbon.

SEPTEMBER 17TH

Today comes the disastrous intelligence of the back-stabbing of

97

G

Poland by the Russians: the foulest political infamy since Bismarck handed over the Polish insurgents of 1863 to the Tsar. Whatever happens now, Poland is wiped out as an entity, and the war must end with a negotiated peace or we go on against the heaviest odds. Already the Turks have sent a special envoy to Moscow. Played a round of golf in the afternoon, hoping to cease from thinking for a little—and played rather well! I hear it is now proposed to shift us to Cardiff, which would be the devil. I go to London next week to try and press Manchester as an alternative. There at any rate are studios we can use. J. looked like a character out of Murger, when we walked on the lawn after rehearsal, wearing a pink shirt and sponge-bag trousers. She very depressed and faintly defeatist. It's queer how people react to these lunatic conditions. Most of our secretaries, with of course honourable exceptions, are going all to bits, rather like spoiled school-girls. On the other hand the engineers have turned up more than trumps, which immensely eases our working difficulties.

SEPTEMBER 21ST

Just back after twenty-four hours of acute depression in London. Eric lunched with me, hopeful of getting an Intelligence job. He tells me Philip Jordan is to be a war-correspondent. I think I have managed to get Manchester substituted for Cardiff, which is something, and to make the point that our output must include other things than footling Variety sketches, and that some recording facilities are really essential. Dined with Norman at the Aperitif, both of us, I fear, feeling quarrelsome, and after to my parents in Queen's Gate. They begin to look pretty frail. I fancy that my father feels the Polish collapse and absence of all news from the family in Cracow a lot more than he will admit. Back to Evesham in a Corporation car with a chauffeur who talked board school socialism at me all the way, and was surprised to get rather more than he gave in reply! Mary Somerville had produced a yarn that the real reason why the war hangs fire is that owing to American pressure another Munich is being thought up, but I hardly see any government bringing that one off. On duty here tonight, and at six have to rehearse two short plays to go on the air at eleven. We seem to be adopting American broadcasting methods and standards wholesale, and Adrian Boult is as cross about it as I am. These nights of full moon are incredible in their beauty. With no street lighting one can see the sky, and the phrase 'silver-washed' takes on a meaning more than literary. The Wilfred Blunt *Diaries* remain a consolation and a charm.

OCTOBER 1ST

Principal hate at the moment is a plague of flies which, growing sleepy, make their way indoors and flop all over everything in the foulest way. Whatever else may happen it is clear that the Soviet-Nazi tie-up is complete. If Germany wins the result is clear. If she loses I should expect her to go red, and the democracies to face an embattled communism from Vladivostock to the Rhine. One only hopes there is nothing in the rumour that the inactivity in the West, the black-out business, and the general depression of civilian morale, are all designed to make the average man so gloomy and uncomfortable that he will be prepared to settle for almost any sort of peace.

OCTOBER 7TH

I have been up to Manchester for a preliminary reconnaissance. Coatman and Fitch both extremely pleasant and helpful, and as to offices and studios we shall be much better off. On the other hand I shall have to live in a hotel, which will be hideously expensive, and black-out conditions seem worse even than in London—being by so much farther away from hypothetical bombs! A vile journey, which took up most of one day, including a wait of two solid hours at Worcester where I heard the broadcast of Hitler's so-called peace offer. A letter from Katherine Kelly, who is working as Hore-Belisha's War Office *chauffeuse* and was amusing about sitting at her wheel outside the Savoy Grill and watching her theatre acquaintances through the big window. Came across a *Times* photographer in the canteen, who was complaining bitterly that he could no longer get any good photographic gear—it was all German.

OCTOBER 12TH

X. down from London to take issue with me about my continued complaints about programme standards and content. I got the

99

faintly sinister impression that both he and Y. are sympathetic to a negotiated peace, which would explain many things. I was very outspoken, the more so as both made it obvious that they were engaged in an intrigue to 'out' Q., which is hardly a testimonial to what should be the motivation of the Programme Division in these circumstances. I think they realised that my more elementary demands must be met. Heard from N. that he is pleased with his new flat, and in consequence is not going out in the evenings. I must try and send him some etchings! What a capital actor Cecil Trouncer is proving himself to be. He never puts a foot wrong. Lectured last night to some sixty moon-faced rustics and evacuees at Pershore: the first entertainment—save the mark—they had had since the war began. Coffee afterwards with the inevitable hearty-vicar type which no amount of stage caricature has availed to kill. I spoke in a tin tabernacle whose elderly verger bemoaned the death of 'serenity in the countryside'. I could sympathise with him. They seemed unreasonably and pathetically grateful, which made me feel properly small. Keynes cracks the left-wingers in the *New Statesman*, pointing out that the intellectuals, having screamed for years for forcible resistance to the Nazis, now realise that they may get hurt and must rely for their defence on Colonel Blimp and the Old School Tie. It is hard indeed that anyone should have to die on behalf of such pickers and squealers. Missed cue-lights and fluffed lines made a horror of our last production. It is the natural result of rushed rehearsals and exhausted actors. It is infuriating none the less.

OCTOBER 21ST
Considerably cheered up by my last visit to London. Lindsay Wellington helpful. St George's Hall to be at my disposal for an occasional show. Longer times for plays. Even a certain appreciation of what I've been doing and arguing for! The black-out improved by better lighting on cars, and the general atmosphere much improved. Dined at the Hanover with Grizelda Hervey and Pat Hoffe, where we had a capital partridge and a good bottle of claret. On the journey back one had to sit and brood in the dark, as there were no lights in the carriages and it was perishing cold. Found a chaos of work on my desk on return. I hope and believe that we

have got Harry Ainley for our opening at St George's Hall, and Leslie Banks for the second of the series—*Henry V*.

OCTOBER 31ST

In London for *Julius Caesar* until yesterday afternoon. Ainley put up a typical but good show, and the crowd—apparently determined to compete successfully with the Repertory at Hogsnorton—worked like mad and were excellent. The previous evening I went to the new Priestley play at the Westminster and was pretty bored. Not even Lydia Sherwood swathed in scarlet chiffon could help it much. I go to Bristol tomorrow for a programme board. The decrease in London traffic is now very evident. One could see almost the whole length of Bond Street clear at midday. Woken by a false air-raid alarm. The noise is singularly disagreeable, and one's immediate reaction a rather acute sense of apprehensive exasperation. There seemed nothing to do except go back to bed. My train back forty minutes late.

NOVEMBER 8TH

The office a hell of packing and general discomfort, and weather vilely wet and windy. Lunched with R.W., who was full of some high-falutin plan for a programme to celebrate this war's Armistice Day when it comes! I found it hard to take the idea realistically or him seriously, even though complete inanition seems to have settled on the battle front. I shall quit Evesham tomorrow with little regret. It has been an uncomfortable, and often beastly, period, but above all else boring. With the weather breaking Manchester can hardly be worse.

MANCHESTER. NOVEMBER 16TH

I am quartered for the time being in the Midland Hotel, which is comfortable enough, if expensive. Tucker McGuire, Frances Clare, and Celia Johnson are all there at the moment so that one has the illusion of renewing some sort of social existence. Eric came over from his mysterious Liverpool existence last night. I have to go to London every week-end, which with the journey lasting eight hours on the average and unheated trains is exhausting and comfortless.

Hair-raising stories from Francis Czarnowski of conditions in Poland: the shooting out of hand of land-owners: the removal of the whole academic staff of Cracow University to a labour camp; literal starvation in Warsaw. I am trying hard to find time to get back to some writing, but with little result.

1940. JANUARY 7TH

Just back from ten days in London, during which I produced *The Butterfly that Stamped*—good—a revival of *Testament of Beauty*—pretty good—a horribly potted *Macbeth* with Godfrey Tearle and Cathleen Nesbitt—not so good—and the second Polish Programme, which was, I believe and hope, a real corker! Immediately I got back I had to cope with the radio version of *Africa Flight*, which went better than it had done in the theatre, with Belle Chrystall and Tony Ireland both excellent. I have been grieved and shocked by Humbert Wolfe's sudden death. He was one of the few people with whom I had been able to make friends in recent years. He was always most kind to me, apart from being delightful to work with. I shall not lightly forget all the fun we had in our party at Boulogne at Easter last year. I shall miss him sorely.

MAY 2ND

My first entry since my fortieth birthday—and not a very propitious occasion as it is marked by the news of our withdrawal from Norway. With the last Budget I was forced to look my economic situation straight in the eye, and found that with a salary of £1,750 a year I could only count—taxes, school fees, and provident fund deducted —on £600. For any addition I must look to writing, and I foresee a complete change not only now but permanently in one's standard of living. For the moment I am back in London, with my flat reopened, though warned that we shall scuttle again at the sound of the first bomb. The resultant splitting of the Department is a mixed blessing, but fortunately I'm too busy to concern myself closely with internal B.B.C. politics, which get 'curiouser and curiouser'. Spent an amusing evening the other day with Z., who told me that she had in fact never been married to the husband with whom she had lived for seven years. She is now engaged to a husky New Zealander, and wonders if I think he is likely to be economically reliable! I find I have handled fifty-five productions personally since the war began, and that I would like a little leave, though it would be against my conscience.

MAY 28TH

Since last I wrote the war has blown up in the biggest possible way: Holland overrun, the Channel ports as good as lost today with the inexplicable ratting of Leopold of Belgium—though Longland, back from France today, tells me that it was not unexpected. Gamelin, Chamberlain, and Ironside all scrapped in favour of Weygand, Churchill, and Dill—but whether the apathy of the last months can now be recovered only God knows. The Baldwin tradition has much to answer for if civilisation goes down. It's a grim situation, and seemed all the grimmer at Alfriston where I spent a week's leave. The quiet and beauty of the countryside against the occasional distant thudding of gun-fire got badly on one's nerves. Theatres are in a poor way, plays coming off right and left, and too many people thinking and talking of evacuation—how and whither? I pretend to no more courage than the next man, but I confess that at the moment I feel it sound to sit tight and say as little as may be. My mother sounded very shaky on the telephone this morning. Churchill faces an Augean stable and no mistake. His feelings must be queerly mixed—if he has time for such.

JUNE 8TH

Weygand's last order speaks of 'the final phase'. Ed Murrow said last night that he gives the French three weeks before they pack up, I didn't agree, partly out of sheer cussedness, partly from a belief, probably romantic, in Belloc's tradition of fighting Gaul. But Ed was firm that Churchill was speaking literally when he talked of our fighting on our own beaches, and there is a considerable under-current of hysteria regarding a Fifth Column and parachutist landings. Simultaneously a most awkward situation in the office where Ogilvie has promised Duff Cooper that there are to be no more features dealing with military subjects—this the result of the row over the Narvik programme—while I am bidden to plan a new

103

series of topical features! I am to go to a programme board to-morrow at Bristol to thrash out the matter, but my position is as near impossible as doesn't matter. I have managed to finish the opening of a new historical novel, but with little heart or conviction. Writing seems a little inadequate to things as they are.

JULY 2ND

Ed Murrow was only too right, and the French collapse is the most lamentable and humiliating *exposé* of so-called democracy in living memory. Happily Lewis—who had been with a military mission in Paris—got away on a tramp steamer from Bordeaux, escaped five torpedo attacks and was landed at Milford Haven. I hear that 8,000 Polish troops in France have got out, and de Gaulle has made the right gesture. But as far as the Continent is concerned we are back in 1803. I should expect Hitler now to go east and deal with Russia while the going is good in the great European plain. The general view seems to be that we will now get the big air-raids at last with perhaps invasion in form. I caught a violent cold from sitting on guard with a shot-gun in the Control Room at Broadcasting House for five hours and a quarter in a draught of refrigerated air. Talking to J. B. Priestley last night, I found myself agreeing strongly with his contention that the attitude to the war should be more highly coloured; that the garrison should be allowed its banners and its bands; and that our own bureaucracy is more dangerous than any Nazis. One is becoming acclimatised to living almost literally from one day to the next, in the hope of proving that if hopes are dupes fears can also be liars.

SEPTEMBER 21ST

The war has just entered a new phase with the materialisation—just a year late—of the so much advertised *Blitzkrieg*. Intensive raids on London began roughly a fortnight ago after the German attacks on the south-coast aerodromes had come to grief. I still don't really believe in the invasion possibility, and the morale of the country seems on the whole sound. But there has already been bad damage in the East End, and there are some bad patches of *laissez-faire* even now. Yesterday the Post Office—which is after all supposed to be

104

responsible for general communication, which has so maddeningly broken down—announced with a flourish of trumpets that its offices would continue to work *after warning sirens had sounded*. This a week after Churchill's speech on the subject! I am back in Manchester, as conditions of production in London had become impossible. I did my last two plays there in sub-basement studios about the size of a small bathroom, with little air and no listening-room. I produced in the same room as the actors, wearing head-phones. Once our guns started up sleep in Long Acre was out of the question. Neal Street had two houses rubbled. Odham's was hit. The flat was bracketed by incendiaries, one on a motor-car just under my window. For some days I wandered between Norman's sofa in Kensington and an armchair at the Savile, snatching two or three hours' sleep at my flat about five in the morning. Bad bombing in St John's Wood and Earl's Court, while apparent shots at Broadcasting House knocked hell out of Oxford Street, Bruton Street and Berkeley Square, including the Langham Hotel and Lewis's Store, which I watched blaze at close quarters. The civilian services quite superb. My parents, who insist on staying firmly 'put', are astonishing, but, as Marie Tempest said crisply the other day at lunch, that generation was brought up to know how to behave. She might have added that they were also brought up in a world in whose stability it was possible to believe. Every theatre of course closed. John is filming in *Disraeli* at Kingston. I told him that unless he made up as George Arliss no one would recognise the character. I spent all of one day on a trip with a commentator and a recording-van scouring south-east England in search of the Battle of Britain. Considering what was so soon to follow, I might have spared myself the trouble. But I did see one ninety-second dog-fight at some fifteen thousand feet, and the fires along the Thames estuary on my journey back to London—five hours from Margate, which was boarded up, derelict, apparently deserted. Dover showed little sign of damage. 'Hell-fire Corner' in fact seemed largely the product of journalistic imagination plus whisky.

SEPTEMBER 30TH
In London for the day, and had a good view of the afternoon raid from Broadcasting House: eight German machines flying at not

more than ten thousand feet above Regent Street, simply surrounded by shell-bursts. Took seven and a half hours on the journey back, blacked out all the way from Rugby to Crewe; no heating, and no food obtainable. Not pleasant.

OCTOBER 1ST

Dined with Moray McLaren and a charming Frenchman of the Foreign News Service, one Thierry. He confirmed the stories of Mme. de Porte's responsibility for the French collapse as Reynaud's evil genius, and of the rivalry between her and Daladier's mistress as the cause of the failure of Daladier to back Reynaud at the critical moment. Thierry said he had had it from Mary Churchill that W.S.C. had got Reynaud to agree to go to Algeria and hand over both fleet and air force to Great Britain when the lady turned up and played the ace. Rather an eighteenth-century story it sounded.

OCTOBER 4TH

My last trip to London rather too exciting to be pleasant, as I had to leave Manchester during a raid with flares falling disagreeably near the station, and we were kept in a siding till it was over. Only got in to London at eight in the morning—no sleeper of course—and found the old hotel adjoining Broadcasting House, in which my last London office had been, had been bombed and was sending up a malodorous cloud of thick black smoke. I gathered that a mass of margarine had been stored in its cellars. Met John Dickson Carr for lunch at the Ivy. He has come back from the States—a gallant and quite uncalled-for gesture on his part—to see the war through in a country he is fond of, and I've good hope of fixing him up with something in my department. His house was hit almost as soon as he had got into it! But he, his wife, and the ms. of his latest serial were all got out all right. For once I was able to sleep in Long Acre undisturbed, and the train back to Manchester made history by running on time. A letter from Cathleen Cordell, touring in Canada, saying that American feeling seems to be moving steadily towards war. I wonder.

Yesterday was a bad day. B.B., who was handling *Hamlet* with John in the part—our first full-length Shakespeare since the war—over-ran the allotted time by twenty minutes, panicked, and had the production faded out before the last act just as London rang up to say that it could go the limit. Disastrous from a professional point of view, and equally so as it puts me on the wrong foot in coping with the present Head Office set-up, which will certainly exploit it. Today we had our first performance in the emergency studio under the Central Library, which went quite well. After to see a film with Edana Romney and we were caught in what was probably the worst raid in Manchester to date. So we sat in the dark for two hours, while the audience sang popular songs of the Boer War to keep up their hearts, took the wrong turn in the black-out on the way back, and found ourselves at Old Trafford at one in the morning! Home finally about half-past two, very footsore after walking on cobbles. Laurence Gilliam rang up to say that he was eating oysters in Wheeler's when a bomb landed between the Palace and the fire station in Shaftesbury Avenue. Very much of a near-miss.

Czarnowski and Kamienska came up for the fourth of the Polish programmes. I'm inclined to think that these—with the *Just So Stories*—have been the best things we've done since the war. Curiously neglected by the censorship and almost entirely motivated by the heart. Michael Arlen lunched with me to discuss his scripts. There was a certain pathos in his evident feeling of his world having vanished—emphasised by the fact that when he wanted to do war work the Ministry of Information declined him on the ground that he was a Bulgarian! As a good Armenian he was considerably affronted, and I gather he will probably go to the States. On Tuesday Broadcasting House had its first direct hit—in the Music Library inside the Tower, bringing down most of the sixth-, fifth- and fourth-floor studios, including of course our Drama suite on the sixth. Six people in the Monitoring Service were killed, including a Pole and two firemen, and twenty-three hurt. K. tells me that the Defence people muddled the job and that the bomb lay inside the building for ten minutes before it exploded without people being warned to clear out.

OCTOBER 20TH

The Broadcasting House bomb affair seems to have been worse than it seemed at first. The bomb lay inside the Tower for over half an hour before it went off, and eight were killed, including several women. The Defence Executive had just been promoted to Defence Director! I find one of the hardest things to bear continually is the intolerable sequence of teashop food. One should of course be grateful for food of any kind, but egg and chips, sausage and tomato sauce, and indifferent coffee repeated *ad infinitum* tend also *ad nauseam*. Home Guard duty, and it is mighty chilly on the roof above Manchester with the autumn fog.

OCTOBER 29TH

In London on Saturday had something of a close shave. I was getting out of a bus outside the Café Royal when out of a clear blue sky and with no warning came a sound like twenty expresses going together through a wayside station. I shot like a rabbit into the nearest doorway—a shoe-shop—and found myself covered with blue paint! An h.e. landed just the other side of the Regent Palace Hotel, which was quite near enough. Went on to lunch with my mother at the Ivy. Very empty.

NOVEMBER 4TH

London again, and the office atmosphere pleasantly improved. To Wyndham's in the evening where the London theatre flag flies alone under the gallant impulse of Edith Evans. Joyce Grenfell, and a clever fat girl, Vida Hope, quite excellent as a nude on the dole. Dined at the Café Royal late afterwards. Food still good, but service, as everywhere else, vile. The theatre very full. To the flat through quite a stiff barrage. My admirable taxi-driver, warned by a warden, merely remarked that we could take care of ourselves, and went on his way. Peter Cheyney writes that he has been bombed out of his flat and lost three of his scripts for us. A blessing in disguise?

Rather exhausted after the production of *Merlin*. This the first of Clemence Dane's series *The Saviours*, which was the result of our Ivy conversations, and promises every sort of excitement. In spite of alarum and excursion it really went pretty well, largely owing to Muir Matheson, who handled the music like a wizard. But I feel inclined to take some credit, for it was as complicated as any pre-war production and yet was done with only three rehearsals, orchestra and all. Winifred seemed pleased—she had typically insisted on coming up to Manchester in the teeth of all discomfort— and we all went back to London at midnight afterwards with high hearts and a good deal of whisky in a party including Dick Addinsell, who had written the enchanting music, and Victor Stiebel, only to go straight on to Bristol with Michael Standing for a programme board. As it turned out, Bristol had had a bad raid the night before. We got to Bath at two and to Bristol at five! The central shopping district still burning, and the high-ups had not arrived, so we had journeyed in vain. Put up at a vile hotel most vilely run with a fire blazing cheerfully a hundred yards away. I gathered that casualties had not been too heavy and that the aeroplane works were all right. Two nights with Eric in his London cellarage on the way back, including a rather alcoholic party at the Savoy with Carroll Gibbons.

Prompted by Ed Murrow, put up a suggestion that the Christmas Day programme—with the King—might be introduced by Roosevelt if he were properly approached. Frigid reception by Broadcasting House, but suggestion ultimately passed to Ministry of Information. Their reply—it savoured too much of a publicity stunt! I wonder what Goebbels would have done in similar circumstances. We have all taken to the playing of table-tennis in the office as a diversion and get our heads beaten off by the *expertise* of the office-boys.

Malcolm Keen turned up over the week-end and entertained me royally after his usual fashion. He wants me to try my hand at a comedy-thriller for Jack Buchanan, but I feel horribly disinclined for writing work at present. I hear there are 14000 homeless as a result of the Sheffield raid, which is serious enough, and Broadcasting House has had its second hit with a hole about the size of a bus blown in through the Portland Place side to the Concert Hall. I have decided reluctantly on economic grounds that I must give up the Long Acre flat. I find I must live on £29 a month—once other commitments have been met—which is less than I earned on the *Radio Times* in 1928: a grimmish outlook.

DECEMBER 25TH

Back to Manchester—a ten hours' journey—and staying in the office to cope with routine arrears had the experience of the second big raid from the viewpoint of the roof: all the big warehouses facing our Piccadilly building in flames shooting up to a couple of hundred feet in great rolls of yellow shot with scarlet—a high wind throwing the blaze across the narrow streets between to catch the curtains as the windows blew out—with feeble fire-pumps and indifferent fire-service, possibly due to the fact that the first fire-party was wiped out by an h.e. on a tobacconist's shop on the corner by Lewis's. G.B., who was on Home Guard duty, went out to give a hand and came into our shelter under the Bank building with his trousers soaked in fresh blood. Glass smashed everywhere over the stairs, and a noise as if Creation was coming down over our heads. Standing behind the roof parapet, the heat on one's face was so great it was hardly bearable. Below the waist, in spite of one's overcoat, one was freezing cold! As a result our production of Edgar Wallace's *The Squeaker* had to go out from the Bank shelter —the land lines to the Library Studio had gone—with gear miraculously lashed up by the engineers, but with no more rehearsal than a preliminary read-through. The dynamiting of wrecked buildings made a curious background to Christmas Day.

DECEMBER 31ST

In contrast London almost a relief, though Bow Street caught it the evening I was in Clemence Dane's flat in Tavistock Street, listening to her reading of the fourth of the *Saviours* series. Everything rocked. The wall behind Winifred's chair bulged ominously.

She merely pitched her voice rather higher and went on reading. In the circumstances I could hardly advocate the advantages of a shelter. Ed Murrow turned up the other night and gave me a capital dinner; the more welcome as my last meal in our canteen had consisted of two aged rolls, some silver-papered cheese, four biscuits and some tepid coffee. He remains sceptical about invasion possibilities, which I found consoling as our Home Guard detachment seems to be expected to defend our offices with First World War hand-grenades.

1941. FEBRUARY 2ND

X. up here for the third of the *Saviours*—which went pretty well—on leave from his unit had two queer yarns: one that a patrol of our own people went out to make a bogus landing in full kit to test our defence arrangements, and got fifty miles inland before they were challenged; the second that the battalion next to his own in the Thames estuary area were given an hour's warning of a hostile motor-boat approach, that fifty Germans were landed and none went back. One can take one's choice. His orders were no retreat and no prisoners. His people are expected to stand for at least three hours, after which they can expect mobile armoured supports.

FEBRUARY 25TH

The Dickson Carr serial has started well. A good repeat performance of Arlen's *Three-cornered Moon* in London last Saturday with Ronnie Squire and Fay Compton. Back here on Sunday for the serial and again to town tonight so that I feel like the Wandering Jew, the more so as I recently lectured at Morecambe and Lytham on two of the coldest days I can remember.

MARCH 17TH

My efforts to achieve a single production unit to supply both Home and Overseas seem to have succeeded against all expectation, largely owing to the common sense and help of Tony Rendall. Whether the gear and facilities needed to do the job properly will be forthcoming is another story. Grieved to hear that P. was in the Café de Paris disaster the other night. Sixteen out of her party of eighteen were killed, and she has had to have a leg amputated, which is tough on a young and attractive girl. Hugo and Rupert had the house in which they were boarded out blown down over them, and emerged from a linen-cupboard coal-black, unhurt and spitting defiance at the Luftwaffe! Collins have shown interest in *Confident Morning*, but God knows if I shall ever find time to finish writing it. As a busman's holiday I produced *The Importance of Being Earnest* in the theatre at Hanley for Nigel Patrick's battalion of the Rifle Brigade. Evelyn Laye made an appeal and it went like a bomb, and we had a wonderful party afterwards in the mess. There is now a scheme afoot to repeat the performance at Leeds for Leo Genn's gunners. I wonder if that play has ever been produced before with only four rehearsals!

MAY 29TH
I have at last got myself back permanently to London, hovering between a room in Manchester Street and Norman's flat. A relief, too, to have been found a pigeon-hole in Broadcasting House after a purgatorial fortnight in Egton and an office with neither light nor air owing to bricked-up windows. I made a running commentary for Leslie Howard to read for a Polish propaganda film, and several of last month's shows were pretty good: a revival of *The Bread-winner*, in which Freddie Lloyd stole the honours from Ronnie Squire; and *The White Cliffs of Dover*, in which Constance Cummings gave a quite lovely performance. It's a satisfaction to have persuaded people like Arlen and Monckton Hoffe to write original pieces for the microphone at last. Saw Ed Murrow last night, who was gloomy, prophesying the imminent fall of Crete, the possible loss of Suez, a probable push by the Boche into the Ukraine, followed by a peace offer 'which would split this country and even more the United States wide open politically'. He has been proved right too often not to be taken seriously. He and Janet are two of the nicest people I know. Our amalgamation with Overseas is at last a *fait accompli*, and we start a new Shakespearean series on Monday: scripts prepared by Clemence Dane; Fay Compton and Marius Goring for the first; Leslie Banks for the second; Sarah Churchill and Robert Helpmann for the third. I spent one week-end at St Austell to see my son and lecture to King's School ex-Canterbury.

Weather superb and the war seeming very distant. I took him and two of his friends out to lunch on the Sunday and we found a perfectly good French *bistro* run by refugees and had excellent soup, a first-rate omelette, salad and cheese for 2/6! Saw something of the Plymouth shambles on the way. Masses of children still there after weeks of intensive raids.

JUNE 24TH

At last the hot weather has arrived, and with it Hitler has thrown the iron dice and invaded Russia. All turns now on whether the bloody-minded Muscovite—for whom after Finland I have neither pity nor sympathy—can and will fight. If he can hold for more than three months—which I understand to be our War Office estimate— the Boche should be in something of a jam. Various Merchant Navy representatives turned up today to 'vet' their programme, and we had to be a little firm about knowing our own business! Eric wired me from New York that he had seen C. and J., who were missing me. *Où sont les neiges . . .* ? And what wouldn't I give for one evening in a city with lights?

JULY 8TH

Last Saturday night out to Stanmore to Fighter Command with Ronnie Squire to see him with Connie Cummings and Marie Lohr in *On Approval*, which R. had put on for the R.A.F. It was a little fantastic to meet men there who had been 'sweeping' over northern France the same morning. Portal and Sholto Douglas both there, and a gay and very cordial atmosphere. Michel Saint Denis came with us, very entertaining about the Churchill broadcasts to France, particularly the famous one from the underground shelter when Michel had to sit on Churchill's knee, there being only one chair. To Winifred's in Tavistock Street on Sunday, when Coward came in with Joyce Carey and we talked about the Navy and E. Nesbit whose books Coward seemed to know by heart, which endeared him to me. We broke up at a quarter to five in the morning after the best party I remember for a long time. I have decided to quit Manchester Street and take over Norman's spare room. A long and sweet letter from S. in the States who seems to think we are starving

H

and promises supplies. The Americans are as generous as they seem to be ill-informed!

SEPTEMBER 25TH

It has become harder and harder to keep this record written up with any consistency. One tends to feel just too tired to be able to convince oneself that it's worth while. Kiev has fallen, and it looks at the moment as if Armageddon might find its setting against the mountains of the Caucasus! I have been doing a lot of production, including *The Pot of Marmalade*, which was violently criticised on the grounds of its immorality, and *St Joan*, in which Connie Cummings played marvellously without a script and with perfect *sang-froid* which the rest of the cast did not share! Alan Wheatley being sick at the last moment, I had to play Warwick myself—not too badly if Shaw's letter of congratulation can be believed. Life continues very unreal with so much attention fixed on food, and the streets dead as mutton after ten o'clock at night.

DECEMBER 16TH

Much grieved by the death of Ian Rankine, who seems just to have turned his face to the wall and died in despair at the end of the only sort of world in which he could bear to live. He was one of my few intimate men friends, though I had hardly seen him since the war. The handling of Pat Hoffe's musical serial, *Night Lights of London*, at Kidderminster—of all queer places—provided diversion with both Harry Ainley and my cousin Phyllis Neilson-Terry being very sweet—and very good—and giving me the opportunity, for which I have always longed, to conduct an orchestra playing a Viennese waltz! Found quite a good hotel there run by a henna-ed lady who might have come out of a Compton Mackenzie novel, and was very good to me when I caught a couple of the most shocking colds. The railings have gone from the parks, and restaurant cars finally from the railways. We ended *The Saviours* series on Armistice Day in something of a blaze of glory, Winifred turning in a quite lovely script, but I feel rather foully devitalised, having done fifty productions myself this year. Find to my surprise that I've also completed 50,000 words of *Confident Morning*, and that I rather like it!

114

I suppose I must mention that the Honours List at New Year brought me the O.B.E. which fourteen years, mostly of industrious clerking, possibly deserve. In a way I find the absence of bombing worse than last winter's horrors. The latter produced a general gutfulness and an almost 'front-line' sense of *camaraderie*. Instead one now sees increasing ill-temper, irritability, and selfishness. But, then, everything gets steadily more comfortless: no decent food to be had outside one's club, and bad news as an almost continual depressant. One must count the blessing of one's work. From Dane to Sayers—after a riot of controversy, correspondence, press articles and meetings of the Religious Advisory Committee the B.B.C. has stuck to its guns, and we go forward with the series *The Man Born to be King* with Bobbie Speaight as the Saviour. I was only involved because D.S. refused to let anyone else handle them, which was something of a compliment—and a consequent headache. Luckily I feel a good deal fitter than at the end of last year, though I foresee complications in the supersession of Ogilvie by a dyarchy of Graves and Robert Foot. John is touring *Macbeth*, of which I hear dubious reports, and my son is now twelve, which makes me feel a hundred.

MAY 7TH

I think *The Watch on the Rhine* the best play seen in London since the war began. Miss Wynyard and Walbrook excellent, and three remarkable children. Ed Murrow is back, to my pleasure. But he tells of a secret agreement supposed to have been signed with Russia and due to break within the next fortnight by which we have guaranteed the Soviet the Baltic countries—and all Poland up to the old Curzon line. This is ghastly news, apart from driving a tank slap through the Atlantic Charter, with infinite implications. He denies rumours of unrest in Italy and any chance of our attacking the Continent this year. I have got myself a suit of corduroys for work in the studio. Largely owing to Graves's good offices the Corporation has agreed to my taking three weeks off to produce a revival of Maugham's *Home and Beauty* for Ronnie Squire. Cast: Isabel Jeans, Tony Holles, Barry Jones, Ethel Griffiths, and a very glamorous young person, June Willock. First rehearsal the end of next week.

The novel is finished, and I confess I find it a creditable piece of work, a view, I'm glad to say, shared by Winifred, who has joined one of the Old Vic companies and gone off touring northern industrial towns. She is an astonishing person, but I shall miss those long evenings of talk in Tavistock Street. I think I've fixed to get into another Long Acre flat next month. I must say I long for my own belongings and my books and a cat and a door I can slam! But noisy nights seem to be starting up again and may well upset the apple-cart. *Home and Beauty* goes to the Playhouse on November 12th.

1943. JANUARY 29TH

For some weeks have been disgracefully lazy over this record. *Home and Beauty* died the death after a ten days' run—too out of tune with the times. A nice flavour of Edwardian hangover with one of the backers trying to insist on the inclusion of his lady friend in the cast! But it was a sad disappointment for me. Collins will publish *Confident Morning* on March 8th. I have hopes—but books are getting almost as difficult to procure as drink, and too often appear in miniscule on vile paper. I am delighted to have got into my new flat. Evil rumours of growing ill-feeling between Poles and Russians as the latter approach the old Polish frontiers. Beaverbrook and the *New Statesman* still singing their singular duet about the need for an immediate landing on the Continent. I could wish them included in the first commando group to land. After Stalingrad and the chasing of Rommel beyond Tripoli one feels that the pendulum has swung and that there is a chance of the thing ending before one is old and worn-out, but I don't like the growing feeling that all is over bar the shouting, the more so as it's combined with so much anti-American prejudice.

FEBRUARY 8TH

An astonishing suggestion comes to me from del Giudice of Two

Cities Films that I should leave the B.B.C. and join his organisation as a producer! The money is attractive enough. Less so to involve myself with an industry which I distrust, and rather despise, with only the remotest connection with the war effort. Nor do I believe myself competent to start at such a level with the minimum of technical know-how, and del G. seemed to think I was mad when I suggested it would be as well if I began much lower down on the ladder. I must try and keep the iron warm, and see what develops. Spoke today at a luncheon of the Interval Club, which was somewhat depressing in an atmosphere of hearty clerics and soft drinks.

MARCH 16TH

Confident Morning started out with a 2,600 subscription, and the first notices are rather encouraging. I'm convinced myself that it's the best thing I've done so far in the writing line. A drink in Harley Street with Leon Lion and found Eleanor Farjeon there smoking a large cigar. Very complimentary about the novel. Lionel Brown brought me no fewer than eighteen eggs from the country: such is real wartime currency.

APRIL 29TH

I am forty-three and feel every day of it. For the moment I have succeeded in stalling del Giudice, but he says firmly that he will have a good job for me when the war is over. I wonder. Ed Murrow back from North Africa, for once quite cheerful, speaking well of the French Foreign Legion and our men, less well of his own people, who tend to forget that they've still a good deal to learn. It seems pretty certain that the Russians butchered the Polish prisoners at Katyn, or they could kill the story by producing some of them alive. However, they seem to have got our press nobbled, the prisoners being officers not private soldiers, and Ed says that the Polish Government's official statements are censored, so that public opinion is swung the wrong way. Spent a couple of days in Brighton with Malcolm Keen, where he had gone for a rest, to find ourselves drinking a good deal of Margaux in the intervals between alerts and volleys from Bofors anti-aircraft guns. Fire-watching tonight. My doctor is trying to tone me up with vitamin injections, but without much effect.

MAY 25TH

Lunched at Quaglino's with Leon Lion, Nesta Sawyer and one of Churchill's personal staff, who mentioned two more years as the probable length of time still needed to settle with Germany. I liked his yarn of W.S.C. at Casablanca on being faced by the mutual intransigence of Giraud and de Gaulle: '*Si vous deux continuez m'obstructer, je vous liquiderai*!' But he would not guarantee its authenticity! Comment by one of our B.B.C. Governors yesterday to Laurence Gilliam: 'I think I should like to have a look at the kitchen end of broadcasting for once.' He referred to a visit to a studio! Oddly enough, the recent raids have cured my insomnia, so that I could tackle the production of Linklater's *The Great Ship*— John and Jimmy McKechnie both excellent in their very different ways—with reasonable success. No other radio play has ever gone out three times in a single week.

JULY 5TH

My mother's seventy-fifth birthday, and she remains quite wonderful through everything. Just back in the office after a month's sick leave. Insomnia again to the point at which the doctor ordered me away. We seem to be pounding the Ruhr and Southern Italy into rubble from the air, which rather sickens such of us as remain at all civilised. There is too much striking both here and in America. Democracy's sons persist in proving that their creed and background are inadequate to the waging of all-out war, while popular song-writers encourage them in the belief that their behaviour is magnificent. It's a sad contrast to the days of the big raids here, when the heroism of civilians was a reality and not a headline. Yet, tired and bored and irritable as we all are, we are getting used to the bloody thing almost as if it were natural. Winifred of course calls me over the coals for my low opinion of human nature!

JULY 14TH

The invasion of Sicily seems to have begun well, but popular

118

reactions singularly flat. Or is it just the same lack of imagination that in 1940 helped so much to save us from the fate of France?

JULY 18TH

My parents' golden wedding day, and the four of us, all together by in the circumstances outrageous luck, able to give them a lunch at the Savoy. If anyone deserved good fortune to mark the occasion it is my mother. Though we have never been specially close, I am only too well aware of her incredible unselfishness, patience and affection—indeed of what I owe them both on all counts. They deserve to see peace return, and to enjoy a few years of tranquillity again. The thought of another winter of war almost insupportable. To get on with any writing at the moment quite impossible.

AUGUST IST

Our democracy persists in proving just how fit it is to conduct great affairs by ignoring all official requests not to go away *en masse* for conventional holidays. It crowds into railway stations and on to beaches, though there may be no trains, and no food or accommodation at journey's end. Was it Talleyrand who said that the majority of mankind always has been and always will be composed of imbeciles? Irving Reiss, once of Columbia Workshop, lunched with me and surprised me with his opinion that since 1940 the average American's view of this country has fundamentally changed for the better. I only hope he is right. Ted Liveing back from Cairo with fantastic stories of Basil Dean in the Near East. Too weary the other night to notice that my black-out curtain was not drawn when I got in late. Summoned to Bow Street in the mildly depressing company of various ladies of the town and was fined five shillings! John Dickson Carr's *Appointment with Fear* series has turned out a winner to my pleasure. Much distressed by poor J.C's suicide, though he may well be fortunately out of everything. His case is a clear demonstration of that fatal philosophy of the Thirties: admit to every failing, and pretend that the admission means that the failings don't matter. But it is horrible to think of the state of mind into which anyone must get before taking such a step. Not very pleasant to get more than one anonymous letter accusing me of responsibility. Told yesterday, under a pledge of deadly secrecy, that a separate Russo-German peace was well on the cards, and that the first clause allowed for ten million Germans to be scheduled for the rebuilding of devastated Russian towns! Anyone who believes that will believe anything.

OCTOBER 14TH

The Luftwaffe came back over London last week, and I was forced to shift one of the *Appointment with Fear* plays down from Studio 8A to the basement of Broadcasting House within twenty minutes of the warning. Both actors and the girl studio assistants behaved admirably, and all went well.

DECEMBER 8TH

Much talk of German secret weapons, ranging from batteries of rocket-guns which will destroy London to a tunnel to be driven under the Channel and lined with some terrific explosive! The B.B.C. is taking it seriously enough to produce a fresh set of evacuation plans. A most interesting dinner the other night with X. who—in connection with our projected railway feature *Junction X*—took me to the subterranean communications headquarters under what was once Down Street tube station. We had a superb meal 1750 feet below ground in a room reminding one of a miniature liner saloon decorated by Woolworth. Our host and his wife seemed content with the life of almost complete troglodytes. I gather that W.S.C. used the place on occasion for sleep in bad raids.

1944. JUNE 22ND

We are once again under fire. With the arrival of the buzz-bombs— *alias* doodle-bugs—London is once more a danger zone. I confess to a certain feeling of stimulation combined with considerable alarm! The risk is of course not great, but the suspense factor is considerable, and they have come as close to Long Acre as the corner of Endell Street, which is too near to be pleasant. X. just back from Normandy with a cargo of smuggled, and delicious, butter and cheese, and hideous stories of Montgomery, Coningham, and

Leigh-Mallory behaving like a cast of rival prima donnas! The Werth book on the siege of Leningrad is good and moving.

AUGUST 14TH

It looks as if this last lap is going to be a bad, grim business. The reaction to the flying-bombs shows how raw people's nerves are and how low resistance has fallen. People rush into and out of London like scalded cats. Railway stations are crammed and trains made hideous by crowds going to and fro without rhyme, reason or much in the way of objective. Things not helped by the situation being monstrously over-written in the papers, and scare stuff churned out daily regarding the so-called V2. I admit to being scared by the beastly things. But people should either admit that they can't take it, get out, and stay out—or they should hang on and put on something of an act. The other day at the Hanover three-quarters of the clientèle went under the tables and wallowed there like captive balloons. S. and I sat tight over our coffee, which may have been foolish but at any rate was not ludicrous. At the moment I can think of little but the second Warsaw tragedy. It seems obvious that the Russians have successfully promoted the rising with the aim of putting the best Poles on to the barricades where the Germans may dispose of them before the Russians move in, which is *Realpolitik* with a vengeance. Even the *Daily Mirror* jibbed at the notion that it wasn't possible to fly ammunition and airborne troops across the width of the Vistula. The del Giudice possibility has cropped up again.

1945. JANUARY 9TH

I have been monstrously idle over this record, but the close of 1944 with the war reviving with Rundstedt's counter-stroke in the Ardennes and the arrival of the V2's has also from my personal point of view been busier than ever. To my surprise the stock of the Department, which had been deplorably low, suddenly and surprisingly rose with Lindsay Wellington's appointment as Controller of Programmes. To be given some credit, and to have one's advice taken, made a most agreeable change! Notable were a production of *Ghosts* with Gladys Young and James McKechnie both superb;

a serialisation by Norman Edwards of *Barlasch of the Guard*, with Freddie Lloyd in the name part; and Howard Agg's excellent adaptation of Maugham's *Gentleman in the Parlour* with delightful music by Antony Hopkins. Dallas Bower and I duly made a film treatment of Duff Cooper's *Talleyrand* for del Giudice, which has resulted in our getting the assignment to tackle Churchill's *Marlborough*, which is frightening in its complexities and implications. I still don't really see myself as a producer of films. Meanwhile, between one thing and another this diary suffers from almost consistent neglect.

MAY 2ND

The European war seems for practical purposes over, with the Russians in the centre of Berlin, Mussolini lynched, and Hitler reported killed last night. At the other side of the world, however, the shadows seem to be lengthening over San Francisco with relations between Russia and the West worsening daily. Not the least evil aspect of this is the general refusal to face the fact that this is the case. There is every sign that the majority of human beings are capable neither of logical thinking nor of truthful memory. Already there is talk of 'a next war' in tones of a dreary hopelessness. Of course everyone is weary to death, but it seems as if the victory has come too late, and that its taste is somehow not all that sweet. The office has been a chaos of writing and rewriting topical victory programmes without much conviction, let alone inspiration; and I seem to have put a cat among pigeons by my memorandum on television and its likely effects upon my department.

MAY 8TH

The Germans threw in their hand yesterday, and there was a certain amount of mafficking last night—crowds, drunks, a bonfire in Coventry Street, and a good deal of mixed bunting with Polish colours conspicuous by their absence. The principal reaction, I feel, is of flatness and weariness. It went on too long, and whether the destruction of the German economy by Bomber Command will not also result in the starving or death from disease of thousands all over Europe only time can tell. Is appeasement of Russia now to be the cry, as was the appeasement of Germany in 1938? It's a grim and sobering thought. I can feel no urge to join in frolicking in Piccadilly. I don't even experience the gratitude I should for having survived the Second German War as successfully as I did the First. At the end of the latter I was eighteen with everything before me. At the end of the former I am forty-five, and can only anticipate formally a promised new world by abandoning this journal for good, hoping that the happiness which has no history is still attainable.

CHAPTER SEVEN

Round and about Television

IN THE course of my professional life I was so fortunate as to be offered two outstanding opportunities. The first was in 1929, when I was made Productions Director at Savoy Hill. The second was almost exactly twenty years later, when I was made head of all B.B.C. drama, including television. I think I am entitled to claim that I took the first of these opportunities with both hands. I am bound to confess that I threw the second disastrously away. The pages that follow are intended to provide explanation, not excuse. Inevitably they contain a good deal of criticism of other people, both direct and implied. I must state without equivocation that fundamentally I blame myself most of all. I could have taken the opportunity. I could have done the job. I failed because of my own weaknesses and shortcomings. It is small consolation that someone with the talent and integrity of Michael Barry was to find, in his turn, that it was beyond him.

Two comments were made widely when the appointment was made: that it was impossible for a single individual to tackle the different problems of sound and television drama, particularly with the former in Portland Place and the latter in Alexandra Palace or at Shepherd's Bush; and that I was really not qualified because of my ignorance of television.

Neither comment was justified. It was perfectly well understood after discussion in Broadcasting House that for a year at least, and probably longer, I should give all my attention to television, leaving my old department in the hands of my deputy. After which the problem would be reconsidered. As to being a television 'new boy', most people seem simply to have forgotten what had happened before the Television Service closed down at the beginning of the Second German War. I had in fact been vaguely associated with television from the earliest beginnings of the Service, when Eustace

Robb and Cecil Madden were doing their best to make bricks without straw in the basement of Broadcasting House, and my principal recollection is of their importation into the studio of a sea-lion and of its pungently fish-like smell. I had taken part in the rehearsals of the first television play ever transmitted. This went out on the Baird system from the Baird studio, which was situated within a stone's throw of my flat in Long Acre. Lance Sieveking produced, with his typical combination of imagination and ingenuity; and I would have played the title role in *The Man with the Flower in His Mouth* but for an unfortunate attack of influenza which necessitated my replacement by Earle Grey.

From the first moments of that rehearsal I was a convert to belief in the future of television drama, and profoundly interested in its development. I realised it was bound to come. I believed that when it did come it would prove a serious competitor to radio drama, even that it might ultimately supplant it. These convictions were in my mind when I suggested my secondment to Alexandra Palace in 1939. I went, as I have said, as an individual producer with no sort of departmental authority, merely to learn the elements of the business. I thought that it was likely, if not certain, that my future might lie with television drama, and I wanted to be prepared. I had not forgotten the state of abysmal ignorance with which I had been handicapped in 1929. This education was curtly interrupted by the war. Of course I had not become an expert. In terms of producing *expertise* I could not hold a candle to people like Michael Barry, Royston Morley, or Dallas Bower. None the less I learned my ABC. And I fancy that those with most experience of the medium would have agreed with me at that time that the techniques were so fluid and experimental that those who knew most knew also that for practical purposes everything still lay in the future. Enthusiasm had worked miracles in the face of incredulity, obstruction, and lack of facilities. But, with all praise to the enthusiasts so determinedly running before they had learned to walk, the foundations of a genuine service had still to be laid.

During those few summer months of 1939 I produced two plays for television: *Mr Jones Dines Out* and a short piece of my own, *Ending It*. I was involved in rehearsals of Somerset Maugham's *The Circle*—in a mews off Marylebone High Street—when I got the message to drop everything and leave for Evesham (code-wor —Hogsnorton), where Drama Department and an embryonic repertory company were to be quartered during the early months of the war. The Television Service was closed down. And for five years I had too many other things on my mind to give much consideration to its hypothetical future.

When that future materialised in 1945 I, like a good many other people, was tired, suffering a good deal from nervous reaction, and feeling that most virtue had gone out of me. More than anything else I wanted a change. From my point of view it was a thousand pities that, if I was to go to television at all, I did not go then. I only learned, when I read Maurice Gorham's book *Sound and Fury*, when I was in America in 1948, that this had been the original intention of the powers that were. However, Gorham, who was the new Controller of Television, vetoed the appointment. He set his face rigidly against the addition to his staff of 'people who had earned their positions in sound radio'.

The point was arguable—but I was not given the opportunity to argue it. From the date of his appointment until his resignation in 1947 Gorham, with an enthusiasm and determination worthy of a better cause, laboured and sorrowed to achieve his own *imperium in imperio*, to destroy any vestige of Broadcasting House control over the Television Service. He certainly had a hand to play. Unfortunately he consistently overplayed it. I believe that his Irish temperament set him on principle 'agin the Government', no matter what the government might be. It apparently irked him profoundly that he should be expected to address the Director-General as 'sir'. Also he had gone too far rather too fast. We had been friends and colleagues when we were both under Eric Maschwitz on the *Radio Times*, of which ultimately he became editor, and I preserve pleasant recollections of draught stout and ham rolls consumed in his company at Mooney's in the Strand. But during the war he was given charge of the North American Service, and later of the Light Programme. He was referred to as 'Haley's rocket', and referred to himself as being 'one of the two B.B.C. live wires', the other being Norman Collins. He became opinionated and dictatorial to a degree which made working with him more and more difficult. We clashed a good deal when he was in charge of the

Light Programme; first, because he did not conceal his intention to Americanise it as far as he was able, a process which I thought both vulgar and stupid; secondly, he insisted on the soap opera as a permanent programme-item because it could be counted on to produce satisfactory listener research figures. These things, no doubt, were in his mind when he refused to have me at Alexandra Palace.

The personal angle is of little importance. What was significant about it was that it was symptomatic of an attitude that basically bedevilled B.B.C. television. I would emphasise at once that Gorham, and those who agreed with him, were by no means entirely to blame. In its early days not even the personality and drive of Gerald Cock could prevent television from being regarded at Broadcasting House as the Cinderella of the B.B.C. It was thrust away out of sight. It was neglected. It was starved. Everything possible was done to settle chips on the shoulders of everyone who worked at Alexandra Palace, so that many of them came to think of themselves largely in terms of nuisance value. It was an attitude that incited the Television Service to cry up its wares too soon and too loudly; to tackle subjects like ballet and opera and elaborate full-length plays at a time when both gear and technique had only reached a stage suitable for quite elementary programme-items. In 1939 this Cinderella was loudly proclaiming her presence at the Ball, in spite of the failure of the Fairy Godmother to provide her with the appropriate costume and slippers.

The reopening of the Service in 1945 was an opportunity to forget such bad old days and start afresh. It might be true that television had little to learn from the successes of, or the experts in, sound. It was certainly true that television could have learned something from the mistakes that had been made in sound. To widen the gulf fixed between Broadcasting House and Alexandra Palace, to establish as a Median and Persian law that practitioners in sound must automatically be both suspect and incompetent, may have seemed a fine gesture of independence to Maurice Gorham, flushed with his new Controllership which gave him access to the inner councils of the Corporation. At less exalted levels it produced ill-feeling, bad blood, and much misunderstanding. I was to experience the results to my cost, when I ultimately went to

Alexandra Palace in 1949. Individualism is a virtue. Rancid individualism can be the devil.

My opportunity when it ultimately came could not have been less expected. It reached me in New York towards the end of that 'year of grace' which I had been offered by Sir William Haley as an alternative when I had suggested to him that the time had come for me to resign. Norman Collins had succeeded Gorham as Controller of Television, and paid me the compliment of asking my advice regarding the choice of a head for his Drama Department. I replied with one or two suggestions—of which I remember that Tyrone Guthrie was one—and at the end of my letter asked, not very seriously, whether he would consider me *faute de mieux*. I was completely staggered to discover on my return to England that the idea had proved acceptable both at Alexandra Palace and at Broadcasting House.

The omens seemed fair. I did not know Norman Collins well, but I enjoyed his novels, and, following upon one or two disputes, we had, I believed, achieved a mutual respect for each other's work when he was in charge of the Light Programme. My immediate programme chief would be Cecil McGivern, whom I both liked and admired enormously. He had been the most brilliant of features producers in sound during the war, and there are still people who remember his *Junction X* and *Bomb Doors Open!* Since those days he had done a stint in films only to meet with frustration and disappointment. I knew him well, and looked forward to the prospect of working with him again. I set myself grimly to the job of learning to drive a motor-car, and in the fulness of time—if something to the public danger—drove myself to Alexandra Palace in pretty good heart. I hardly thought of Muswell Hill as one of the Delectable Mountains. It turned out to compare unfavourably with the Hill Difficulty.

I was prepared to enter an atmosphere quite different from that of Portland Place. To an extent I even welcomed the prospect. But until I got there I had no idea of just how different that atmosphere was going to be. As far as television drama was concerned I found myself back in almost precisely the same situation that I had faced at Savoy Hill in 1929. Apart from occasional and spasmodic suggestions from McGivern—who was supposed to be frying more important fish—there was no sort of direction. There was no policy. There was a collection of producers of very varying merit, who were supposed to, but did not, form a department. There was an officially acknowledged Senior Producer in the talented person of George More O'Ferrall. There was a Drama Coordinator, with ill-defined responsibilities, who had expected to get my job and resigned when he failed to do so.

As I saw it, the case was one of starting again from scratch with two main objectives in view. The first was to make a genuine working Drama Department for the Television Service. The second was to produce a workable television drama policy. In my innocence I found myself running my head against a brick wall both above and below.

This was sufficiently discouraging. In my previous experience I had found that when on occasion I had trouble with my producers I could always count on support from my Controller or, if the issue warranted it, from my Director-General. When I felt that I had to argue an issue with my Controller I could count on the backing of the professional opinion of my department. This war on two fronts simultaneously was something new to me. Apart from overweighting the odds against my getting what I wanted it made me feel lonely and miserable. If McGivern did not want a policy for his drama, and if drama producers resented a representative spokesman, I could not help but feel that I was wasting my time.

My situation as it developed *vis-à-vis* Cecil McGivern distressed me particularly. Nothing could destroy my admiration nor my personal liking for him, but I was compelled swiftly to realise that he experienced a profound discomfort in being in a position to give orders to someone who had in the past been largely responsible for bringing him from Newcastle to London, and under whom he had worked as a producer in Features. I failed to persuade him that I did not in the least resent the change in our relative positions in the hierarchy. Having once been trained for service in a regiment whose tradition is that all orders, however seemingly fantastic, impossible or unreasonable, are simply acknowledged with the word 'sir', I have never objected to authority as such. And so long as authority has known its business I have welcomed it. Such an attitude was as incomprehensible to McGivern as it had been to Maurice Gorham.

I

What happened in practice was that McGivern saw as little of me personally as he could, preferring to send me curt directives in writing to decide issues which could only have been settled satisfactorily in discussion. This resulted in misunderstandings, in mutual exasperation, in interminable correspondence, and in a hideous waste of time.

He agreed that both a policy and planned schedules were necessary for television plays. Both depended on foresight, forethought, and consistency. The policy problem was far more difficult than it had been in sound, where alternative programmes made it possible to channel different types of play to differing types of listener. With only a single programme to achieve a balance which should satisfy the philistine and the highbrow, devotees of thrillers and lovers of the classic drama, the difficulties of framing a policy and creating schedules which should implement it were formidable. For McGivern it was simply a question of 'doing as much good stuff as possible', of sensing when the main body of viewers was getting restless, and then of whipping into the schedule an Ibsen, a Shaw, or a Shakespeare, to satisfy the critics and bolster up prestige. It is an attitude which, both with the B.B.C. and the independent companies, has persisted with the years. I still find it inadequate.

He was also passionately addicted to off-the-cuff and last-minute changes. He would hear of a new *diseuse* in Paris or a remarkable comedy duo just arrived from the States, and I would be told that a play, often already in rehearsal, must be changed for one costing less money because the budget was strained—it always was—and he needed the balance to pay for his new enthusiasm. The general programme may have been vitalised and brightened up: the drama schedule was knocked to pieces, its balance ruined. That this was bound to happen he could not or would not see.

Worse than this was the tradition among producers, crystallised under the Gorham *régime*, of that individualism which I have called 'rancid'. With no established script unit, and with no departmental control worth the name, it had been left almost entirely to each individual producer to choose the plays that he would handle according to his own tastes and whims. This obviously made balanced scheduling impossible. And while I am strongly averse from compelling a producer to handle any play with which he is not in sympathy, and while it is true that a producer will naturally work more enthusiastically on a play which he particularly wants to produce, I know from experience that producers are by no means the best judges of the type of piece they produce best. Clowns long to play Hamlet. Admirable producers of Ibsen yearn to handle light comedy. The assigning of the right play to the right producer seemed to me always one of my most important responsibilities at Broadcasting House. It seemed to me even more important at Alexandra Palace. I was not surprised that the producers themselves disliked the change. I was bewildered and affronted when to that dislike was added the disapproval of McGivern.

While determined to get my own way over choice of material, I was able to sympathise to some extent with the producers' feelings in the matter. Their inability to see eye to eye with me over another principle of our work was far more serious. Even in Broadcasting House I had always felt that our output of drama had increased unduly, was still increasing, and ought to be diminished. A groan would run round the programme board when at regular intervals I pleaded for 'fewer and better plays'. Quality as opposed to Quantity was known as my King Charles' head. Still the point was taken, and I was never pressed into commitments for which there were inadequate production facilities or inadequate rehearsal time. (I except the early period of the war, when all broadcasting was governed by considerations of emergency.) At Alexandra Palace, with only two studios—one of which was much too small—at our disposal, the regular production of two full-length plays a week was beyond our capacity, if a proper professional standard was to be maintained. About one piece in every three was properly rehearsed. Again and again one heard described laughingly how a play had been televised with a final act unseen by the cameras until the actual transmission.

I expected to find that producers would dislike this state of affairs as much as I did. I was wrong. I have never seen the adage that 'everything will come all right on the night' so monstrously abused. Not only had television producers been expected to work under such handicaps and surmount ensuing crises by improvisation and ingenuity, they had come to pride themselves on this state of affairs. It was part of the *mystique* of the Television Service, naturally incomprehensible to outsiders.

This was a straightforward professional issue—there was of course more than one aspect of the policy issue—over which I believed I could tackle McGivern, and, if necessary, Norman Collins, with confidence. In fact my preliminary approaches were sympathetically received. McGivern, however, wanted to know if my point of view was supported by producers whose experience of work in television studios had been longer and more varied than mine. This was reasonable enough. I put the question to a producers' meeting accordingly. My proposal amounted to this: that we should, as a department, give our opinion in writing that no play should be televised without a minimum of three camera rehearsals, even if this implied cutting our output of drama by a third, which I anticipated it would. Two voices were raised in my support. A few were silently disapproving. Most were outraged, and made no bones about saying so. I was asking them to admit that their present production standards were not as good as they ought to be. (They were not.) To subscribe to my opinion would imply that they knew they were falling down on the job. (It would not have done anything of the sort.) Of course facilities were inadequate, but if they had allowed themselves to be held back by that sort of thing, television drama would never have got anywhere. (This was at least arguable.) What about all the 'rave' notices gained by television plays in the press? (Few of such notices were written by recognised critics, and any 'new thing', with the publicity interest of television, can count on plenty of newspaper coverage.) In short I had grievously offended their *amour propre* and was proposing to denigrate their professional capacities. McGivern, who could hardly have been expected to welcome a smaller output of plays for the sake of his programmes as a whole, concluded that I was trying to rush my fences; that I was trying to act with insufficient knowledge of the facts. Things went on as before. And though in my own production of *St Joan* I got my three camera rehearsals by flatly refusing to handle the play without them, an average of two or one and a half day's camera rehearsal remained the convention. I get the impression that even today it has not been significantly extended.

I should perhaps make it plain for the benefit of the layman that a play can be rehearsed *outside the studio* for three weeks or a month. *The camera rehearsals are the only ones that really count*, except for the learning of lines and the rough plotting of moves.

Concerning the operation of gramophone records of music and effects from the Control Gallery and the use of microphones in general I was more positively critical. In these instances it could hardly be suggested that I did not know what I was talking about. I objected to gramophone operators knitting socks while they were on the job, and I thought, and said, that there was more to the use of microphones in television plays than taking care to keep them 'out of shot'. The implication that Alexandra Palace had anything to learn from current Broadcasting House practice in these matters was hotly resented.

Such was the atmosphere in which for eighteen months and during seven days a week I worked harder than I have ever worked in my life with—as far as I could and can judge—no good effect whatsoever, except the quite fortuitous result of the *Party Manners* row which seems to have freed the B.B.C. permanently from any danger of political censorship.

But let me repeat that I was principally to blame. I should have been more patient, more prepared to temper the wind. I could have been much more tactful. I should probably have insisted on a personal show-down with McGivern, or at worst gone to Norman Collins over his head. I should have been more courageous and much more far-sighted. I should have thickened my skin and stuck to my guns. After all, I had been through much the same sort of thing before, and all had turned out for the best.

Unfortunately now I was twenty years older. Even more unfortunately my private life during this period was complicated by a state of affairs which nagged at my conscience, excoriated my nervous system, and lowered such self-esteem as I possessed. When I could escape the Alexandra Palace frying-pan, it was to find myself in a fire of personal problems and self-reproach. Between the two I felt that I was making a misery of my life for no apparent purpose.

I said as much to Sir William Haley, who was as kind to me on this occasion as he had been over the *Party Manners* imbroglio and my 'year of grace'. My face was saved handsomely. It appeared that

I had been missed at Broadcasting House. There seemed to be still plenty of life in the old dog, radio drama. Even nominal responsibility for sound and television drama combined had been proved too much for one man. I could take my choice. So I returned to Broadcasting House, taking no sheaves with me, and leaving, I imagine, a good many hearts the lighter in the Television Service for my going.

The disaster was not unrelieved. There had been the enchanting friendliness and wonderfully adept co-operation of the camera-crews. There had been the excitement of the move to Lime Grove from Muswell Hill and the first sight of four big new studios. There had been the *St Joan* of Constance Cummings, which lives among my memories of great acting performances. There had been the outstanding production work of Michael Barry. There was, in occasional moments of calm and reflection, the realisation of all that the medium could do; what ultimately it was bound to do no matter how it might for the time being be mishandled.

For what my opinion may be worth, the greatest danger that faces television today is precisely the same as that which faced it in the days when I saw it at close quarters. Even more than sound radio television is a Moloch. Its capacity for devoration is terrifying, and the eye is more easily and more quickly surfeited than the ear. In its early stages television tried to do too much owing to the enthusiasm of devotees determined to show how much they could do and how quickly they could do it. The same motivation has today been supplied by competition with the commercial companies. That the cry should continually go up from viewers for more and more television is natural enough. Listeners in their time did the same thing. When the same cry is taken up by responsible programme executives it is necessary to look the ensuing problem very straight in the eye: the problem of the supply of adequate programme material. With the evidence before our eyes of the present output, can anyone be sincerely convinced that the writers, the actors, the personalities, the music, even the gimmicks, exist to provide material for the B.B.C. Second Channel, let alone the alternative envisaged in the future for the independents?

The answer is that no one can. But I cannot remember having seen the fact stated in the House of Commons debates on the

Pilkington Report, in correspondence in the press, in the official hand-outs that have been issued from time to time both by the B.B.C. television moguls and the executives of the independent companies. And when existing programmes have to make do with mildly fetichist absurdities like *The Avengers*, formula-ridden hack-work like *The Third Man*, the domestic sedation of *Compact*, and a steady supply of out-of-date films, the prospect for the Second Channel looks, to say the least of it, dim. Nor is the intelligent viewer much consoled by the occasional *Hedda Gabler*—cut down to fifty minutes and both over-starred and miscast; a *Cherry Orchard* with its last act played as though the dialogue had been written by Mr Coward; or a *Lysistrata*, also cut to ribbons, and as a result largely unintelligible apart from its 'nubbly bits'.

So far it has been impossible to convince the people responsible for programmes both in television and sound of the attraction of rarity. If the B.B.C. Second Channel would confine itself to the production of one absolutely first-rate programme each evening— play, documentary feature, musical, or opera—or if one of the independent companies would experiment under the slogan 'High quality advertising for high quality goods', I think it might be agreeably surprised by the result. The prestige acquired by such a programme would inevitably be enormous. Television as a whole would be relieved of the reproach that the greater part of it is directed at a public almost self-consciously moronic. Writers, actors, and producers, would get the same kind of 'shot in the arm' that was given them when the Third Programme was first launched by B.B.C. sound. It is no adequate answer to say, as might justi-fiably be said, that the Third Programme has become too academic too *avant-garde*, too intellectually snobbish. If practice has fallen short the principle was sound. Must television always be too proud to learn from the older medium's mistakes?

CHAPTER EIGHT

The Second String

ONE OF my recurring difficulties during my period of service with the B.B.C. was to persuade my colleagues to believe that I was in some sort a professional writer. This was the more strange because my first novel, *Black Gallantry*, was published by Constable just before I joined the Corporation, and I had made a gentleman's agreement with my superiors that I should be at liberty to continue private writing, no matter what the official regulations on the subject might be. Between 1928 and 1963 I had published seventeen novels, two volumes of autobiography, and four books written in collaboration with Eric Maschwitz. During the same period I also wrote a number of stage plays.

This considerable output raised unworthy thoughts and suspicions in certain quarters. Either, it was whispered, I must be employing a 'ghost', or I must be misusing my office desk and the Corporation's time. I confess that when I look back at the scope and volume of my B.B.C. activities during those years I am a little bewildered by the consistent industry of someone as congenitally lazy as I know myself to be. But the explanation was simple. First and most important, I liked writing. Secondly, I spent neither time nor energy on any form of physical exercise. Thirdly, until the war changed the whole pattern of my living, I seldom felt the need for more than six hours' sleep. Last and by no means least, I depended for my little luxuries, and largely for my holidays abroad, on whatever money I could earn apart from my official salary. There also hovered vaguely at the back of my mind a theory, which with the years became a conviction, that when I should ultimately leave the B.B.C. I should need a second string. I can never be sufficiently grateful that I yielded to that conviction.

I admit that it irked me that the Corporation made the least possible use of such talent as I possessed in this particular field. I had been able to persuade the powers that were that it was an actual advantage for the head of a producing department to handle productions personally, thereby familiarising himself with the details of the business for which he was responsible and with the problems which faced the individual producers on his staff. On the other hand my inclination, natural to any writer closely connected with a new and fascinating medium, to write radio plays was discouraged and even on occasion frowned upon. Of course I did in fact write a number of such plays, even though for many years I received no payment for them. (This was neither as unreasonable nor as ungenerous as it sounds. It was clearly undesirable for outside writers to be given matter for genuine grievance by my being in a situation in which I could accept and pay for work of my own.) I believed in the writer for radio who was in a position to produce his own work. In the cinema M. Clair and Mr Chaplin—not that I would class myself for an instant with men of such outstanding gifts —have shown the immense advantages and opportunities for experiment offered to the producer who can also write a script with all the knowledge that comes from intimate association with the technicalities of the medium. It was a theory that was not to be accepted in British broadcasting until Laurence Gilliam established his team of writer-producers in the post-war Features Department, and Louis MacNeice—to take only a single example—made history with *The Dark Tower*.

It well may be that my own attitude to my writing was insufficiently serious for it to be taken seriously by other people. Whether in terms of drama or novel, I did not look beyond the telling of tales. I thought of myself as a story-teller, not as a psychologist or a social reformer. During my formative years I had had the greatest pleasure in my reading from Kipling and Maugham, Galsworthy and de Maupassant, Anthony Hope and Seton Merriman, John Buchan, Rider Haggard and Conan Doyle, Dumas and Victor Hugo. I knew that I had neither the talent nor the inclinations of 'the writer for writers'. I found little appeal in the gathering of self-conscious intellectuals about the base of their ivory tower. My creative approach tended to remain that of the small boy who had managed to escape the more unpleasant attentions of his little playfellows by telling them stories in the dormitory after lights-out: serial stories which it was inadvisable ever to bring to an end.

There had been a period—during my time at Oxford and two or three years afterwards—when, largely influenced by Hugh Walpole, then at the height of his popularity, I wrote three novels of devastating tedium and adolescent self-searching. Fortunately they were never published. More fortunately one of them caught the eye of Michael Sadleir who, over an exceptionally good luncheon, advised me to stop writing about things I knew and didn't like, and try tackling subjects which I would find sympathetic, however ignorant of them I might be. Accordingly I abandoned the fringes of bohemian London for the marches of Poland as the background to *Black Gallantry* and enjoyed the change immoderately. I invented a family, largely a sublimation of my Polish forebears, whose offshoots and adventures kept me busy according to the best Ruritanian traditions until Hitler's War destroyed Poland and seemed finally to put an end to the possibilities of fictional romance.

The books written with Eric Maschwitz were even more frivolous an occupation. The first—the only one that achieved much success —was *Death at Broadcasting House*. I have mentioned elsewhere how Eric, convinced that there must be a market for a story whose subject, willy-nilly, was being advertised twelve hours a day, wore out his generous impulses by trying to persuade his more indigent friends, one after the other, to make use of the idea. All refused. It was then that I, who had always felt a certain exasperation that such a 'natural' should be handed on a plate to an outsider, induced Eric to combine the writing with a holiday with me in the South of France. We took with us—I thought rather foolhardily—one of the Corporation's secretaries, and all of the book's seventy thousand odd words were dictated in sixteen days. As we anticipated, the result was satisfactory. It was serialised. It was published in the United States. Lord Reith accepted a copy and wrote a charming letter of commendation, finding fault only with our invention in that we had described him as calling a special meeting of the Board of Governors to consider the results of murder on the sacred premises! This, he wrote, he would never have dreamed of doing.

We imagined, in consequence, that we had a fool-proof film property on our hands. We were mistaken. For the best part of a year we besieged one established British film company after another with requests that they should make some easy money for themselves, and incidentally for us. The deafest of ears were turned —until three imaginative individuals brought together by Mr Hugh Percival formed a company specially to make the picture with a capital of some sixteen thousand pounds. (This was of course in 1930-31.) The film was made, in one day over a schedule of twenty-eight, for rather more than eighteen thousand pounds, and eventually grossed—so I was informed—ninety thousand. Our share, alas, was not proportionate. But I had the added fun—and salary— of acting myself as Director of Drama in the picture with a cast that included Jack Hawkins, Ian Hunter, and a galaxy of contemporary radio personalities.

The publishers, less hide-bound than the film industry, urged us to make *Death at Broadcasting House* the first of a sequence of thrillers. Unfortunately we were both too busy with other things to cope adequately with this suggestion. We had on a shelf the script of a play dealing with a dope-ring which used the underground rivers of London for its nefarious activities. It had been produced, hopefully and disastrously, in Blackpool in the middle of winter, and we had attended the first night, wearing tails and white ties, to find an audience of about two hundred in an ice-cold theatre which should have held about two thousand. This tragic disappointment was the basis of *Under London*, which was received more charitably than it deserved. In *Death as an Extra* we made shameless use of the experience we had acquired in the film-studio during the making of *Death at Broadcasting House*, while a holiday in the Hungarian capital provided the setting for *Death in Budapest*, which turned out as a far better tourists' guide-book than detective story.

By this time Eric Maschwitz, as the result of the huge success of his musical *Balalaika*, had forsaken Portland Place for Hollywood. Further practical collaboration was no longer feasible. This I regretted for a variety of reasons, but the likelihood of an unwritten masterpiece was not one of them.

During the war years time for private writing—leaving aside all question of inclination—became increasingly difficult to find. *Confident Morning*, to which there are a number of references in my diary, took the greater part of three years to complete. Perhaps for that very reason it is, in my prejudiced view, by far the best of my books. It is certainly my favourite, and I still think it was unlucky in that its publication coincided with a shortage of paper which forbade its reprinting. As an amateur student of the Napoleonic period I had always been fascinated particularly by Elba, the Hundred Days, and the final squalid tragedy of the epilogue on St Helena. Also I believe that as a subject for fictional treatment there is nothing more promising than the historical character of whom almost nothing is known apart from some brief harlequin-like appearance. One such is the Polish Captain Piontkowski, who turned up so mysteriously and so unwelcome at Longwood with an invented past, only to vanish again into obscurity. In these cases imagination can be given free rein without doing violence to Clio. So I fictionalised the story of Piontkowski in *Confident Morning*, and for once felt genuine indignation when it achieved neither commercial success nor *succès d'estime*. I find comfort in insisting to myself that *Confident Morning* dawned untimely.

With the return of peace the problem of defining some new writing objective became acute; Ruritania, together with other less picturesque eastern European states, had vanished into the limbo behind the Iron Curtain. As far as adventure, espionage, and deeds of derring-do were concerned Truth had reduced Fiction to the level of an inadequate and poorly-rehearsed understudy. Most readers had had enough and more than enough of the sensational, often in the unpleasant shape of personal experience. I was the more fortunate, when I was granted my year of grace by Sir William Haley, to have the opportunity of spending it in the completely strange environment of the United States. Eight months spent in an apartment in Greenwich Village, and journeyings which took me under most agreeable auspices from Charlottesville to New Orleans, from Dallas to Los Angeles, from San Francisco by way of the Grand Canyon to Santa Fe, blew away accumulated cobwebs and fixed ideas to the extent of stimulating the writing of two plays and a critical survey of the contemporary American scene. I came back to England with a certain contempt hardening in my mind for the manufacture of thrillers in a cloud-cuckoo land.

My publishers did not altogether agree. For them my reputation, such as it was, was that of a writer of thrillers, and I could produce no evidence to show that I was capable of better things. In any case, however the case might stand at the moment, the market for sensational fiction would certainly come back, and it was one of steady reliability. Little or no enthusiasm was evinced for the idea that I might be added to the number of established 'general list' novelists. Nor was my agent any more encouraging.

I have the impression that over the last forty years or so relations between authors and their various publishers have changed considerably; have even, to some extent, deteriorated. No doubt this is due to altered conditions in the book trade rather than to personalities, but a certain intimacy—I had almost written 'cosiness' —seems to have vanished with the rose. In the Twenties when I met my first agent, and Michael Sadleir took me under his wing, I would go to their offices in much the same mood of expectancy and friendliness as I felt when visiting my solicitor or my family doctor. One's present welfare and future well-being were as high on the agenda of such meetings as arguments concerning economic detail. No doubt a good deal of time was wasted. Everybody seemed to have more time to waste. No doubt so much tempering of winds to shorn lambs was unnecessarily indulgent. Today one's interviews are with courteous, eminently pleasant, but almost always also eminently brisk business-men. Probably they sell more of one's books, but the feeling creeps in that one would be no less highly regarded if one happened to produce cheese or cutlery instead of writing. However, I would not wish to seem ungrateful, and the old-fashioned publisher with the peculiarly personal touch is probably as out-dated under contemporary conditions of publishing as is the old-fashioned general practitioner under the National Health Service.

In the event my publishers were justified. The first two books that I wrote after my return from America were in fact novels, as opposed to being thrillers or detective stories, though it is true that one was flavoured with espionage, and the second described the background and influences that led ultimately to murder. *The High Jump* appeared in a general list and sold indifferently. *Cat*, which was given the imprint of the Crime Club, did better than any of my books to date. So I resigned myself, at any rate for the time being, to being labelled as a 'crime-writer', joined the Crime Writers under the genial persuasiveness of Julian Symons, and made up my mind that, until my retirement from the B.B.C. at any rate, I would chronicle the adventures of a single detective. Hence *Gallows' Foot*, *To Bed at Noon*, *And Died So?*, and *The Goggle-Box Affair*, each of which was a Crime Club Choice. I will not deny for a moment the considerable pleasure and satisfaction that I have found in the company of Detective-Inspector Gregory Pellew, Humphrey the Viscount Clymping, and Lady Hannington. At least two of their joint experiences remain to be told. But writing this in the quiet of the country, looking out at the curve of the Downs against the sky, I begin to believe that before very long I shall find myself handling a different type of story—and to hope the result may not be too analogous to the efforts of the clown who at long last finds himself playing Hamlet.

I have occasionally been asked—as what author has not?—how I do my writing, and I am almost persuaded that it is a question to which laymen, and particularly voracious readers, genuinely want to know the answer. In the first place—though circumstances have too often compelled me to break the rule—I believe that one should try to write regularly and according to some sort of set routine. To wait upon inspiration is a snare and a delusion. When undistracted by other activities, I find that four hours of writing a day is about my limit, and an output of some two thousand words a day a reasonable average. Away from London I like to work for two hours in the morning and two in the afternoon with a break for a light meal and—if on a Mediterranean holiday—a siesta. In defiance of doctors I smoke, almost continuously, both a pipe and cigarettes. (Apprehension of lung cancer is modified by my recollection that only a few years ago medical opinion condemned pipes as likely to cause cancer of the tongue as vigorously as they now indict cigarettes.) As I write in longhand with a stiff wrist and the result is largely illegible, I work directly on to a typewriter. This, I fear, aggravates a natural disinclination to revise or rewrite. In the past and under pressure, as in the case of *Death at Broadcasting House*, I have dictated three books, but I do not wish to repeat the experiment. I am quite unable to use a dictaphone; and the critical eye of a typist, however personable or amiable, as she waits for the next sentence, I find quelling. Rather curiously, considering the vital importance of plots in all stories of adventure or crime, I am inclined to establish characters in a certain situation and follow up such developments as arise naturally from the impingement of the latter on the former. I do a considerable amount of thinking, for the most part in bed and in my bath, before I sit down to my typewriter, but such notes as I make are scrappy and for the most part discarded. I firmly believe that the characters in a story, if they have any merit, achieve a creative vitality of their own, and that it is unwise to prevent them from doing their fair share of the work. Unlike some authors I find encouragement and not distraction in some wide expanse of countryside or sea on which I can rest my eyes when fingers falter or the precise phrase will not come. I have never worked with such a sense of ease and relaxation as I did on the balcony of a friend's villa just above Taormina, looking down on the sweep of the Sicilian coast-line, the deep blue and glittering silver of the bay, and the black spears of the cypresses ringing the cemetery on a little head-land. At the same time I rather pride myself on being able to work anywhere and under almost any conditions. I wrote what I believe to be my best play in New York in a room so small that it contained with difficulty one chair and a small table; and another in the saloon of a small boat sailing up the Dalmatian coast simultaneously occupied by a Jugoslav students' jazz combination. I prefer to work in an open shirt, and I find a modicum of alcohol almost indispensable. I use an encyclopaedia less than I should, and a dictionary almost never. Finally I prefer to think of myself as a workman rather than as an artist, and I believe I have learned to accept criticism, even when needlessly virulent or ill-natured, with a slightly forced grin. I find that I nearly always like the completed typescript of a book, only to loathe it when I first see it in proof.

What I most wanted to do, like far too many other authors, was to write plays; not only plays, but successful plays. During the brief period when I was an actor and swiftly realised just how bad an actor I was, I found a good deal of consolation in the thought that this experience of the stage's traffic and the player's craft might be expected to prove useful to a would-be playwright. I was not mistaken. But I was to learn that of all the prizes that glitter on the author's horizon and haunt his dreams the stage success most resembles the golden apples of the Hesperides. The play's writing is no more than a first hesitant step. From that point one is engaged in a gamble presided over by the Goddess of Chance, with the odds as firmly adverse as on any table at Monte Carlo. All managers are sceptical. Most managers are capricious. Some managers are illiterate. An occasional manager is dishonest. Yet deprived of acceptance by a manager the play must gather dust in the desk drawer reserved for broken dreams. Star actors are seldom available —never at the right time. Good actors are rare, good producers rarer. Both are temperamental—and both distrust, even if they do not detest, authors on principle. Too often their attitude is justified. A play's chances can be killed by miscasting, by under-rehearsal, by over-rehearsal, by actors' misinterpretation, by a producer's fads. It can also be killed by the weather, a royal demise, political crisis or catastrophe, the illness of a leading player. Over all these factors the author has not, and cannot have, the slightest control. Yet his work is at their mercy. With these things in mind I cannot help feeling that it is something of a miracle that any play succeeds.

This, admittedly, is the conclusion of one who has failed as a playwright. That failure has been one of my bitterest disappointments. I know that when I lay a large part of that disappointment to the account of sheer bad luck I risk the obvious reaction of critical incredulity. Surely I was in a better position than most young men to have my plays read and seriously considered? Surely I had a certain amount of family 'pull' with actors and managers? Surely, once my position in the B.B.C. was established, I had a degree of personal prestige in the theatrical world? Finally every play that I wrote was in fact, and in one way or another, staged. If they did not succeed can I in fairness blame anyone but myself?

I rather wish that I could not. On three or four occasions success was so tantalisingly near that one brushed it with one's finger-tips before it was revealed as mirage. Perhaps it puts a blight upon work to want it so desperately to succeed. Perhaps I had merely over-drawn my good-luck account. I owe so much to fortune that it is only fair that I should have been reminded that there is a balance in these things. And, very occasionally, I managed to remind myself that success does not invariably equate with happiness.

My opening throw promised well. I was understudying in *The Ringer* at Wyndham's when I wrote my first play. At that time there were at least half a dozen reputable Sunday night play-producing societies, most of them anxious to give an unknown author a run for their money. One of these presented two performances of *Self* at the Court Theatre. For a first attempt it was not too bad, though it might fairly have been labelled a cross between the Pinerotic and the Maughamesque. It gained vastly from a cast including Cathleen Nesbitt's brother Tom, Jane Wood, Malcolm Keen and Naomi Jacob, the last two of whom acted in it out of sheer good-nature and personal good-will. Critics of the stature of Hubert Griffith and St John Ervine called it 'promising'. And in spite of James Agate's dismissal of 'pink passion in a pink boudoir' I saw visions and dreamed dreams. Dream almost became reality when for some weeks Margaret Bannerman toyed with the idea of producing *Self* at the Globe as a vehicle for herself. I remember sitting in Anthony Prinsep's office, wherein flew innumerable budgerigars, while he discussed with Miss Bannerman the probable cost of her clothes. Then came the General Strike, and by the time it had ended the Globe had been offered a play by an established playwright—and that was the end of that.

The fate of *Chinese White* was more curious. This was a 'triangle' play set in a riverine station up country in China. It was produced by the Play Actors at the Strand on a Sunday night, and a mild sensation was caused when Robert Harris, who was supposed at a dramatic climax to smash a mirror with a flung ash-tray, missed the mirror and with typical actor's courage put his fist through it. From where I sat I could see blood trickling down over his hand, and no amount of author's nerves could prevent me wondering whether he might not faint before the scene was over. He did not. As it happened, there was among the audience that night an elderly lady, a Mrs Henderson. She was an acquaintance of my mother's. She was also very rich, and the widow of a gentleman who had made a fortune in the Chinese import-and-export trade. The next day she wrote to my mother to tell her how greatly she had been impressed by the Chinese atmosphere of the play: so greatly that she was prepared to back it with a considerable sum of money if a management could be interested. (This to me was as surprising as it was exciting. All I knew of China I had gathered from the letters of an Oxford friend of mine who had been posted with a firm in Chungking for a couple of years.) I met Mrs Henderson, and we became very friendly. She urged me to pursue the finding of a possible management. Being a complete stranger in the world of theatrical 'angels', I sought the advice of an actor friend of mine. In the best of faith he told me that this was a clear case for an agent, and introduced me to one whom I will call 'Mr X'. He professed the greatest enthusiasm, and I took him to meet Mrs Henderson who was impressed by him even more than she had been by *Chinese White*.

So greatly was she impressed that X. persuaded her not only to back the play, but to build a small theatre in which to present it. In fact everything seemed too good to be quite true—and this was the exact situation. As time went on and the building proceeded X's enthusiasm for *Chinese White* notably dwindled. After all, and in spite of good notices, the verdict of a Sunday-night audience was notoriously unreliable. Would it not be as well to try the piece out again? This was done, for a week's run, at the Arts Theatre Club. Owen Nares produced what was essentially a static play of conversations as though it had been a game of musical chairs, and the leading lady's performance was seriously affected by a domestic bereavement. The results were not happy. Mrs Henderson was at last convinced that the play had been overrated, and X found a different piece with which to open the new theatre. I found it sardonically amusing when it failed in its turn, and that new theatre became the famous Windmill over whose 'nudes' Mrs Henderson presided with immense enjoyment, enormous *bonhomie*, and a touching regard for their welfare and their romantic attachments. She liked nothing better than to conduct parties of her dinner-guests to the Windmill and to take them 'behind' after the performance. I was included on several occasions, and I hope succeeded in hiding my deeper feelings.

I must admit that *Red Triangle* and *I May be Old-Fashioned*, both produced on Sundays by the Repertory Players, met with the fates they deserved. The former, an adaptation of a novel by Mary Agnes Hamilton, had little merit apart from an effective trial scene and an outstanding performance by Francis Sullivan. The latter was a farce which, owing to circumstances beyond anyone's control, was seriously under-rehearsed. In consequence, owing to a mistaken cue, the second scene of the second act was played through *twice*, which emphasised its weakness, and an actor called in at the last moment to play a character who appeared at the very end of the play and had four lines to speak 'dried' well and truly over the only one with significance and ruined the final curtain. The only subsequent performance—by the Oxford Repertory Company—proved that in this case the author had really no one but himself to blame.

By this time, at any rate in the eyes of the critics, my promise had been belied by performance. *Africa Flight*, produced at Richmond shortly before the war, did little or nothing to change a view which had veered from benevolence to condemnation with the appearance of *Punch and Judy* at the Vaudeville, where it lasted for five nights.

In this case I was probably served rightly for breaking one of my own rules. I had always believed it a mistake for an author to write a play with a particular actor or actress in mind for the leading part. Actors should serve plays, not plays actors. *Punch and Judy* was written for its leading lady. Worse still, I was emotionally engaged with the leading lady at the time. I made another mistake in accepting the suggestion that I should produce the play myself. Though I say so, I am a rather more than competent producer, and the piece presented no special difficulties. None the less I am inclined to think that it is a mistake for any author, no matter how great his production experience, to handle a play of his own. It is almost impossible for him to see it in proper perspective. There are cherished lines, scenes, situations which their creator finds it next to impossible to cut or alter. It is harder for him than for anyone else to realise obscurities which may prove baffling to an audience. These handicaps were of course exaggerated by the complication. of personal relationship. The leading lady took exception to certain demands of the management, and quarrelled with me when I found it impossible to support her attitude. Argument, which should have been confined to the boudoir, flowered embarrassingly on the stage.

These things were bad enough for the play's chances, but the beam was tipped finally against it by two factors for which I could not be held responsible. In the first place it was presented at the wrong time. It dealt satirically with Ruritania under the fascist rule of a quasi-Mussolini, and it was produced at the moment when appeasement was most in fashion. The appeasers found humour on the subject irritating and out of place. The anti-appeasers found such treatment of the subject intolerably frivolous. In the second place the leading man—a charming person of the highest professional attainments—had spent the last two years of his career entirely in film studios. In consequence he had temporarily lost that indefinable thing, the 'feel' of a live audience. This resulted in an attack of first-night nerves so devastating that throughout the first act he killed laugh after laugh by mistiming. The other members of the cast were inevitably infected. And the play's tempo sounded as if it were being played on a barrel-organ. I forbear to give quotations from the critics. With the amiable exception of Ivor Brown, who managed to give me credit for both good and amusing intentions, they made me feel that in writing a play which had failed to please I had committed a criminal offence. I confess to finding this hard to bear—the more so as a friend of mine with connections in Fleet Street had warned me a week or so before the opening that 'your play had better be good'. It seemed that in some quarters the impression had grown up that as a personality I was growing too big for my boots, that an opportunity of cutting me down to size would be welcome. The almost permanent vendetta which persisted between the press and the B.B.C. found expression in queer backwaters.

During the war years I wrote only one play, *Man's Company*, which dealt with a commando raid on the Normandy coast. I should have known, from experience of *Prisoners of War* and *Journey's End*, that there is no audience for a serious play dealing with war during the period of the war itself. Circumstances had killed for the time being both the Sunday-night producing societies and the 'fringe' theatres. In consequence *Man's Company* had to wait for production by repertory companies in York and Northampton respectively. The performances were excellent. However, the play attracted no metropolitan interest. The chief gainer was the B.B.C. Repertory Company which, as a result of my admiration for their performances in *Man's Company*, recruited Hamilton Dyce and Mary Williams, who gave yeoman service to radio drama.

With the production of *Away from it All* at the Embassy Theatre at Swiss Cottage in the autumn of 1946 I fell foul of the critics once

148

again. In the face of scepticism I claim that this was actually the first of the many plays which have dealt from one angle or another with the problem of the atomic bomb. My approach was similar to the one I had made use of in *Punch and Judy*, the amusingly satirical, and I suppose I should have learned my lesson. However, rehearsals ran smoothly under Anthony Hawtrey's most intelligent direction. I had a capital cast with Raymond Lovell, Avice Landone, and Ursula Howells outstanding, and the response of the first-night audience was all that any author could have wished. Anthony Hawtrey and I were so convinced that we had hit the jack-pot that we sat up all night in the Lyons in Coventry Street waiting for the morning papers to confirm our opinion. We had sacrificed a night's rest in vain. James Agate dismissed the piece as 'a nice dull talkie'. Mr Darlington complained that 'the idea had not been exploited to the full'. Mr Lionel Hale called it 'a theatrical null'. Mr Leonard Mosley referred to 'tinny political theories'. Once again Ivor Brown rallied to the losing side: 'wit in the writing; style in most of the performances', and *The Times* admitted to having been 'lightly amused'. But the majority carried the day, and *Away From it All* was kept firmly away from the West End, though it was to receive considerable acclaim years later when produced first as a radio play and later for the Television Service. Once again a play had been presented at the wrong time. The cloud over Hiroshima hung too closely in the background of people's minds for them to be able to accept what the critics had considered frivolous treatment of such a theme. I feel that today the piece might qualify successfully as an outstanding example of 'sick' humour, and be applauded by *avant-garde* intellectuals and the members of CND!

My disappointment was acute, and I did not try my hand at another play until I was stimulated by the change from the atmosphere of wartime England to the environment of New York. This time I was determined that I would make no bones about tackling a serious theme seriously. Shortly before I left England I had renewed contact with one of my oldest and dearest friends. She had been a home student at Oxford, where I had been unblushingly in love with her, and had been trapped in Occupied France, where she had managed ultimately to join one of the *maquis* groups of the Resistance. Later she had joined U.N.R.R.A. as a welfare officer, and my imagination was stirred, and horrified, by her first-hand stories of the camp for displaced persons in Austria in which she had worked. About the same time I read a newspaper story of how a train full of unhappy Ishmaels had been side-tracked into a siding on the frontier between Italy and Jugoslavia, and left there to freeze to death while the bureaucrats on both sides tried—and failed—to make up their minds what should be done with them.

Of this combination *Iron Curtain* was born. With unusual courage—as the Russians who appeared in the play were presented as hard-headed human beings rather than as monsters—Anthony Hawtrey produced the play at the Embassy shortly after my return from America. Its reception was respectful rather than enthusiastic, which was only to be expected on a night which was almost as cold outside the theatre as the snow which fell on the stage during the second act. But this time to my surprise the critics were both impressed and flattering. The *Tatler* went so far as to claim that it was the best play in London and demand its immediate transfer. Mr Harold Hobson wrote of it in terms so lyrical that I forbear quotation. Alas, the bad weather persisted. The political and economic atmosphere was gloomy. West End managers felt, reasonably enough, that the moment was not propitious for the presentation of a sombre piece calling for some heart-searching by audiences seeking only to be cheered up. Not one of them risked being proved mistaken.

On this occasion I was not cast down. I had written what I believed, and still believe, to have been my best play. It had demanded and received serious consideration. Radio and television audiences were in due course to approve it. And I found myself in correspondence with quite a number of excellent people of various nationalities who almost succeeded in persuading me that I had made a tiny contribution towards the improvement of international understanding and the realisation of essential humanities. It irritated me to have to admit to myself that I was irked by another failure to achieve the accolade of the West End, but it was true.

While still in New York—and possibly as a reaction from the earnest reality of *Iron Curtain*—I had also written a trivial little comedy called *Party Manners*. To be honest I did not think much of it, with the exception of one scene, and after *Iron Curtain* my sensation was that of shifting from the almost sublime to the nearly ridiculous. The last thing that crossed my mind was that it would become not a nine days' but a four months' wonder; that it would shake the B.B.C. to its foundations; that it would be discussed in both Houses of Parliament; and that it would be the subject of editorials and correspondence in almost every newspaper in Great Britain from *The Times* to the *News of the World*. I have already sketched the outline of this singular story in the preface to the printed edition of the play. I hope I may be excused for repeating it here in rather greater detail.

The explosion, when it came, was all the more remarkable because the original stage production at the Embassy passed almost unnoticed. I could not have felt less intimately associated with the political scene. I believed, in the words which I put into the mouth of the seventh Earl of Eltham, that 'the only consistent political belief held by the English is that all politicians are funny'. I also believed in more serious moments that by and large the country was sick of party politics, longing only for less and better government. To my pleasure and surprise the critics were almost without exception favourable, including both *The Times* and the *New Statesman*, drawing attention to the 'urbanity' of its approach, the absence of any malicious intent, and its fundamentally 'comic slant'. Transfer to the West End was only prevented by the difficulty of getting a theatre at the time of a temporary theatrical 'boom', and by one of the leading actors having to fulfil an engagement in America. But I still did not rate the play at all highly, and I was particularly busy owing to my recent transfer from Portland Place to Alexandra Palace. I thought little more about it.

A few weeks later one of my B.B.C. colleagues, who had visited the Embassy, asked me if I would consent to a production of the play in the Home Service. The broadcast took place with once again the minimum of reaction. Two letters of objection were received from listeners who thought that the play had *left*-wing bias, and from one who objected to the one really funny scene on the ground that in it too much alcohol was consumed. I did not know at the time that one of the Governors of the Corporation had heard the play and taken exception to what he conceived to be a malicious attack on the Labour Party. As this opinion was not passed on to me, I can only assume that the critic's colleagues did not agree with him.

Four months later I produced the play myself for the B.B.C. Television Service. I had been urged to lighten the dramatic schedule with comedy, and *faute de mieux* I submitted the script with the notices of the Embassy production to the Controller of the Television Service, and was authorised to go ahead. The first performance took place on Sunday October 1st, and a second was planned for the following Thursday. As a rule telephone messages of protest on one ground or another are received before the transmitters close down. On October 1st, 1950, there were none. On the Monday morning the *Daily Herald* adorned its front page with the headline: *We Don't Want Any More of This, Mr Gielgud*, and a vigorous accusation that I had indulged in a deliberate propaganda attack on the Labour Party. On the Tuesday Lord Simon of Wythenshawe cancelled the second performance.

What was the reason for this example of autocratic panic? The Labour Party Conference was sitting at the time, and it was widely rumoured that Mr Herbert Morrison, now Lord Morrison of Lambeth, had seen and been so affronted by the television performance that he had personally telephoned to Lord Simon. This rumour was never confirmed. The *Daily Herald* could hardly claim the credit on any grounds of passionate conviction as its then editor told me himself some time afterwards, with friendly and engaging cynicism, that he had not seen the TV performance himself. Wearied out, no doubt by his labours of the day, he had gone peacefully to sleep in front of his newly-acquired set, to be woken by his wife during the play's last five minutes. Her outraged reaction had persuaded him that *Party Manners* provided one of those sticks, so beloved of the press, with which to beat the B.B.C. dog, and a headline which would serve in default of anything more sensational. I also learned later from an authoritative source that the Governor aforementioned on being informed that the play against which he had protested when it was broadcast had been repeated on television made urgent representations to Lord Simon. In any event the deed was done, the cancellation stood, and practically every newspaper in the country, apart from the *Herald* and *Tribune*, opened a violent campaign against suppression of individual opinion.

Personally, in a state of bewildered apprehension, I lay low and said as little as possible. For a time I thought it likely that I should have to resign. But I was given both support and encouragement by Sir William Haley and Mr Norman Collins, who were considerate and remained admirably unmoved by the tea-cup storm. It was said that Mr Collins's resignation from the B.B.C., which shortly followed, was partly due to the *Party Manners* incident. This I believe to be entirely false. For some weeks I was able to appreciate the feelings of persons who, for reasons reputable or disreputable, find that their lightest word, their most insignificant action, makes news. I was rung up at all hours of the night. If I went out to dinner I was liable to find a reporter on my host's doorstep. I was followed to York—where the Repertory had staged the play—and subjected to inquisition in the hope of catching me out in some spoken indiscretion. I was urged by Lord Simon to admit, in writing, to folly if not to malice prepense, and with difficulty refused. I was chivvied from pillar to post, and I hated it.

The most important result of this singular outcry was a remarkable, and most desirable, relaxation of restrictions regarding TV drama. Within a short time of the *Party Manners* incident an attempt was made to raise a similar storm over the production of Orwell's *1984*. It failed dismally, and the failure was generally attributed to the precedent set in the case of *Party Manners*.

Less important, but to me equally interesting, was the effect on the play itself. A well-known publicity agent told me with rueful envy that I had been given a free quarter of a million pounds' worth of personal advertisement. This sounded promising at the moment when *Party Manners* had just been announced for production in the West End. As usual there was a catch in it—in fact, two catches. First the management was impatient to cash in on the publicity. Instead of waiting for a theatre of the size that intimate comedy demanded, it grabbed the Prince's, which was the first house available, and on whose vasty stage all wit sounded forced and all subtlety disappeared. Secondly the play's attraction had inevitably become that of something scandalous. Audiences went, expecting to be shocked by an explosion, only to find themselves mildly titillated by a squib. The new notices reflected this impression, and in spite of a 'celebrity' first night with Lord Montgomery

153

of Alamein in a stage-box the run only lasted just over three months.

There was a certain irony in at last seeing my name in lights outside a West End theatre as author of one of the least considerable plays that I had ever written. And it well may be that some theatrical purists may have felt that I had been outrageously favoured by fortune. If so, the balance was well and truly restored by the fate of my next play, *The Bombshell*. This was tried out at Croydon, imaginatively produced by Anthony Pelissier and most excellently acted by a largely unknown cast. Such criticism as it received was favourable, and when it was accepted for production at the Westminster with a cast including Leo Genn, Rachel Gurney, and Malcolm Keen, my hopes were high.

They were quickly dashed. In the interval Charles Morgan's *The Burning Glass* had stolen much of whatever thunder the theme possessed: that of the problems inevitably facing the conscience of the atomic scientist. Neither production nor acting fulfilled the promise of Croydon, and I was too ill to be able to be present at the first night. None the less the piece was designed as a serious contribution to a serious question of wide interest, and I still do not understand why it should have been not so much condemned as execrated. Probably the tone of the notices was exaggerated by an incipient nervous breakdown, but I cannot read them even today without blinking a little at their virulence. If a playwright's rewards appear sometimes excessive when compared with the labour involved, the punishment for his failures can be proportionately exaggerated.

Of the other two plays for which I have been responsible there is little to say. *Mediterranean Blue*, an entirely frivolous little comedy based upon personal observation during a Sicilian holiday, was presented by several repertory companies with some success, particularly at Sheffield. *Not Enough Tragedy*, written as a retort to Mr Osborne's *Look Back in Anger* and with the requirements of repertory companies particularly in mind—it called for a single set and a cast of seven—was treated by most of the said companies as a Greek gift. Its most appreciative audiences were probably those who saw it performed by the Old Stagers at Canterbury. But by this time *Look Back in Anger* was 'old hat', and the Hungarian rising against the Russian occupation old bones.

154

There remains in a drawer in my desk one piece at the time of writing unproduced, and likely to remain so to judge from the amount of interest in it I have found it possible to rouse. I am not particularly surprised. *Georgeous George* is constructed conventionally. There is no possible doubt about what it means. Its setting, though simple, is luxurious. All the characters wash as a matter of habit. Sex is not treated seriously, let alone tragically. And the only object of the play is to provide an evening's light entertainment. So far I have found no management prepared to take the risk of exposing themselves to the charge of trying to turn back the clock of theatrical progress by staging an example of what was once known as 'high comedy'. It is of course difficult to cast this type of play when so many fashionable actors have been trained in the Littlewood stable and in consequence can neither speak the Queen's English nor wear a gentleman's clothes.

Reading back over this record, I find it rather a dismal tale. I got plenty of fun out of it for all that. I also got, which was far more valuable, considerable experience of adversity, hope deferred, actors' virtues, actors' temperaments, human idiosyncrasies, and practical stage problems. Most important of all, I learned that no judgement of any play is reliable until that play has been seen acted.

I doubt my continuing to write plays. One should know when to stop, and I find prevailing fashions in the theatre profoundly unsympathetic. I wish it were not so. I wish that I did not find the Theatre of Non-communication anomalous and incomprehensible. It is no doubt my fault and not Brecht's that to me his work appears old-fashioned and above all boring. I wish I could share my friend Martin Esslin's enthusiasm for the Theatre of the Absurd, and that I could feel an Arts Council subsidy desirable for the Theatre of Cruelty. I wish that I did not draw so many breaths of relief over the fact that it is no longer an essential part of my professional business to visit the theatre. Glamour and illusion have gone together, symbolised perhaps by those bare stages on which no curtains rise.

No doubt the elder generation among audiences which had flocked to applaud Irving at the Lyceum and Alexander at the St James's felt much the same when the town was first scarified by Bernard Shaw and Granville-Barker, and the Theatre of Ideas

CHAPTER NINE

Round and about the Theatre

I HAVE confessed myself as a failure as a playwright, and as the worst actor of my generation. (Mr Lionel Hale has on occasion disputed with me over this title. Never having seen him act, I cannot give him the lie. However, when I recall a performance of Mr Kenneth Tynan's as the Player-King in *Hamlet* I am not sure that I can justify my claim absolutely.) This chapter is not written from the point of view of player or author, but of someone whose situation *vis-à-vis* the contemporary Theatre was, owing to circumstances, unique and perhaps a little remarkable. During thirty years of my service with the B.B.C., the Head of the Corporation's Drama Department was in fact responsible for the only existing National Theatre. He had no competitors. His audience was vast and ready-made. His plans were not qualified by the demands of a box-office, nor by the assistance of expert advisers, requiring only the endorsement of his Controller and his Director-General. Most important of all, his productions could be made available to the nation as a whole. It was not until the late Fifties that this position came to be taken over gradually by the Head of Television Drama, whose problems were complicated by two new factors: commercial competition, and the fact that by a rough estimate a television production cost six times as much as its equivalent in sound; much more in the case of complicated or costume pieces.

It was therefore part of my professional business to see every play I could; to be acquainted with a wide range of authors, producers, and actors; to read theatrical criticism, both significant and insignificant; to try to keep abreast of matters theatrical on the Continent and in the United States. These activities sprang from my fortune not my virtue. They resulted in my being very much 'in' the Theatre if not 'of' it, almost as if I had been given a regular seat in the wings. I found myself in the position of that onlooker who proverbially sees most of the game: a game by turns moving, exciting, amusing, exasperating, puerile, magnificent, and always interesting. I represented the B.B.C. on the advisory panel of the Arts Council, and frequently attended the meetings of the Council of Repertory Theatres. I was in a position remarkably favourable for a study of the general theatrical scene during a period when the English Theatre was being affected by one of its periodical revolutions.

It is frequently stated, and too often accepted, that this revolution began with the phenomenal success of Mr John Osborne, representing the Angry Young Men of the Fifties, with his play *Look Back in Anger*. I feel that it is time for this particular red herring to be put into the discard. *Look Back in Anger* is in many respects a capital play. It tells a story—though the story is not very original. Its dialogue is vigorous, fluent, eminently speakable. Like *Journey's End* it has been demonstrated actor-proof. Its situations are most effective in theatrical terms. For audiences who can swallow the protagonist's rancid self-pity and nauseatingly bad behaviour—not to mention its *Winnie-the-Pooh* sentimentality—it makes a good evening's entertainment. But to pretend that what it has to say is new, let alone revolutionary, is absurd. And, to do Mr Osborne justice, I doubt if he has ever claimed so much. *Look Back in Anger* is an example of the well-made play dealing with a contemporary sociological problem in the tradition of Ibsen, Somerset Maugham, and Stanley Houghton. Its explosive success, its violent impingement upon theatrical consciousness, have been compared with that of Mr Coward's *The Vortex*. It would be more accurate to draw comparisons with the effect of the first productions of the Manchester School. Jimmy Porter and his masochistic outpourings were effective because the details and background of his existence were unfamiliar in terms of their place in the social scale. The revolt of a younger generation is commonplace as a subject for the dramatist. What was new—and to some extent shockingly attractive—about Jimmy Porter was his justification of sleazy living combined with lower-middle-class consciousness. This hit the bull's eye for audiences which, however reluctantly, were beginning to adapt themselves to the development of a classless society and the Welfare State. The play was a symptom, not a cause. In many

158

respects, notably its conventionally solid stage-craft, it was old-fashioned.

The importance of the production of *Look Back in Anger* was not the play itself, but the effect of the play's success upon the Royal Court Theatre. The Royal Court became fashionable, and it also made a good deal of money. The Theatre does not live by its experimental, 'fringe', or *avant-garde* theatres. On the other hand it cannot live healthily without them. For what he has done in this field a great debt is owed to Mr George Devine, his actors, and his collaborators. Without the success of *Look Back in Anger* it is possible that the Royal Court might not have survived. It would certainly not have been able to lay the foundations of that alliance between the intellectuals and certain among the critics which mounted the astonishing campaign to make such authors as Brecht and Ionesco acceptable as popular, as opposed to significant, dramatists; to point with enthusiasm to Method acting and the Theatre of the Absurd as guiding-lights towards a new and splendid future; to stigmatise 'entertainment' as a dirty word.

The reader will probably have gathered that personally I have little sympathy with the enthusiasm displayed for the Theatres of the Absurd, of Non-communication, and of Cruelty. To an extent I have been able to admire, while not pretending to understand, the Absurd, although after reading Martin Esslin's capital book on the subject I almost believed that I could do so. Certainly I have received both pleasure and stimulation from the plays of Ionesco. But I remain convinced that one Ionesco, one Samuel Beckett, does not make a school of dramatists, and that most of their imitators are both boring and inept. Over Non-communication I can feel nothing but exasperation. In my unsophisticated mind the business of writing plays is inseparably connected with the job of a writer to *communicate with* his audience: to be able to do so is the author's primary justification. If, on the other hand, by Non-communication is meant the expression of the incapacity of any human being to communicate with another human being across a bridge of words, I would suggest that far from being a revolutionary or interesting idea it is the dreariest truism. Every man knows in his heart that he must travel alone on the journey from cradle to grave—unless he attains to the grace and the mercy of God. And there have been plenty of writers before our contemporary dramatists who have made the discovery and pointed its sombre moral. As for the philosophy of the desirability of annihilation for its own sake, it seems to me that the Stoics made less fuss about accepting the consequences of the realisation that life was not worth living.

Mr Harold Clurman has described the Absurd as 'tragedy which has put on the mask of farce. People are no longer individuals because the world has lost all meaning. Having lost our identity, we cannot communicate with each other. Our conversation represents nothing but vestigial impulses expressed in language void of original force because without roots in reality. Reality itself has become a dubious concept.' I can only comment that for me the world has by no means lost all meaning, and that conversation representing 'nothing but vestigial impulses in language void of original force' is boring, and is certainly not dramatic. I repeat that such 'fringe' activities in the Theatre have a useful, even a vitalising, influence, but they are a trend, not a revolution. If intellectuals succeed too well in making such a trend fashionable, they risk doing the Theatre a good deal of harm. On the one hand they risk antagonising audiences who expect to find entertainment in theatre-going. On the other they risk exaggerated encouragement of authors who find in the Absurd and in Non-communication excuse for neglecting such elementary aspects of their business as workmanlike construction, intelligible dialogue, sympathetic characterisation, and basic plot-invention.

Not so long ago a well-known critic of a Sunday newspaper directed 'every manager's attention' to a first play which he summed up as follows: 'An Irish tart, professing to suffer from a rare disease of the lung, beguiles a rich young drunk into offering her a free trip to Switzerland. The action, set in a Soho bar, is frail and static, but the dialogue, haunting and ironically repetitive, has a fascination that is part Beckett, part Tennessee Williams.' I fail to see why any manager should follow such direction, unless he is determined to find a monumental flop on his hands. The production of such a play at a tiny experimental theatre may have been worth while. To transfer it to the West End would have invited massacre.

Nor can I believe that the best interests of the Theatre were served by the antics and exhibitionism which were so broadly displayed—and so unfortunately publicised—at the 1963 International Drama Conference at Edinburgh. Many worthy citizens of Scotland's capital were outraged by the appearance on a balcony at the final session of a young lady in the nude, and apparently forfeited sympathy by denouncing such goings-on as not respectable. What should have upset them was not so much a vulgar publicity-gimmick as the fact that the proceedings could be called, in the *Sunday Times*, 'an uninhibited effort to demonstrate the Theatre of the Future', and explained with apparent seriousness as 'a Happening, giving a new conception of Time and Place'. This mixture of adolescent bad manners and schoolboy bad taste did not augur particularly well for the Theatre either of the present or the future. And if any of the money of the rate-payers of Edinburgh went towards subsidising the Conference, those rate-payers had a considerable cause of grievance.

As for the Theatre of Cruelty, Mr Roger Gellert in the *New Statesman* put it in its place—I hope once and for all. Reminding us that the title was 'reverendly filched' from Antonin Artaud, Mr Gellert quoted Artaud's own description of his meaning: 'Instead of words—cries, groans, apparitions, surprise theatricalities of all kinds, magic, beauty of costumes taken from certain ritual models; resplendent lighting, incantational beauty of voices, the charms of harmony, rare notes of music, colours of objects, physical rhythm of movements whose *crescendo* will accord exactly with the pulsation of movements familiar to everyone, concrete appearances of new and surprising objects, masks, effigies yards high, sudden changes of light which can arouse sensations of heat and cold . . .' Mr Gellert added that 'apart from its grand . . . imprecision this may strike you as fresh and charming'. In my view he might have added that it may also strike you as pretentious balderdash.

What Mr Gellert did add, with much point, was that Artaud was protesting against a stuffy *bourgeois* theatre which no longer holds sway. Messrs Peter Brook and Marowitz, the sponsors of Cruelty, were beating against an open door. *Avant-garde* theatre is the idol of the intellectual press, and it appears that the Governors of the Royal Shakespeare Theatre, which has seldom ceased pleading passionately for the increase of its Arts Council subsidy, 'have subsidised this experiment up to the hilt. We have a small theatre

L

and our subsidy can therefore be *total*: it covers us even if every seat were empty at every performance.' This of course gives the game well and truly away. Messrs Brook and Marowitz seem to agree with the producer who expressed the view that in the ideal Theatre subsidies should substitute for audiences, that without the hampering and possibly critical presence of the latter, the writer, the actor, and particularly the producer could work in absolute freedom. In other words such writers, actors and producers claim to enjoy their private fun and games at the expense of people who have no desire to share in them. It seems a pity that such a lofty, if grotesque, ideal should have been blurred by the 'Cruelty' presentation of a sketch with an actress in the part of Miss Christine Keeler, thereby ensuring the filling of every seat at every performance.

Mr Gellert finally reminded us 'that Artaud, a brilliant, un-balanced man, was finally (rightly or wrongly) certified as mad'; that consequently 'he is an unreliable master'. We can be grateful to Mr Gellert for this breath of the fresh wind of sanity.

What I believe to be far more revolutionary, and far more important, than trends typified by *avant-garde* theatrical experiments or the plays written by Young Angries is the largely unquestioned acceptance as axiomatic that the Theatre, like Grand Opera, can only survive if subsidised by public money. The view seems to be generally held, first, that this is true, secondly that it is desirable, symptomatic of progress and the spread of popular culture. Whether the masses desire or deserve the spreading of culture among them is a question concerning which I would not dream of pronouncing, nor dare to lay down any law, though I confess that I shudder with apprehension at the shadow of that old Trojan horse, a Ministry of Culture and Fine Arts, darkening the plain outside our city walls and ridden by Mr R. H. Crossman. Still, the more closely and the more frequently that I have witnessed in operation the subsidising of the Theatre, the less I have liked it.

The arguments of its supporters seem, on first consideration, irresistible. Civilisation is a good thing. The Theatre is part of civilised living. If payment at the box-office is insufficient to pay actors adequate salaries, to encourage authors of the first class, to stage plays as they should be staged, to make a repertory of classic

162

drama generally available, then public money must be provided to make up the difference. It is as easy as that. It is irrelevant whether it be provided directly through the appropriate ministry, or indirectly through the medium of a body like the Arts Council. The assumption is so easy that putting it into practice should be simple. It has turned out to be nothing of the kind.

There has been the unedifying spectacle of the Royal Shakespeare Company and the new National Theatre complaining querulously about the amounts of their respective subsidies, while hotly denying that they were competing with each other. There has been the establishment of the undoubted, if unacknowledged, fact that in the minds of those responsible for the direction of repertory companies up and down the country the prime consideration is no longer the production schedule, the standard of the company's acting, the requirements of local audiences, but the size of subsidy which can be wheedled, blarneyed, or just demanded from the Arts Council. There have been embarrassing cases of actors engaged on foreign tours subsidised by the British Council objecting to their being expected to add commercial-travelling on behalf of national exports to their professional duties. There exists considerable feeling, for the most part without adequate expression, that there is something wrong with a National Theatre which signalises its opening by raising its prices and diminishing the number of its seats; that the Royal Shakespeare, while trumpeting—with a good deal of reason —its artistic triumphs, is coy in revealing details of its business management and both arrogant and extravagant in implementing certain personal foibles of its producers. There was the unfortunate incident of the 'punch-up' at the opening of the new Nottingham Theatre, which showed only too clearly the great gulf fixed between the directors of a theatre and the representatives of the municipality which had largely paid for its building.

There is of course much to be said on both sides. Talented and well-known actors, producers of international reputation, are temperamentally impatient of any questioning or control, still more of cheese-paring economies which hamper their cherished schemes. Justifiably enough, they claim that they know their own business, and that it is a business unlikely to be sympathetic or even intelligible to the mentality of bureaucrat or accountant. On the other hand a ministry, a municipal corporation, even the Arts Council naturally claims some voice in the use of the subsidy which it provides. The theatres would like to be given the money, and to do what they like with it. The subsidisers protest that they are at least entitled to consideration of their wishes by the subsidised. The result is only too often irritation, exasperation, bad feeling, and unsatisfactory compromise. And occasionally a still small voice can be heard asking how it was that the English Theatre survived so long and achieved so much when its audiences paid its expenses, and the National Theatre was no more than a dream in Geoffrey Whitworth's mind.

I have no doubt that the subsidised theatre has come to stay. I am convinced of its many benefits. But if those benefits are not to be seriously qualified both subsidisers and subsidised will have to achieve a less selfishly subjective point of view. Individuals, however brilliant, who accept and spend other people's money will have to be prepared to account for its spending. Public bodies which finance the building or the running of theatres will have to be prepared to break away from habits of supervision and criticism appropriate to the building of public lavatories or the running of elementary schools.

In addition to the subsidised theatre and the new school of dramatists we have also experienced during the last decade the products of a new theory of acting. Most publicised, and least significant, of such products is the notorious Method. Fathered, libellously and monstrously, upon the great Stanislavsky, the Method was originally devised as a means by which the 'clothes-horses' of Hollywood could be induced to act. Players, lacking in both technical equipment and normal imagination, were treated literally like children. Acting was reduced to the elementary dimension of a game of 'let's pretend to be so and so'. If a character was required to appear in a scene in a state of exhaustion, he would be exhorted to prepare for his entrance by running swiftly round the block. This, if puerile, was harmless or nearly so.

It was not long, however, before the Method extended to embrace a psychological *mystique* of acting, which was a godsend to actors who preferred interminable discussion of the significance of their parts and their problems to the wearisome round of normal rehearsals. Such discussion could be enlarged indefinitely, affording infinite opportunity for the evasion of straightforward producing direction. Admirable instinctive players muddled their minds and spoiled their performances by thinking about acting instead of just acting. Less admirable players trusted to confusion of mental process, debates conducted in language which they hardly understood, the introduction of vast and high-sounding irrelevancies to cover up their deficiencies and explain away their shortcomings. I have known of one actor who demanded release from rehearsal on the ground that he needed time to commune with the Almighty concerning his interpretation of a part; of another who, naïvely unaware of practical considerations, informed a startled radio producer that he never began to give a performance until he had studied the part's atmosphere and implications for at least six weeks. It is a far cry from this attitude to the traditional roguery and vagabondage of the Profession. Hard things were said in the Twenties about actors and actresses who pretended to be ladies and gentlemen, who liked to be seen in fashionable restaurants, and to see their photographs in the *Tatler* and the *Bystander*. They were blamed for not taking their work seriously. I doubt if these concessions to the amiable human vices of mild snobbery and vanity did their work much harm; certainly not as much harm as the humbug and hot air which have been spoken and written by devotees of the Method.

Fortunately in this country the Method has had little influence and less success. But I do not think it is unfair to find a link, albeit a tenuous one, between it and the school of acting and production inseparably connected with the name of Miss Joan Littlewood. This is a very different, and very important, pair of shoes, because Miss Littlewood is a professional of professionals. She came up the hard way by unobtrusive persistence, unostentatious self-confidence, unquenchable enthusiasm, and hard work. She can point with satisfaction and pride to a record of success which was certainly both earned and deserved.

Unfortunately Miss Littlewood's name is as inextricably bound up with *A Taste of Honey* as is Mr Osborne's with *Look Back in Anger*. I believe that Miss Delaney admits that without the help of Miss Littlewood's guiding and revising hand her play would have been a different and a less triumphant thing. Certainly most of the critics attributed the piece's success largely to Miss Littlewood's production. As a producer her virtues are undeniable and outstand-

165

ing: immense vitality, abounding vigour, fertile invention, originality of approach. Miss Littlewood in her theatre at Stratford East was an inspiration to her actors, a second self to her authors, and a tonic to jaded West End audiences and critics. Miss Littlewood with her name in lights above two or three West End theatres was an anomaly; she has too openly expressed her contempt for non-proletarian audiences, her belief in a style of acting admirably suited to experiments 'on the fringe' but inadequate for the centre's hard core.

Unless I have gravely misinterpreted the work of hers that I have seen, and misunderstood her *credo* in interviews that she has given and articles that she has written, Miss Littlewood's theatre is a theatre of professional charades designed strictly for the underprivileged both among her players and her audiences. The basic idea for her play should contain a certain sociological significance. Details both of dialogue and construction should not be left to the author. They should be worked out on a basis of co-operation during rehearsal between players and producer. The theory is an interesting one, worthy of both attention and respect. In practice it has paid off in a number of notable instances. Without her contribution the London theatre would have been a less vital and a poorer thing.

None the less the example of Miss Littlewood has been something of an *ignis fatuus* both for writers and for actors. Deprived of her directing hand and her individual personality, author and players alike have discovered that an idea by itself is not enough; that qualifications for acting include other things besides vigour, enthusiasm, inventiveness and an off-beat accent. Critics who have solemnly written of Hamlet as 'an Elizabethan Jimmy Porter', and of King Lear as 'a Jimmy Porter grown old', have merely revealed lack of perspective and humour. But the management which did not realise that a young actor's success in *Fings Ain't What They Used to Be* did not automatically qualify him to play Edmund in *King Lear* showed itself up as following a fashion as opposed to knowing its own business.

It seems to me that the basic trouble, as far as the theatre is concerned, with the intellectuals and their critical allies is their determination to divorce culture from entertainment. By this I do not mean that I think that our theatre should consist of transatlantic musicals, shockers, and the type of farce generally associated with the Whitehall. I spent a large part of my professional life in arguing against giving the public what a number of know-alls asserted the public wanted. My experience proved that in fact public taste is considerably in advance of what it is believed to be by professional *entrepreneurs*. But my experience also taught me that to stamp a play with the educational label was to kill it stone-dead from the point of view of popularity. I believe it to be equally true that the average English audience shrinks instinctively from Culture with a capital C. Most people go to the theatre to enjoy themselves in terms of laughter, tears, sensation, or purgation emotional or intellectual. 'Enjoy' is the operative word. If the theatre, fortified by subsidies, is enabled to disregard audience reaction; if the pretentious, the self-consciously obscure, the dreary but sociologically significant, can rely on the backing of critics who forget that they exist to represent as well as to influence public taste, then the theatre will operate in a vacuum of its own creation.

Am I altogether mistaken in thinking that what is called for is a sober reappraisal of our theatrical values? In Olivier and Gielgud, Richardson and Wolfit, Michael Redgrave and Stephen Murray, Peggy Ashcroft and Vanessa Redgrave, Flora Robson and Edith Evans, the English Theatre possesses a wealth of acting talent— talent matured, experienced, at the peak of achievement—which it would be hard to parallel anywhere in the world. But Mr Tynan persists in using as his yard-stick the work of the Berliner Ensemble, and in endeavouring to persuade us that Berthold Brecht—it is typical that so many of his devotees like to refer to him cosily as 'Bert'—in his time an exciting polemical dramatist, is nowadays something other than an outdated and monumental bore. Similarly Mr Hobson has made himself almost a resident alien of his Parisian theatrical home. Mr Tynan's attitude towards team-work on the stage is unexceptionable. It might be more usefully applied to criticism of the present lamentable standard of small-part-playing both in the National and in the Royal Shakespeare companies. No one would dream of quarrelling with Mr Hobson for his adoration of the beauty and talent of Mme Edwige Feuillère. Still, there are beauties and talents nearer home. I feel it is a pity when the cream of the English acting profession can be heard wondering uneasily whether it is possible any longer for them to be 'with it', wondering whether there is any longer place for technique hard-won by experience, for the naturally beautiful and properly trained voice, for the genuine professional article.

It has become 'the done thing' to denigrate playwrights of the ability and tested craftsmanship of Mr Coward and Mr Rattigan in favour of such tyros as Miss Delaney and Mr Livings, whose undoubted promise will only achieve performance if they are sufficiently and authoritatively adjured to do a great deal more home-work in studying the alphabet of their business.

I have listened to a discussion of the design for the National Theatre during which only two out of the twenty-odd persons present raised eyebrows at the claim made by supporters of the Chichester-type stage that the latter should be adopted, not because it particularly suited plays in a classical repertory, not because it was a good thing from the point of view of the audience's seeing and hearing, but because it 'gave freedom' to the producer and the scenic designer. Is it hopelessly old-fashioned to suggest that it is not freedom which is lacking so much as common sense and self-discipline?

Nothing is more vital to the future and well-being of our theatre as a whole than a healthy and economically sound body of provincial repertory theatres. This is generally admitted and agreed. Help from the Arts Council has been made readily available for as many of these organisations as have been able to show that they can attract and are needed by audiences, and that they are prepared to help themselves. Yet their representatives waste time and effort in declaiming against television, which in fact has done them little harm beyond putting weekly rep. out of business—which should have been done by the repertory movement long ago for its own sake and for the sake of so many ill-paid and exploited actors. Sir William Williams, as the result of his long experience as Secretary-General of the Arts Council, did his best to persuade the provincial repertories that they would never achieve real economic stability without adopting his 'grid' system, according to which the better repertories would cover regions as opposed to staying put in their own localities. He got next to nowhere. I remember an argument I once had into the smallest hours with the producer of one repertory company in the

South-east of England who had made a notable success of her own theatre. Within twenty miles are at least half a dozen other theatres, some of them barely managing to exist, in a region crowded with rich potential audiences and better served than most by public transport. I urged that it was almost a duty—it would surely have been a pleasure—for this talented lady to extend the sphere of her operations by the 'grid' method. Her reply was that the town in which she had worked for ten years would never forgive her, and that without her continuing physical presence her own theatre would collapse within a matter of months. I have also been told that the different sizes of various stages make such touring practically out of the question, but I seem to remember that in the days when touring companies were the rule and not the exception this difficulty, if it existed, was overcome as a matter of course. No doubt it is more comfortable for actors to quarter themselves as best they can in one locality on a semi-permanent basis. To this the only reply must be that acting is no more a comfortable than it is a secure way of making a living. The player who places his or her comfort and security beyond the demands of the job would be well advised to try something else.

Personally I owe much to repertory companies, in particular to York, to Northampton, and to Sheffield, which have not only taken the risk of performing plays of mine, but have done them more than justice. My admiration for their hard work, their cheerful refusal to be daunted by every sort of harsh circumstance, their ingenuity, and their basic contribution to the theatre as a whole is immense. On every count I wish them well, just as I sympathise with their problems. None the less their directors—*not their producers*—suffer too often from an ingrained and parochial conservatism. For its success a provincial repertory depends principally on two things: a suitable choice of plays, and its public relations. As far as my experience goes, both of these things are considered to be part of the normal business of the producer.

The result can only be that either they are neglected or the producer works himself to death or into a nervous breakdown. The P.R.O. has become accepted as an essential cog in the machine of any up-to-date organisation sensitive to public tastes and public demands. I know of no provincial repertory company which employs one. Yet if that personal link between a theatre and its audiences does not exist, or exists only in so far that the producer does his best to maintain it in his exiguous spare time, the theatre is in grave danger of forfeiting the prestige and good will which are both vital to its continuing health.

Again how many times have I heard hard-driven producers proclaim simultaneously that the finding of good new plays and their inclusion in schedules are of high importance and value, and that, owing to pressure of work, they cannot guarantee reading of and decision upon such plays within a period short of several months? It is not an encouraging state of affairs for the would-be playwright. Two professional play-readers—more than two are unnecessary, and any sort of committee is futile—should form part of the permanent staff of any repertory theatre of consequence. With their help the producer would have the job of winnowing the grain from the chaff done for him. He would have time and concentration left for the business of ultimate selection. Authors would not have their hearts broken by interminable delays. Producers would not be driven to fall back upon the list of Messrs Samuel French's acting editions, or the inclusion in their schedules of plays which have been favourably noticed by West End critics, but which the producers in question have never had the opportunity of seeing.

The English theatre has so regularly been accused of dying that it may seem ungracious, even unreasonable, to find so much fault with it at a time when it is so obviously and aggressively alive. But while an invalid needs compassion and cosseting a healthy organism requires stimulus and criticism if it is not to wax fat and smug. Trends should not be exalted into revolutions. Subsidies should be justified and earned, not demanded as of axiomatic right. The new playwright and the up-and-coming actor should of course be encouraged—but in reasonable perspective, and with less emphasis upon personality news-stories. A certain chastening is proverbially allied with love. Those of us who love the theatre, and cherish the highest hopes for its future in the light of the promise of its present, are compelled sometimes to wonder whether the gravest menace to the theatre today is not a plethora of indiscriminate admiration and self-satisfaction.

CHAPTER TEN

The Last Lap

IN APRIL 1952 I returned to Broadcasting House to resume my old post as Head of Drama (Sound). My state of mind at that moment was not a happy one. I was smarting under the realisation of failure over my television assignment. I had almost managed to convince myself that the future of the broadcasting of plays lay with TV rather than with radio. Also I had realised that as far as personal existence was concerned I was 'over the hump': what is generally supposed to be the best and most productive period of life was now behind me. When I compared what I had done with what I had hoped to do I felt ashamed and inadequate. There seemed little left ahead of me but the gradual running-down of the machine, one's acceptance by one's colleagues as the sort of person who deserves a certain indulgence as the result of long service and past promise; a tolerant shelving. It was a disagreeable prospect.

It worked out otherwise. First of all, to my astonishment as much as my pleasure, I was received back, if not with open arms, with smiling faces. Quite a number of people seemed genuinely pleased to see me again. This attitude, after a period when I had felt every man's hand against me, was remarkably uplifting. In the second place TV competition, instead of reducing the staff of my old department to defeatism and despair, had given it a most efficacious shot in the arm. The good old days when twelve million odd listeners heard *Saturday Night Theatre* might have gone for ever. With them they had taken that vast body of moronic listeners whose innate and unalterably conservative tastes had always acted as a brake upon the adventurous, the novel, and the experimental in radio. Our future audiences would be much smaller, admittedly. There was every hope that they would also be more intelligent. This in itself was encouragement. In addition there was the natural stimulus rising out of the determination to prove that the people who had already labelled sound 'a dead duck' might be mistaken. In the third place there was the Third Programme.

If he had contributed nothing else to broadcasting, Sir William Haley would have earned a notable place in its history by his sponsorship of the Third Programme and his determination that it should go on and prosper. If he ever glances back from Printing House Square to Broadcasting House with regret, I dare swear that the regret is due to the fact that he is no longer intimately concerned with a programme that has become the envy and admiration of every cultivated person in the international radio world. A good deal of humour has been expended upon Sir William's theory of 'the pyramidal audience', according to which intelligent listeners would move by almost imperceptible stages from the broad base of the Light Programme to the central reaches of the Home and ultimately to the comparatively rarefied heights of the Third. In fact there was nothing wrong with the theory. It was not Sir William Haley's fault if certain among his practitioners failed to interpret his intention aright. As things turned out certain heads of the Light Programme proved so determined to down-grade their output— one of them once took forty minutes to explain to his dazed colleagues that he saw it as his real business to compete favourably with Radio Luxemburg—as to make any consistently upward movement very difficult indeed. Also at the top of the pyramid it was occasionally forgotten that it is possible to equate the popular with the good, that in the Third's original brief it was laid down that its programmes should include the regular performance, on the highest professional and technical level, of acknowledged classical works of both music and drama. On the one hand the Third tended towards the bloodlessly academic—I have heard it stigmatised too often as presented by dons for dons. On the other it has occasionally fallen into the trap of sponsoring the esoteric, particularly if the esoteric's author were a foreigner, for its own sake.

But whatever its shortcomings in practice nothing can blur the programme's original grandeur of conception, or destroy its very real record of astonishing achievement. Most of its critics find themselves in the position of small boys throwing pebbles at the Sphinx. Certainly the opinion of civilised Europe is against them.

To radio drama the programme gave an inspiration, a tonic, and unrivalled opportunity. Producers of the calibre of Raymond Raikes, Douglas Cleverdon, John Gibson and Louis MacNeice, who had experienced frustrations and disppointments common among unusually talented individuals faced with too many routine assignments, enjoyed a greater freedom and achieved notable reputations. It became possible to commission new plays from young authors of promise on a scale much greater than before. Such pieces as Ibsen's *Brand* were no longer frozen out of schedules because of the time factor. For the first time it was possible to offer the productions of a genuinely intellectual theatre to an audience which, in terms of the average intellectual theatre, operated on a shoe-string in a side-street, was fantastically large.

I would not wish to overstate the claim for the effects of Third Programme drama. None the less it is merely fact that such authors as Adamov and Audiberti, Ugo Betti and Michel de Ghelderode, Diego Fabbri and Malraux were little more than names to most people in this country before their work was broadcast; that such authors as Robert Bolt and Harold Pinter, Giles Cooper and L. R. Adrian, H. A. L. Craig and James Forsyth, James Hanley and Errol John owe to broadcasting much of their basic technique and of their subsequent reputation in the Theatre. I am inclined to doubt whether without the stimulus of the Third Programme the so-called New Wave would have climbed the beach as far as it has.

I can back this point of view the more easily because my own contribution was for the most part a negative one. The positive credit should go to Donald McWhinnie and the younger generation of producers who for the most part found the new plays and bear-led the new writers. It will be obvious from my chapter on the Contemporary Theatre that my personal enthusiasm for the New Wave is, to say the least of it, limited. Much of it I did not understand. Some of it I frankly disliked. I seldom myself produced plays of this kind, because I felt myself incapable of interpreting to actors pieces with which I had little sympathy and of which my comprehension was limited. For all that, I had the greatest admiration for McWhinnie's intelligence and enthusiasms, and I conceived it my business to do what I could to give producers such practical help as I could in my capacity as their responsible professional head.

173

Also I believed that it is an essential part of the business of broadcasting to represent all kinds of current trends in artistic output. And no doubt it was good for me to discipline my prejudices, to try to learn from my youngers and betters.

In fact this Young Guard owed less to me than to the various Controllers of the Third Programme. Unlike the heads of the other Home Services of the B.B.C., the Controller of the Third has complete editorial power of approval, veto, and commissioning. He can flatly reject the recommendations of the heads of his producing departments. He can accept material against their advice. His responsibility is absolute. It was for the most part shouldered with wisdom, with imagination, with sensitive appreciation of possibilities, and with quite remarkable tact. There are few recollections of the B.B.C. that I cherish more warmly than my relations with Howard Newby. We disagreed almost invariably. We argued lengthily and inconclusively. I have never known a man prepared to go to such lengths and spend so much time in making sure that justice was done to an opposing point of view. His courtesy was completely disarming. I have no doubt that he found me tiresome, just as on occasion I found him obstinate. But he never exploited his position in the official hierarchy, and I did my best to encourage personal relationships between him and producers more in tune with his ideas than I was. I enjoyed working with him almost as much as I have enjoyed his novels—which is saying quite a good deal.

The contrast between my last ten years of service with the B.B.C. and the pioneering period and wartime years was considerable. I was no longer fighting for personal or professional recognition. My colleagues seemed prepared to tolerate my foibles and prejudices as personal idiosyncrasies. Actors seemed pleased, indeed almost privileged, when I could include them in my casts. With a department that over the years had become staffed almost entirely after my own thinking and my own desire I found myself able at long last to do a certain amount of sitting back and thinking. With my arms upheld, as it were, by Donald McWhinnie on the left and Martyn C. Webster on the right, I found it possible to plan the output of radio drama on more solid and comprehensive lines; to worry less about next week and more about six months hence; to exploit properly what had been so painfully established. I find the record of those years pleasantly free from those feuds and crises which in the Thirties had been exciting, but which in the Fifties would have been intolerable. In its own small way my position had become that of an elder statesman. And though a good many people must have shared my own feeling that I had sat in the same chair for quite long enough, they seemed to appreciate certain compensations in the consistency of attitude of the devil they knew.

These years were signalised by the planning and production less of individual plays than of various series of plays conceived in terms of a definite all-over pattern: series designed to give the regular listener to broadcast plays the opportunity to follow developments and to draw comparisons. *English Theatre 1900-1950*, presented in 1953, *20th Century Theatre*, presented in 1954, and, most interesting and significant of all, *Between Two Worlds*, presented in 1955—largely on the impulse of Donald McWhinnie—can, I think, be held to justify to some extent my claim to have established a national theatre before any such thing existed in stone and concrete. Lists of names tend to make tiresome reading. Still, it is with a certain pride that I recall that in 1953 the English listener could have heard representative works by Stephen Phillips, John Galsworthy, Sean O'Casey, H. M. Harwood, James Elroy Flecker, Henry Arthur Jones, John Masefield, Alan Monkhouse, Granville-Barker, J. B. Priestley, Christopher Fry, and T. S. Eliot; that in 1954 he could have heard works by Eugene O'Neill, Lilian Hellman, Strindberg, Chiarelli, Pirandello, Anouilh, Gaston Baty, Sartre, Molnár, Afinogenov, and Carl Zuckmayer; that in 1955 he could have followed the dramatic expression of social history between the two German Wars from Shaw's *Heartbreak House* to Robert Bolt's *The Last of the Wine*; that the same years included festival series of the plays of Somerset Maugham, of J. B. Priestley, and of Noël Coward; that in 1956 radio drama could offer a festival of its own with pieces written for broadcasting by Richard Hughes, Tyrone Guthrie, Eric Linklater, Philip Wade, D. G. Bridson, Louis MacNeice, Edward Sackville-West, and Patrick Hamilton. The list is by no means comprehensive—and enough is enough.

Lapped in an atmosphere of comparative stability and calm, I found it much easier to select my own productions with greater discrimination, to approach them with a more judicial mind, to

175

handle them with greater attention to detail. I could throw my net more widely and confine my attentions to the bigger fish.

Ever since my collaboration with Humbert Wolfe over *Cyrano* I had toyed with the idea that one day *L'Aiglon* might be brought to the microphone. I had only seen the play once—when Miss Marie Löhr presented it for some special performances at the Globe Theatre with herself in the name part—but I had been fascinated by it. I had also been daunted, as in the case of *Cyrano*, by the practical problems of broadcast presentation of a play of such length, requiring such a large cast, not to mention an orchestra and three actors of the highest calibre. Solutions were found as a direct result of having worked with Clemence Dane, Dick Addinsell, and Marius Goring on *The Saviours* series during the war. Each of these seven plays had been extremely complex to handle. Each of them had owed much of its success to Dick Addinsell's music. Marius Goring had given outstanding performances in all of them. When I discovered that Clemence Dane had made a translation of *L'Aiglon* my way seemed clear at last. She, as always, met me more than half way in the preparation of a radio script. Dick Addinsell brought some enchanting music back from a visit he had paid to Schönbrunn. In contrast with *The Saviours*, all of which had been produced within forty-eight hours, it seemed almost child's play to tackle *L'Aiglon* in a week. Marius Goring as the Eaglet, Leon Quartermaine as Metternich and Arthur Young as the old grenadier, Flambeau, could not have been bettered. And I am prepared to claim that the Wagram ghosts scene, like the ghost scene in Flecker's *Hassan*, was infinitely more effective on the air than it could hope to be when visualised on a stage.

During a visit to Zürich early in 1953 I saw, and was immensely impressed by, a performance of *Iphigenia in Tauris*. Not only did the production seem to be in the finest classical tradition, but I believed that in Miss Maria Becker I had seen an actress of quite unusual quality and power. When I discovered on acquaintance that she spoke English well, apart from being a most modest, straightforward and co-operative personality, I could not rest until I had arranged for her to appear as Iphigenia for the B.B.C. She did so with immense success—a success which owed much to Sir Donald Wolfit's performance as the King. Harsh things have been said of Sir Donald regarding his choice of actors for his companies, his determination to stand first with the rest nowhere. I can only state the fact that I have never seen a better example of unselfish co-operation, of courteous helpfulness to a stranger in a strange land, than Sir Donald gave in *Iphigenia in Tauris*. It removed once and for all a mutual misunderstanding between us which had lasted far too long.

Less significant certainly, but for me no less interesting, was the result of one of my visits to Stockholm. For the first time I was able to see at close quarters a National Theatre organised and working on sound practical lines, combining the classic with the experimental in two buildings that adjoined each other, and with companies that graduated from the latter to the former. With due apologies to Sir Laurence Olivier, that Swedish *Richard III*, with Lars Hansen in the name part, was the finest I have ever seen. (It was greatly enhanced by the fact that every actor who played one of the 'bloody baronage' gave the impression of standing about seven feet high and looking about three feet thick.) I was even more interested by one of the representative pieces of the little experimental theatre: a play to which, when it was adapted later for the air, I gave the title of *The Shadow of Death*. Its author was a young man called Stig Dagerman, who at the time was being spoken of as a contemporary Strindberg and was to die with most of his promise unfulfilled. It was a queer, morbidly fascinating, intensely atmospheric play dealing with the mentality of a condemned murderer. When, some time later, it was presented by a tiny experimental theatre in London, it was criticised as pretentious and obscure. In Stockholm, where both acting and production were superb, it was neither one nor the other. I shall never forget a scene in which one of the most beautiful girls I have ever seen had to play the frankest possible undressing scene with the greatest possible deliberation, ostentatiously sexually provocative. She managed it with an exquisite artistry and a mastery of timing which made any reaction of titter or leer impossible.

Nearer home I owed to Mr Montgomery Hyde, whom I had met briefly during the war, the opportunity to offer to B.B.C. listeners the famous 'lost scene' from *The Importance of Being Earnest*. Originally this scene was placed after the second act, and described how a solicitor, a certain Mr Grisby, called upon Algernon

M

Moncrieff to arrest him for a debt owed to the Savoy Hotel. It was supposed that the scene was cut by Sir George Alexander during rehearsals on the ground that it would make the play twenty minutes too long. It was also said that Oscar Wilde's reaction was to shrug his shoulders, remarking, 'You may be right my dear Alec. I can only tell you that it took just five minutes to compose.' Mr Hyde secured a copy of the script of the scene from America, and it was broadcast with my brother John as John Worthing, Richard Bebb—who took over from Rex Harrison at very short notice—as Algernon and John Ruddock as the semi-mythical Mr Grisby. It proved entertaining enough, but hardly sufficiently so to demand its restoration to the conventional text.

One of my greatest regrets is that I have only twice met Mr Somerset Maugham. Both occasions were rather large luncheon-parties, and I doubt if we exchanged more than a dozen sentences. I regret this because there are few authors to whom I owe so much or to whom it would have given me so much pleasure to try to express gratitude. As a reader I found in *Of Human Bondage* the only English equivalent to a Dostoevsky; in many of the short stories a rival to de Maupassant; in *Cakes and Ale* a little master-piece. As a playgoer I believe that *The Circle* stands comparison with the best of Sheridan or Congreve; that *For Services Rendered* was, if not the best, certainly the worst neglected of dramatic comments on the First German War; that in his sense of construc-tion, his tautness of dialogue, his instinct for effective dramatic situation, Mr Maugham remains extremely hard to beat. He has said that he considers himself out of date, and that that is why he abandoned the Theatre when he did. Personally I shall be much surprised if *The Circle* is not still being played long after *Waiting for Godot* is forgotten. With the exception of Laurence Sterne—and possibly of Edward Whymper—he has written the best travel-books that I know, assuming that the object of a travel-book is to bring the country visited alive with its sounds and smells and curious incidentals of things and people. He has eschewed humbug so that he appears neither as cynic nor sentimentalist. I would recommend close study of his work to any aspiring young author.

I am grateful to him also on two more personal grounds. Most established authors, especially in the early days of broadcasting,

178

were the reverse of forthcoming in the face of requests that their works might be adapted to the new medium. Some declined to have a phrase or a comma cut. Some demanded fees far outside the B.B.C.'s capacity to pay. Others hedged hypothetical consent about with stipulations regarding casting or times of performance both impractical and exaggerated. Mr Maugham's attitude was always the same: a courteous agreement combined with the expression of a bland astonishment that anyone should wish to present in one medium what had been written originally for another. Nor, as far as I know, was there ever the smallest argument on the subject of fees. Mr Maugham was not among those who imagined that to make his works familiar to the largest possible public was likely to diminish the number of his readers or the size of his theatre audiences.

As a master of dramatic story-telling he might have been thought of as God's gift to an adapter; an impression which the acknowledged popularity of radio productions of his work seems to confirm. But I am inclined to think that he was fortunate in his adapters, and particularly in one of them whose friendship I achieved largely as the result of our mutual feelings on the subject of Somerset Maugham.

Howard Agg entered the broadcasting field in the first place as co-author with Mabel Constanduros of several successful plays, and later as a producer in the Variety Department. When he left England to live in Sicily he became one of the most regular, dependable, and professional adapters to work for my department, making almost a 'corner' in Mr Maugham's novels and short stories. He was daunted neither by *Cakes and Ale* nor by *The Gentleman in the Parlour*. He proved—as Eric Maschwitz had proved with *Carnival*, as Muriel Levy proved with *The Forsyte Saga*—that the only real basis for satisfactory adaptation is genuine love of the original without which perfect understanding of it is impossible. For a freelance writer he is fortunately situated. The balcony of his modest villa outside Taormina looks out over one of the finest views in Europe. Sitting there, his face terra cotta-coloured beneath hair prematurely white, behind a barrier of cactus plants and with *gecci* scuttling briskly along his walls, he resembles rather some benevolent bonze contemplating the outside world with a withdrawn distaste which only occasionally becomes explosive. To his intimates the most generous of hosts and most entertaining of com-

panions, he is generally reputed—and I fancy enjoys being reputed
—unsociable and even a trifle alarming. I know few experiences to
be preferred to sitting in one of his long chairs with one of the
martinis which he mixes so skilfully in my hand, watching the
distant flashing of a Calabrian lighthouse and a great red moon
climbing the sky out of the sea. More than once on that balcony I
have felt at one with the eaters of the lotus. More than once I have
had to resist the temptation to forget that London was no more than
a day's flying-time away. Yes, I owe much to Somerset Maugham
besides his books.

A subject which was frequently debated on that balcony, and
which consistently occupied my mind when I was back in England,
was the problem of productions of Shakespeare for broadcasting.
Needless to say, Shakespeare had been represented in B.B.C. drama
schedules from days previous even to the Savoy Hill period. *Romeo
and Juliet*—with Cathleen Nesbitt and Ernest Milton—was broadcast in July, 1923; and the general directive given me by Roger
Eckersley in 1929 included the stipulation that at least eight of
Shakespeare's plays should appear in our programmes each year.
This stemmed from the unexceptionable point of view that representation of Shakespeare should axiomatically find a place in the
Corporation's general cultural and educational policy. It was
hardly qualified by any detailed consideration of the suitability to
the medium of the plays themselves. The vague notion existed that
it would be a good thing if the whole canon were ultimately broadcast, and repeated from time to time as opportunity might serve.

While justifiable in terms of publicity and good intentions, this
was neither satisfactory nor practical. I remember being mildly
rebuked for contending that *The Comedy of Errors* was wildly
unsuitable for an audience unable to see the play. I think it was
largely due to early TV productions of Shakespeare that it became
clear how great a gulf was fixed between the plays that made superb
radio material and those that could be no more than readings at the
microphone. Trial and error taught us that in general terms the
plays of fantasy and imagination—in particular *A Midsummer
Night's Dream* and *The Tempest*—might almost have been written
for the 'insubstantial pageant' of 'thin air'. It is difficult, if not
impossible, to make magic convincing against the painted flat or

under the all-seeing eye of the TV camera. Contrariwise the realistic historical plays with their big casts in which, *sans* eyes, it was nearly impossible to distinguish Warwick from Talbot or Salisbury from Gloucester made for difficult radio presentation and depressingly dull listening. Between the two extremes came the great tragedies and the classic comedies, depending for success on the air—as in the theatre—upon outstanding performances and finely intelligent speaking of the verse.

Three Shakespearean productions of the Fifties stand out vividly in my recollection. The first was one of *Othello* in which Mr Alfred Drake played the Moor. I must admit to having approached this assignment with mental reservations. I had seen, enjoyed, and admired Mr Drake playing *Kiss Me, Kate* in New York, and knew him to be an actor of charm, intelligence, and huge vitality. I had no experience of his capacities as an actor in tragedy, and my apprehensions were considerable when he arrived at the first rehearsal carrying a large volume of Shakespearean commentary, in which the theory was put forward that the truth of the Othello-Iago relationship was that it was a homosexual one. However, all was well that ended well, and with a cast including Coral Browne and Stephen Murray we coasted safely home.

Incidentally I have never been able to understand why Stephen Murray is not recognised as being at the very top of his profession. I would say without hesitation that he is the finest actor in broadcasting with whom I have ever worked. Again and again—in Granville-Barker's *Waste*, in *Brand*, as Captain Shotover in *Heartbreak House*, as Odysseus in *The Rescue*—he carried almost the whole weight of the play on his shoulders, playing a long and exhausting part with skill, subtlety, certainty, and insight—and with a minimum of fuss. Essentially introvert rather than extrovert, I have heard him called 'difficult' and even 'unapproachable'. I can only say that I never found him either.

In the production of *A Midsummer Night's Dream* I had the opportunity to do something which, as far as I know, had never been risked by any producer in the English Theatre: to make use of the complete Mendelssohn score of incidental music. The suggestion came from John Hollingsworth, who conducted for me. In *The Saviours* series during the war Muir Matheson had destroyed the prejudice existing in most radio producers' minds against working with a live orchestra. His co-operative flair combined with acute professional *expertise* had succeeded in mastering all the difficulties arising from inadequate rehearsal time and Musicians' Union rules. When Muir ceased to be available owing to his film commitments John Hollingsworth took his place. In spite of the handicap of his persisting ill-health I have never met anyone so indefatigable, so conscientious, so practically helpful. On his musical side he never made difficulties. On my production side, as difficulties arose he was the first person to suggest or improvise some way through, round or under. He shared my own detestation for waste of time. And his control of his orchestra was marked by a mixture of such firmness and charm that again and again he persuaded his players to break their own rules for the benefit of the production as a whole, and to break them with cheerfulness and good-will. Apart from the performances of Sir Ralph Richardson as Bottom and Frank Duncan as Puck, I remember nothing with more pleasure than the fact that when, at the close of the broadcast, I went out of the control-cubicle to thank John and his musicians for their superb playing the orchestra broke out in a burst of spontaneous applause. It was one of the moments which made worth while months of routine and trayfuls of departmental memoranda.

It was also in collaboration with John Hollingsworth that I experimented with the wedding of Tchaikovsky's music for *Romeo and Juliet* to Shakespeare's play. It was no fault of John's that the result was only a partial success. I was at fault in failing to realise that the personalities and approach of composer and author were too individual to blend satisfactorily, while neither June Tobin nor Gabriel Woolf—fresh from their triumphs in *Salome* and *The Persians* respectively—quite succeeded in fulfilling my expectations as the lovers. Still, I believe the experiment was worth trying, and, as in the case of *A Midsummer Night's Dream*, it proved that radio production of Shakespeare gained much from being broadcast from a theatre that had been adapted as a studio: that theatre in Camden Town which faces the statue of Cobden in unbecoming Victorian stone trousers. At the time, apart from the vasty desert spaces of the Maida Vale studios which had once been a skating-rink, we disposed of no accommodation large enough to contain both a big cast and a full symphony orchestra. In the Camden, with the plaque of Ellen Terry in its vestibule and the atmosphere of gilding, red plush seats, and plaster caryatids still hanging about its auditorium, the actors seemed to breathe more freely, to achieve a greater breadth and attack than they found possible in an environment more contemporary and more sternly functional.

Indeed there were occasions when I was to think of the Camden with nostalgic regret. His determined preference for the acoustic properties of the Maida Vale studios caused my only difference with John Hotchkis, who wrote and conducted the music for the sequence of Greek plays which I produced in Constantine Trypanis' transla-tions. An enthusiast, a perfectionist, and a delightful companion, John Hotchkis contributed enormously to the success of a project which for years had been close to my heart.

I had always believed that there was magnificent microphone material in classic Greek drama. In the circumstances of the con-temporary stage not even the ingenuity of Michel Saint-Denis had been able to solve the perennial problem of the Chorus in robes regrettably reminiscent of a Turkish bath. The only quite satisfying stage performance of a Greek play I ever witnessed was one of the *Antigone* one afternoon in the open-air theatre in Syracuse, when—in spite of being played in Italian, too soft a language for the stark tragedy of Attica—something of the original spell was woven by the proximity of rocks and sea, by the frieze of Creon's guards in their great crested helmets with their armour black against a slowly darkening sky. We had of course presented a variety of broadcast productions since that first Gilbert Murray *Hippolytus*, of which I have already written. But the chorus-speaking had always left much to be desired, and available translations had always seemed either too dully academic or too lusciously free.

Then on a visit to Oxford I saw an amateur performance of the *Hippolytus* in which I was immensely impressed by the handling of the Chorus and the simple accuracy and unpretentiousness of the translation. I found that the latter had been made by Professor Trypanis of Exeter College who had been helped in the production by a Miss Colette King, who had specialised in the unison speaking of verse. The result of that visit was an association which I shall always remember with gratitude and pleasure. Miss King tackled

183

the choruses with an indefatigable enthusiasm which began by frightening her actors almost to death, went on by driving them almost to the pitch of nervous exhaustion, and ended by infecting them with her own perfectionist vitality. Constantine Trypanis—as friendly as he was handsome, and with a most delightful and hospitable wife—produced a succession of new translations, working over the details of each draft script with John Hotchkis and me and enduring with a marvellous patience our suggestions and emendations. The collaboration proved as fruitful as it had been agreeable. *The Persians*, with Gwen Ffrangcon-Davies and Gabriel Woolf, *Oedipus at Colonus*, with my brother John and Joan Plowright, the *Antigone*, with Joan Plowright and Brewster Mason, the *Oresteia* trilogy, with Mary Wimbush, June Tobin, and Margaret Whiting, made a sequence of which I believe even the Third Programme could justifiably be proud, and one for which, if for anything, I should like to be remembered.

Looking through my scrap-books covering that last decade of my B.B.C. service, I get the impression of a gradually quickening pace checked by and interspersed with the occasional 'still' picture. There was the dramatic adaptation of Malraux's famous novel of the Chinese Civil War, *La Condition Humaine* (I had seen it in Paris and been greatly moved in spite of my companion of the evening succumbing to a bad oyster during the performance). There was Audiberti's play *Le Mal Court*, broadcast—its first performance in this country—under the title *Alarica*. I tried, and for a time thought I had managed, to persuade the delicious Mlle Suzanne Flon to repeat her Paris success. I had greater luck than I deserved when Miss Joan Plowright stepped into the breach and gave immediate proof of personality and outstanding intelligence. There was June Tobin's Salome. Of this I was particularly proud; first, because Miss Tobin was a discovery of my own, in whose talent and future I had every belief from the moment when she first arrived in England from South Africa; secondly, because I had always been convinced that *Salome*, while an impossible proposition for the stage, would broadcast most effectively. June Tobin and Malcolm Keen proved that I was right. There were two of the plays specially written for broadcasting by R. C. Sherriff, *The Telescope* and *Cards for Uncle Tom*, with their masterly technique so cunningly

184

concealed behind their deceptive simplicity. There were Anouilh's *The Lark* and Mlle Sagan's *Castle in Sweden*. In the case of both these plays I had felt that their stage production in London had been quite inadequate, and got considerable, if arrogant, satisfaction out of calling upon the microphone to redress theatrical shortcomings. There was the Polish political play *Silence*, whose translator felt it wise to remain anonymous. There was Mr Michael Kelly's play about the Dreyfus Case, written as a result of his meeting with me during which he told me that he had seen Esterhazy's tomb in the churchyard at Harpenden with its singular inscription from Shelley: 'He has outsoar'd the shadow of our night.' There was Mary Renault's *God of the Crossroads*, in which Peter Claughton distinguished himself as Alcibiades. There was the first performance in English of Anouilh's *Foire d'Empoigne*, under the title *Animal Grab*, with Peter Bull and Malcolm Keen. There was a revival of *The Seagull* in which Virginia Maskell gave what I believe to have been the most touching performance of Nina since Miss Valerie Taylor played the part at the Little Theatre in the Twenties.

As I have said, the pace remorselessly quickened. Colleagues to whom I had owed so much for so long—Lance Sieveking, Mary Hope Allen, Wilfred Grantham, Peter Watts—followed each other into retirement. The B.B.C. Repertory Company celebrated its twenty-first anniversary, and in doing so made me very glad that for once I had been forced by circumstances to change my original opinion that such a company would bore listeners by repeated appearance and lower the standard of microphone acting. I could not have been more wrong. Whatever might be thought of our selection of plays, I found that, wherever I went abroad, B.B.C. acting was taken as a standard for envy and admiration. Nothing contributed more to the setting of that standard than the work of the B.B.C. Repertory Company. I used its members in my own productions whenever they were available. I cannot remember an instance when they let me down.

When finally my retirement became imminent the Home Service and Ronald Lewin made the charming gesture of inviting me to choose my own valedictory production. I chose to revive Ibsen's *Brand*—another of those plays which in my opinion broadcasts infinitely more satisfactorily than it can ever be staged. And maybe the choice was influenced to some extent by a personal sympathy for that harsh, uncompromising, indomitable figure with mad Gerd crouching behind him, standing in futile defiance against the white onrush of the avalanche. 'If only,' I thought sometimes during the rehearsals while I listened to Stephen Murray's cruelly moving performance, 'if only I could have found the courage and the certainty to face my problems like that.' I suppose that in today's opinion Brand, like Leonidas, is considered little better than a fool. I find such folly admirable, while only too well aware that its emulation is beyond me.

It was with the voices of Stephen, of Ursula Howells, and June Tobin still ringing in my ears that I walked out into Portland Place after the recording of that production of *Brand*. Next day there appeared in *The Times* a photograph of a hansom-cab, with a single huddled figure inside it, jogging down Portland Place into a misty evening. I found it immensely appropriate.

Looking back at Broadcasting House metaphorically through the rear-window of that hansom-cab, what did I chiefly feel? Sadness over an irrevocable end? A little. Regret for opportunities neglected, for words better left unsaid or unwritten? Perhaps. A lingering glow of occasional satisfactions? Again a little. Most of all, I think, I was aware of a settled conviction: the conviction which had made the business of broadcasting, with its strains and stresses, its excitements and its frustrations, its feuds and its friendships, so immensely worth while as an occupation; the conviction that good broadcasting depends not upon the brilliance of producers, not even upon the personalities and abilities of directors-general, but upon collaboration in the best sense of that word. Producers, planners, engineers, even administrators, are all parts of the essential machine. All depend mutually upon each other for success. This dependence calls for humility and understanding, as well as for vitality and brains, for common sense as much as for imagination. To have learned that lesson, to have watched it in operation over so many years, to have contributed towards it in even the smallest measure, seemed to me at that moment to demand some expression of gratitude beyond the ordinary.

How to express that overwhelming sense of gratitude to so many colleagues, so many actors and authors, who were also friends? Perhaps it can best be done by the payment of a small tribute to some people who never achieve credits in the *Radio Times*, to whom overtime is a commonplace of existence, whose work is often insufficiently honoured by those who profit from it and remains unsung by critics: producers' secretaries, and teams of studio management. Were it only possible, I should like to embrace them all after the fashion of the French *accolade*; recognition by the equivalent of drums and trumpets.

Apart from hard service my secretaries without exception gave me loyalty, tolerance, good-humour, and aspirin. They did not shrink from the occasional necessary white lie. They guarded my privacy. They tempered the wind to many shorn lambs. They endured with patience and without the lifting of an eyebrow my reactions to private affairs which must frequently have caused them embarrassment. They kept their eyes open and their mouths shut. I hope they will forgive me if I add that, like all first-rate secretaries, they were not first-rate typists. (The only first-rate typist who ever worked for me was a 'relief' during the war. She ended by joining the W.R.N.S., in which she became an officer, and I last saw her in the bar of the Berkeley, attended by a commander and two naval lieutenants.) I remember them all—Jean Bartlett and Cynthia Pughe, Anne Webster and Ann Keay, Jean Baxter and Lyn Boucher—with gratitude, admiration, and very real affection. As I write my own letters, forget my appointments, find that I have allowed myself to run out of cigarettes or excuses, I realise how much I miss them and the size of my debt to them. It is one I can never hope to repay.

The same thing is true of those individuals composing the teams of technical studio assistants, whose share in successful production is greater than any outsider can ever know. The contribution of fine actors and musicians is self-evident. But when I think of Stephen Murray or Mary Wimbush, of Brewster Mason or Joan Plowright, I think also of Fred Bell, cool as a cucumber in the face of any crisis, shepherding the crowds in *The Man Born to be King* and *The Saviours*, or the choruses in Greek plays, with a tactful certainty which no difficulty could daunt and no temperament could ruffle. When I think of John Hollingsworth and John Hotchkis, I think also of the patience, ingenuity and skill of Johnny Johnson and Cyril

CHAPTER ELEVEN

Collection of Cats

MY PARENTS' opinion of household pets was quite simply that they were both unhygienic and undesirable. My father was never a sportsman, and his attitude towards all animals approximated to that of the Forsytes: their proper place was in the Zoological Gardens. My mother, I fancy, thought with occasional nostalgia of the lawns and stables of Moray Lodge with their dogs and ponies, and of her father Arthur Lewis driving his dog-cart from Campden Hill to his office in Conduit Street. But there was no room for a dog —let alone a pony—in Earl's Court Square or Gledhow Gardens, and my mother was violently ailurophobe. The mere presence of a cat in a room made her physically ill. Being by nature a perverse child—especially where my mother was concerned—I discovered in cats an extreme fascination, a fascination clinched by my reading *The Cat that Walked by Himself* with its illustration of the Cat Waving his Wild Tail and Walking through the Wet Wild Woods. I found this mixture of isolation and self-sufficiency irresistible. From that moment I longed earnestly to have a cat of my own. It was to be more than twenty years before that longing could be fulfilled.

It was, however, in Gledhow Gardens—in the square itself—that I saw my first Siamese cat. In 1907 Siamese cats were almost unknown. They were certainly not fashionable. I can still remember my sensation of startled wonder when I saw one morning from my bedroom window an extremely attractive young lady with long red-gold hair walking slowly along the path opposite, and behind her on a lead a fawn-coloured cat with blue eyes and chocolate mask and paws. My first thought was that this must be some peculiar quasi-domesticated wild animal. And, if this impression seems impossibly ingenuous, it is the fact that during the Thirties more than one visiting tradesman to my flat asked me whether my Siamese wasn't some sort of monkey; that the family with which I was an unwelcome 'billetee' at Evesham in 1939 objected to the presence of the same Siamese on the grounds that he was obviously unsafe to be at large.

I never made closer acquaintance with the Gledhow Gardens cat, though I watched for his occasional appearances with longing, and developed an extreme devotion for his mistress, who became for me an ideal *Princesse Lointaine*. I did manage to find out her name, which was as unusual as her pet. She was called Nara. If she is still alive she must now be in her seventies, and that wonderful hair—only to be compared with the Princess Flavia's in *The Prisoner of Zenda*—must be grey. I am sure that there never crosses her mind the slightest recollection of a remarkably plain small boy with large, round, steel-rimmed spectacles hovering shyly in the middle distance of that London square, yearning to find enough courage to ask if he might stroke her cat. Perhaps it is as well that my nerve failed me. I was clumsy with my hands as well as being short-sighted. It would probably have scratched me, and my mother would certainly have said, 'I told you so'.

She did in fact 'tell me so' when I was given a Siamese of my own about three years after I had come down from Oxford. Two young ladies, with whom I frequently went dancing, gave me a queen. Her name was Semiramis, and she was most attractive to look at. Unfortunately, like most Siamese queens, she was also extremely vocal. Aided and abetted, as always, by my sister, I had hoped with unreasonable optimism to be able to keep Semiramis more or less *incommunicado* in the decent seclusion of what had been the nursery floor. But Semiramis was not only vocal; she liked attention. When she did not get it she lifted up her voice in no uncertain manner. She also climbed up window curtains and scratched the furniture. She also was fussy about her food. Appreciating that both legally and in my own estimation I was now grown-up, my mother felt clearly that there was no longer any question of imposing a veto. Her reactions were those of sorrow rather than of anger, but they were unmistakable. And my father was disapproving and sarcastic. The resulting atmosphere was anything but comfortable, and I suffered a good deal from attacks of conscience. The house, after all, belonged to my parents, and they had had enough to put up with from me in other ways which need not be specified. I found myself faced with what I absurdly thought of as 'a crisis'. Either Semiramis would have to go, or I would have to leave home and take her with me. In the event she solved the difficulty herself by catching some obscure ailment and dying within two or three days, putting up little or no fight after the oriental fashion of her breed. It was a dismal and inauspicious episode, and it was some years before I could bring myself to risk a repetition of glazed eyes and a limp furry corpse. I felt miserable and guilty and hardly done by.

Then in 1930, as one of the happiest results of the production of the radio adaptation of his novel *Carnival*, I made a friend of Compton Mackenzie. At that time he was living on Jethou in the Channel Islands, and he invited Eric Maschwitz and myself to spend Easter with him. He was engaged upon the writing of *Gallipoli Memories*, and whenever I take down my own copy of that book from its shelf I see again the bluebells on Jethou as I first saw them from the sea, a flare of unbelievably vivid colour; the long study with its westward window framing each evening's sunset over Herm; and the dining-room with the candles on the table, the Siamese cats sitting in the shadows along the walls, and Sylvia, the matriarch of the feline family, stepping daintily between the candle-sticks.

Every evening after dinner 'Monty' would read us the last instal-ment of what he had written, only too often reducing both us and himself to tears by his recollections of the splendours and miseries of that great, yet disastrous, feat of arms. Every morning before breakfast I would go out for a walk through the bluebell coppice, moving as stealthily as I knew how so as to catch sight of one or more of the Siamese, couched *perdu* in ambush or lying flat along a low branch, waiting for a rabbit.

I would not swear to the precise number of Sylvia's tribe. My diary mentions thirteen, which in retrospect seems exaggerated. Enough to say that its members were many, lively and altogether enchanting. But there was one, the runt of the last litter, only to be described as odd girl out. She was small. She looked permanently scared. And her brothers and sisters bullied her regularly and dis-gracefully. Monty confessed that he was worried about her future, and ultimately confided that future to my care. That was how Lulu —she was named after that faintly disreputable character in *Extra-*

191

ordinary Women—came to exchange Jethou and its rabbits for a tiny house and back-yard in the shadow of the water tower on Campden Hill in Kensington.

In that unpromising environment I am glad to be able to say that she flourished exceedingly. She became the feline belle of the neighbourhood, and at appropriate seasons lifted up her voice accordingly so that all toms might listen and attend and yearn. During the early days of our association I was stern with her, being determined that she should only mate with her own kind. But Lulu's tastes were unpredictable, and—it must be admitted regretfully—coarse. Again and again I staggered to Richmond under the weight of a heavy cat-basket, only to be informed a few days later that the chosen sire had either been terrorised or ignored. Ultimately she did produce one pure-bred kitten. (He was named Daffodil after the young Norwegian dancer in *Extraordinary Women*, because of his grace and his good nature.) But Lulu was *amoureuse* rather than mother. After a scullery window had been left open carelessly one night she was neither to hold nor to bind, and the list of her lovers became legion. Like the great Catherine of Russia she chose deliberately beneath her: lean, battered, prowling toms with lustful eyes and ferocious appetites, by whom she had litters mostly black or tabby, only their voices betraying their mother's identity.

Most of Lulu's *liaisons* were scandalously fleeting affairs. But she maintained one 'steady', without question the most ruffianly tom-cat I have ever seen. His colour was indeterminately dusty-grey. He always looked half-starved. He had lost part of one of his ears. And because of a gash across his face I christened him Scarface. Between him and Lulu there was a touching sort of honour-among-thieves understanding: that he would always be around when she was tired of her latest conquest. No doubt the fact that he could rely on a regularly filled saucer in my back-yard had something to do with it. None the less, for the benefit of the cynical it should be recorded that on one occasion, when Lulu was in labour and having a difficult time of it, Scarface was discovered in the kitchen beside her kneading her body gently and helpfully with his paws; and, when she was nursing her kittens, he would leave for her horrible relics of his dustbin forays outside the door that led into the yard.

By 1933, owing to circumstances over which I had little control, I had exchanged Campden Hill for Long Acre. This, alas, implied separation from Lulu, who remained to gratify Scarface—and many successors—with her favours; to produce hybrid kittens with splendid regularity; in fact to live the full feline life in every sense of those words. I saw her from time to time, and she never failed to recognise me or to imply that she regarded my desertion with more sorrow than anger.

In the agreement for my Long Acre flat there was a clause forbidding the keeping by tenants of domestic pets. It was, however, more honoured in the breach than the observance by most of the other lessees, and when I was offered a pair of pedigree Siamese kittens as a birthday present the temptation was irresistible. Christened Rudolf Rassendyl and Rupert of Hentzau respectively, they belied their names by playing and sleeping together in the greatest amity. Unfortunately—and as a result I have mistrusted pedigrees ever since—they were too inbred to be healthy. Rudolf indeed had only been with me a few weeks when he snapped two of his legs as if they had been chicken-bones merely by jumping from a kitchen table to the floor, and had to be destroyed. Rupert, as perhaps might have been expected, was made of sterner stuff. But in due course he too succumbed—to an attack of virulent cat-'flu. I made up my mind never again to put my trust in a West End pet-shop, no matter how fashionable or expensive, and to insist that any Siamese I might have in the future should be country-reared: a decision I have had no cause to regret.

Accordingly Hugo arrived one afternoon at Paddington in the guard's van of a train from Gloucester. He was nearly nine months old, and had had the run of a country garden, so that I was apprehensive of his reactions to comparative confinement in a flat whose main outlook was a view of the roofs about Covent Garden. However, he accommodated himself to the new conditions of his life immediately and philosophically to become the most sympathetic and best loved of all my cats.

Like all Siamese he had marked personal idiosyncrasies. He would always sleep in—not on—my bed, and preferably on my feet, emerging beside my pillow in the morning to bite my ear, purring and quite untousled. He was fussy about his food. He would not touch anything cooked. Nor would he drink milk. He jumped as though propelled by coiled springs, and moved with the most elegant certainty. Yet during occasional bouts of ill-humour he would make the round of the sitting-room along the mantelpiece and the tops of the book-cases, and quite deliberately knock one ornament, ash-tray, or photograph after another off on to the carpet with nervous flicks of one hind leg. He seemed to enjoy being talked to as much as he liked to be stroked, contributing comment and reply in a variety of low-pitched keys. He was always sitting just inside the front door when I came back from work in the evenings, and would trot down the passage in front of me to the kitchen, waving his tail as graciously as any 'painted jaguar' with an air that could only be described as essentially proprietorial.

I do not propose to contribute here to the eternal controversy between the respective merits of cats and dogs as pets, and the equally futile argument as to which type of human being loves the former or idolises the latter. If the dog gives more, he certainly demands more. If the cat demands less, he almost certainly gives less. For myself I would only suggest that in the circumstances of city life it is easier to make things agreeable for a cat, and that my conscience is lightened proportionately. In some ways the Siamese lies somewhere half-way between dog and cat. He tends—Hugo certainly tended—to attach himself to the person rather than the place. He can be happy without 'the wet wild roofs' at night. He has not the self-sufficiency of the ordinary cat. At the same time he never fawns, and he is never servile. He accepts affection as a right, never as an indulgence, and returns it in the same spirit. He knows his place—and it is definitely not below the salt.

On occasion I would find it necessary to leave Hugo alone in the flat when I went away for a week-end. Needless to say, I always arranged not only for him to be fed, but also to be visited. However, he never failed to make it clear to me just how much he disapproved of these desertions on my part. When I came back he would meet me at the door as usual, but after trotting down the passage in front of me he would jump up on to a table and sit down deliberately turning his back upon me. He would not look at me; he would not converse; he would not purr. He would accept no overtures of friendliness or apology. He would remain thus withdrawn, hunched-up, implacable, for hours until he felt that I had well and truly learned my lesson. Then he would suddenly appear, or scratch at the door, or jump on to my bed, without *arrière-pensée* of any kind. He had made his point, and we could go on from there. No woman could have established a grievance more neatly or less hurtfully.

Hugo was with me when the war broke out in September 1939, and when my department was evacuated to Evesham—or 'Hogsnorton' as it was somewhat frivolously termed—I was determined that Hugo should go with me. I made what I felt then might well be my final shopping expedition in London to buy first a cat-basket, and second a bottle of vodka. I was in a considerable hurry, and a fashionable store, which shall be nameless, took advantage of the fact by selling me a bottle of cointreau instead—a fact which I only discovered when it was already too late to be able to do anything about it. On the other hand Harrods provided me with a magnificent basket. It was an eerie experience to walk through one department after another of that vast building, which seemed the vaster because for once it was practically empty of shoppers on that morning and rows of assistants stood about white-faced and empty-handed, as though waiting idly and helplessly for the Wrath to Come.

One of the actresses in the B.B.C. Repertory Company—which had been formed in embryo immediately after Munich in an anticipation of the future which must be admitted to have been reasonably intelligent—had been kind enough to offer me transport to Evesham in her car. Into this car Hugo's basket was packed among the suitcases. It immediately became clear that evacuation was by no means sympathetic to his proud and aristocratic spirit. He proclaimed his distaste *à haute voix* all the way to Reading. It was a distressing commentary upon an experience both humiliating and disagreeable.

The actress concerned had been offered a night's hospitality on the journey by Lord (then Sir William) Rootes in his house just outside Reading. The invitation was extended to include me, and it was sitting on the staircase of that house that I listened to Neville Chamberlain's famous broadcast announcing the beginning of the Second German War at eleven o'clock in the morning of September 3rd, 1939. With a gesture typically kind-hearted Lord Rootes had extended his hospitality to Hugo in the shape of providing him with a complete barn to himself in which to spend the night. It took almost as long to pry him out of its recesses as it took me to drive on to Evesham later in the day.

I have already written of the disfavour, indeed of the alarm, with which Hugo was received by the unfortunate family on which I found myself billeted. Its members proved unsusceptible alike to his charm and my persuasions, to considerations of sentiment or financial compensation. As a result Hugo achieved, I fancy, what must be something of a record even for a Siamese cat. A furnished house had to be taken for him.

So far so good. But with the opening of 1940 the Drama Department was shifted to Manchester, and I had to quarter myself in the gloomy splendour of the Midland Hotel. This implied of necessity separation from Hugo, apart from the fact that I did not feel inclined to invite any Siamese to face the combination of winter and black-out in Manchester. He received both hospitality and affection in the temporary home that I managed to find for him in Ladbroke Square. Alas, he perished in that deadly epidemic of cat-'flu which devastated London in 1942, having survived various air-raid experiences with characteristic *sang-froid*. I hope he is happy in his own Elysian fields.

It was some time before I could steel myself to be unfaithful to Hugo's memory and get another Siamese, but when in due course I returned to London and was lucky enough to find another Long Acre flat, my loneliness was assuaged from time to time by two blacks and a tabby. Both the blacks were kittens, and neither stayed with me long. The first, a regular Covent Garden stray, scratched at my door one night—I christened him Black-Out—stayed for just over a week, and vanished as mysteriously as he had come. The second—I called him Blitz—was found by a friend of mine wandering on an anti-aircraft battery site, and seemed to appreciate regular meals and a roof over his head. But there must have been something inherently adventurous in his disposition. Before long he found the freedom of the adjacent roof-tops irresistible, and one night he, too, did not come back.

The tabby came to me as a gift from Dorothy Sayers, after we had worked together on the play-series *The Man Born to be King*.

Dorothy swore that his mother was a genuine witch's cat and pronounced, with her usual decision, that the only possible name for him was Merlin. Away from the studio floor one did not argue with Dorothy, and certainly Merlin was no ordinary cat. He was aware of many things invisible to the human eye. He would sit perfectly still for hours with great amber eyes fixed unwinkingly upon apparent vacancy. He would bristle all over, and indulge in inexplicable leapings, without discoverable reason. At last I made the mistake of taking him away with me for the week-end to the country cottage of some friends. There he fell victim to the fascination of climbing trees, and when I brought him back again to London nothing could stop him from making the best of a poor alternative and climbing book-cases. I hated to part with him, but if there is anything I cherish more than cats it is my books. So I found him a home in the country, where I trust that he may still be climbing to his heart's content, and, it may be, weaving spells among the topmost branches of an orchard.

After Merlin I had no cat for quite a number of years. My domestic background tended during this period to be complicated and disorganised: a state of affairs which no right-minded cat can be expected to enjoy. Then, one Sunday, I was invited to lunch with some friends of mine who had a house at Strand-on-the-Green, and encountered a Burmese cat for the first time. Completely smitten by the combination of cigar-brown body and beryl-green eyes, I had to confess to infidelity to Hugo's memory, and made up my mind on the spot that at the first opportunity I would acquire a Burmese of my own.

U-Puss, as I called him, when he arrived at King's Cross looking pathetically small in the corner of a large travelling-cage, came from Yorkshire. He lived up to every hope and expectation. In the first place, even as a kitten he was immensely healthy, unlike so many Siamese, who are tiresomely prone to every sort of infantile ailment. He was friendly, lively, and enormously decorative. He was quite fearless. Occasionally I would take him with me to Cowdray Park to watch the polo, where he created something of a sensation, particularly among the dogs who are always present in large numbers. I remember vividly one poodle who, confronted suddenly with U-Puss, gave the impression of being about to turn inside out with surprise and horror. Perched on my shoulder, he would accompany me to the pony-lines, his green eyes contemplating dogs, humans, and horses with an expression of mildly supercilious indulgence. When the game began he would retire with dignity to the seclusion of the car, and go to sleep.

He would astonish and, I fear, interrupt the labours of, typists in the office-block adjacent to my flat by exploring or sunning himself on the flat roof outside their windows. But he would respond immediately to my wife's call or the clatter of a knife against a tin plate, leaping from behind chimney-stacks and across low walls with the speed and elegance of a ballet dancer.

As he was a friendly and conversational—though by no means a tiresomely vocal—cat, we felt that perhaps he lacked the society of his own kind, and we secured accordingly a Siamese kitten—Thai-Puss—to bear him company. The result was not entirely successful. Thai, until he grew up, was delicate and rather neurotic. U-Puss was tough, strong, and inclined to treat the kitten as he treated his other toys, with slap-happy, careless heartiness. A *modus vivendi* was ultimately achieved. They came to sleep in the same basket. But Thai was never really at his ease, and often was frankly terrified. It was only after a tragic night when U-Puss went out across a window-ledge in pursuit of pigeons and never came back that Thai achieved full stature physically and morally, and became the controlling influence in the household that he remains at the time of writing.

Does it seem trivial, or sentimental, or even absurd to recall and describe these things? I think that Carl van Vechten provided the answer when he wrote: 'It is seemingly very simple, such a companionship, depending on scarcely more than a mere propinquity . . . a touch of the cold moist nose, a soft paw against the cheek, a greeting at the door, a few moments of romping, a warm soft ball of fur curled on the knee, or a long stare. It is thus that the sympathy between men and animals expresses itself, but interwoven and collectively. These details create an emotion which it is difficult even for Time to destroy.'

As far as my cats and I are concerned, Time can never destroy it.

CHAPTER TWELVE

Innocent Abroad

As long as I can remember I have liked to think of myself as a traveller. A sightseer I have never been. I must have visited Paris more than a dozen times before I saw the inside of the Louvre. I spent eight months in New York and never saw Grant's tomb. I say this not with any sense of snobbish superiority to the vulgar herd. I am simply not made that way. There is a strain of sheer cussedness in my disposition which provokes a negative reaction to the recommendations of guide-books and the enthusiasms of people who 'have been there before'. Also, to be entirely mundane, I find that churches and picture-galleries make my feet hurt, and that artistic appreciation is not increased by physical exhaustion. For choice I like to go to a place strange to me, and to settle down to live in it for an appreciable time. The covering of ground for its own sake makes no appeal to me, and for the actual business of movement from place to place I prefer a boat to a train and a train to an aeroplane. The latter is of course useful in emergencies, and I am probably prejudiced as the result of a ticklish forced landing as far back as 1935, and of being flown over Budapest in a thirteen-year-old Fokker machine in 1938. I have flown several times since. I have always been frightened or bored.

From 1919 onwards—the years of Hitler's War of course excepted—it has been exceptional for me not to spend my holidays or annual leave out of England. That this became an established habit was due largely to my brother Lewis. During the years between the wars I could always be sure of a welcome and a bed in his flat in Paris, and no city makes a better jumping-off place for a European excursion whether one's objective is east or south.

During the early Twenties it was usually south. In those days the French Riviera was a paradise for the impecunious, when Juan-les-Pins consisted literally of a clump of pine trees and one hotel, Le

Lavandou was an almost unknown hamlet, and Saint Tropez was ignorant alike of film-starlets and bikinis. I can still feel the excitement of the night-crossing from Newhaven to Dieppe—second-class; still taste the first ham-roll, coffee, and cognac in the Dieppe station *buffet*; still hear the arguments with stout French women, who seemed always to be swathed in black garments, regarding the desirability of the admission of fresh air to a railway-carriage; still see the domes of the Sacré Cœur incredibly white in the sunshine of early morning. Discomfort was nothing. Adventure of one kind or another seemed always imminent.

In those days one was not exasperated by the present profusion of travel advertisements at Christmas. It was not necessary to plan the details of a summer holiday in early January. It was still possible to make up one's mind almost at the last moment, hastily to pack a bag, buy a ticket, and arrive without apprehension as to hotel accommodation. In those days too the English pound and the Englishman's reputation for honesty stood higher than they do today. The French *hôtelier* did not look askance at an English cheque. And I remember with gratitude the proprietor of a small hotel in Naples, where I had stayed for a single night on my way to Capri, lending me my return fare and pocket-money with no security of any kind, when I was called back to England by a sudden emergency.

Now, if one seeks to escape the noble army of trippers—especially of red-faced, paunchy, Teutonic trippers with female counterparts unattractively greased and sun-glassed—it is necessary to go somewhere south of the latitude of Rome. Majorca already might as well be Blackpool. And the combination of the aeroplane and the Affluent Society throws menacing shadows across even the less-known Isles of Greece. Mlle Bardot has made her washpot of the Riviera, and Miss Fields has cast out her shoe over Capri. With the destruction of distance and the increase of the travelling public it becomes more and more difficult each year for the seeker after comparative quiet and solitude to find anywhere to go. Looking out at my own little corner of Sussex, where I have found sanctuary after sixty years of living in London, Mediterranean delights begin to pall except in terms of nostalgic reminiscence. And how could I dare to write of Venice—loveliest of all cities I have seen except

San Francisco—with Mr James Morris's superb book on a shelf at my elbow?

It is almost impossible to see those beaches and villas in the South of France, where Eric Maschwitz and I talked and laughed and drank so much cheap wine, except through a haze of nostalgic romance which enhaloes everything from the boat-train platform at Victoria to those tiny Parisian *boîtes de nuit* in which Lewis would help us to celebrate leave's end. There is something of the unreality of an old-fashioned musical comedy about the places and our behaviour alike. Memory holds the door, but only holds it tantalisingly ajar. Did we spend all one night in Montparnasse in the company of a female contortionist and a White Russian *émigré* who earned his living by diving into a swimming-pool through flaming paper-covered hoops? Did I write most of one of my thrillers in the upstairs sitting-room of a little hotel in Le Lavandou, while in the room below Eric and his composer hammered a popular song into what was to prove a riotous success? Did Lewis's Korean man-servant, who brought tea for two to one's bedroom in the morning and left it tactfully outside the door, really belong to a revolutionary organisation, so that he had to be sent out for the evening when Japanese guests were expected? Did we share a villa at Juan with Hermione Gingold, and meet Marlene Dietrich and Jean Gabin before they were world-famous? Did Aldous Huxley, opening out his lanky figure like a foot-rule, forget to eat his lunch while he explained in detail the coition processes of salamanders and Siamese cats respectively? In each case the answer is 'yes'. But it is given hesitantly. Sharp outlines have faded. Relevant circumstances have vanished beyond recall. Perhaps it is that the Twenties were little more than a backwash from the tempest of the First German War; that the survivors were so astonished to find life still going on that the importance of the trivial became enormously exaggerated.

I have said that my favourite means of transport is a boat, and I wonder sometimes why this should be so. I should not care to live by the sea. I doubt there being a drop of sea-faring blood in my veins. But I have never failed to enjoy Atlantic crossings, and I spent four of the happiest weeks of my life on the Danish freighter which took me to Los Angeles by way of Jamaica, the Panama Canal, and various Central American ports in 1938. The omens were hardly propitious, for, although I was looking forward to staying in Hollywood with Eric Maschwitz, I began the journey feeling remarkably ill. Also I found myself sharing a cabin with a nice old gentleman who spent most of the voyage in bed. It took me several days to discover that he did so because he was a confirmed dipsomaniac. When we struck rather a heavy swell off the Azores empty bottles rolled all ways from under his bed. It was off the Azores, too, that I saw one of the loveliest sights in the world: a three-masted schooner under sail.

What completed my cure and, I believe, prejudiced me permanently in favour of sea-travel was the sensation of inhabiting a world tiny and self-contained, completely isolated from that other world in which one lived strenuously, moved neurotically, and had a restless being. Impossible to worry about problems personal or political while one lay back in a deck-chair for hours at a time, one's only occupation the watching of the slow lift and fall of the horizon. Impossible to be concerned with practical affairs, with the state of heart or stomach, while one sat in the bows while the ship ploughed her deliberate way through a sea crawling with turtles, and flying-fish spun and dived like silver flames. Impossible to be startled by those chequered shirts of many colours—with very short shorts to match—sported by a stout New York business-man, who came aboard at Kingston with a cargo of the least funny stories I have ever heard. Impossible to be impatient with the interminable delays accompanying the loading of bananas—15,000 bunches of them— in Nicaragua. Impossible to find active fault with meals of hot soup and heavy meat dishes on top of rum cocktails in tropical heat. Impossible to feel surprise when a lady, with whom one had only become acquainted on the boat, revealed the most intimate secrets of an unhappy married life with the candid abandon of a character in a Somerset Maugham short story. Escapism is neither a philosophy nor a solution, but I am glad to have experienced it during those few short weeks.

The experience remained more vividly etched upon memory when contrasted with the crossing in the *Normandie*, on which Eric and I sailed from New York some six weeks later. I had never been on a big liner before, and this—peace to her rusting hull!—was the biggest of them all, complete with private chapel, lifts and a film-theatre, not to mention a vast and pillared swimming-pool. There was a large theatrical contingent on board, most of whom we knew. We had a first-class state-room, as the result of Eric's Hollywood salary, in which we never seemed to go to bed. For four hectic days and nights we ate almost nothing but caviare and drank little except vodka. There were a few uneasy moments when, looking down from the heights of the boat-deck, one had the impression not of a ship at all but of some great luxury hotel, and asked oneself how it could manage to go on floating with funnels vast enough to contain a railway-engine, propellers the size of windmills, and a rudder as tall as a tree. But this, too, was a world isolated and self-contained and proportionately soothing, though my instincts lean less towards luxury than comfort.

Neither was much in evidence when I crossed the Atlantic in the *Queen Mary* not long after the end of the war. She was still adapted for troop-carrying, and I shared a small cabin with Michael Joseph and five other men. Most of the passengers were the English wives and children of American soldiers on their way to their new homes in the States. Many of them came from country villages in England and Wales and had never seen the sea. Few of them had even the haziest notion of what to expect in the future. I fancy that some of the husbands had had some talent in 'telling the tale' if the girls were to be believed, for some of them anticipated life in a city penthouse with the equivalent of Gregory Peck and Deborah Kerr for neighbours, while others looked forward to being rescued from the perils of 'the frontier' by a posse led by John Wayne. If they were astonishingly unsophisticated, they were also amazingly courageous in facing an unknown future, and touchingly grateful for any help over their present problems, among which the most consistently pressing was their children. These squirmed and yelped like puppies, and vanished into the more obscure corners of the ship with the smooth ingenuity of kittens. Much of the crossing was spent in extracting them from lockers and ventilators, even from officers' cabins. But there resulted neither official exasperation nor maternal hysteria. I hope too much disillusion did not await them in their brave new world. I was only disappointed when, having gathered a party on deck to see the skyline of New York emerge above the morning mist, it chose rather to concentrate on the comparatively squat insignificance of the Statue of Liberty. This these Pilgrim Mothers had heard of—and they were not going to miss it.

There are serious gaps in my journeyings abroad. I have never set foot in Asia—except for one depressingly cold day in Istanbul—in Africa, in South America, in Canada, or in Australia. I have never been nearer to Russia than Warsaw. The Taj Mahal, the Great Wall of China, Table Mountain, Sydney Harbour, the Kremlin, and the Pyramids remain for me, and now are likely always to remain, the illustrations to a book of Never-never Lands. Yet I cannot find it in my heart to envy those citizens of the United States who, insured by Express cheques and carried—almost packaged—in jet-planes, come nearer every year to emulating Puck in putting a girdle round about the earth in forty minutes. I feel no urge to put myself down for inclusion in future holiday cruises to the moon.

Yet I hope that one day I may be able once again to sit during an afternoon and watch the light changing on the slopes of the Matterhorn; to see the sun rise from a bridge over the Seine; to hear the sounds of Venice waking as light spreads across the Lagoon; to hang perilously on the side of a cable-car as it climbs the hill-streets of San Francisco and see each view more astounding than the last until I can drink a Bourbon old-fashioned in the bar on the Top of the Mark; to watch the lights spring up through the falling dusk in New York; the moon climbing slowly out of the sea below Taormina; the silent red hills about Segesta; Gibraltar's lion-silhouette; the eagles of Zeus swooping across the face of Delphi's cliffs; the mysterious and threatening distances of the Hungarian *puzta* and the Polish plains, for so long the marches of Eastern Europe guarding Western civilisation; the grim darkness of the Sangre de Christo mountains against a blood-red sunset.

I would like once more to eat trout in Brussels, sea-food on Fisherman's Wharf, oysters Rothschild in New Orleans, *smörgåsbord* in Stockholm, *scampi* in a restaurant behind the Fenice Theatre, roasted saddle of hare in Paris, *blini* in Warsaw; to drink *goldwasser* in Danzig, apricot brandy in Budapest, a dry martini in New York, *vino bianco* in a *trattoria* beside the little quay at Malcesine, or on the terrace of the Villa Fontana Vecchia where D. H. Lawrence once wrote poems, and vodka—straight—in Warsaw.

In short, I would like to see again almost every place that I have been to—with one exception. I have been twice to Hollywood. In spite of fantastically generous hospitality, much friendliness, and a good deal of fun, nothing would induce me to visit the place again. I have described it elsewhere: its unreality, its false values, its meretricious pretentiousness, its vulgarity, its crazy-paving of talent wasted or misused, of physical beauty exploited and degraded, of jewels and sweat-shirts, of fine intentions and commercialism run mad. To leave Hollywood was for this traveller one of his most satisfying experiences.

Should one travel in company or alone? In theory there is much to be said for Kipling's advice on the subject: 'He travels the fastest who travels alone.' But for me personally speed is not the object of the exercise. I know that in fiction it is the solitary traveller who meets the girl of his nightmares, or outwits the stout and elderly philosopher who proves to be head of some secret international organisation. But in practice I have found when alone that I have been marked down by some unattractive spinster who prefers not to pay a porter to carry her bags, or—as once in America—by a commercial traveller insistent upon revealing the details of his business at inordinate length. (Shortly after leaving Oxford I travelled commercially, and unsuccessfully, first in books and later in typewriters. Of this sombre episode I recall that I could sell only the works of Florence Barclay, and that as a result of my persistence I was thrown out of an office in Ludgate Circus—an office which I was delighted to see was destroyed in the Blitz.) I think that company on a journey, particularly under conditions of discomfort, is not only agreeable but almost essential.

Should the companion be masculine or feminine? A man is likely to be less trouble. A girl ought certainly to be more fun. I am assuming that in either case the choice will possess good temper, patience, an equably polite attitude towards foreigners—waiters, porters, and cab-drivers in particular—interested curiosity, sensitive reactions to the new place and the new thing, a sound digestion, and a capacity for silence. It may be that a girl with these attributes qualifies also for the Kingdom of Heaven, especially if she can be persuaded that the one axiom of successful travel is never to take more in the way of baggage than can be carried in the traveller's hands. Also I may have been beyond the ordinary lucky. But, much as I owe to the companionship of Eric Maschwitz and other men over the years, my warmest recollections are for members of the miscalled weaker sex: for A., who preserved an admirable calm when we found ourselves on an Italian platform between stone-throwing strikers and trigger-happy police; for D., who took me back to my hotel and put me to bed one night in Paris, when a Polish acquaintance's hospitality had proved excessive; for R., who shepherded me across the United States with unfailing tolerance and amiability, and taught me that the only road to good Anglo-American relations is for each nation to treat the other as foreigners—and foreigners who speak a different language in spite of appearances; for J., who reacted to everything—the *wagon-lit*, the meals, the gondolas and galleries, the shrilling of cicadas, the colour of village vegetable-stalls, the cats and the *apéritifs*—with such evident pleasure and excitement as to double my own sensations of well-being and satisfaction.

I do not know whether it is better to travel hopefully than to arrive. But always to travel hopefully—that is the thing.

CHAPTER THIRTEEN

Croquet on Donkeys

APPRAISAL OF men's characters and abilities has been conditioned by a remarkable number of different things: the size of their noses, the set of their jaws, the balance in their bank-accounts, their attitude towards children and dogs, upbringing, education. Mr Sherlock Holmes delivered the judgements which so startled Doctor Watson by observation of every sort of outward and visible sign. Old Jolyon Forsyte believed that 'by the cigars they smoke, and the composers they love, ye shall know the texture of men's souls'. Personally I have found that to know anyone really well it is necessary to be made aware of apparently trivial hobbies, of seemingly inexplicable habits. It is in the light thrown by such things that the real man often emerges with a *persona* considerably different from that established by the masks of professional achievement or domestic conventionality.

It is on account of this conviction that I felt that this self-portrait would be incomplete without reference to such small matters as my cats and my toy soldiers, and my addiction to military history. It is for the same reason that I mention the only sporting interest in my life: an entirely unreasonable and unreasoning passion for the watching of polo.

I have only once ridden a horse—along the sands at Nairn in Scotland, when I was thirteen—and I showed no sort of aptitude for the exercise, nor did I enjoy the experience particularly. It is true that the uncle after whom I was named—he became a Native Commissioner in Rhodesia, after romantic experiences as a cowboy in Arizona and as a trooper in the Matabele War—played polo in Bulawayo, but I cannot believe that a very 'fixed' snapshot of his team fired my imagination to any extent. I can remember tea at Ranelagh with one of my aunts in the picturesque dead days of the Kit-Kat Club and garden-parties on the lawns, with a military band in the background, and a polo-pony from an adjacent ground almost cannoning into the strawberries and cream. But this frightening interruption—I was about eight at the time—might have been expected to have established an inhibition against, rather than a fascination for, the greatest of all games.

I have a shrewd suspicion that, just as my father's reading aloud of *The Cat that Walked* was basically responsible for my collection of cats, my discovery of *The Maltese Cat* in *The Day's Work* on a shelf in the library of my house at Rugby pointed my way to Hurlingham and Windsor and Cowdray Park; which is why I owe a great deal more to Rudyard Kipling than the pleasure which the reading of his books has given me.

I trust I may be acquitted of the fashionable vice of name-dropping if I aver that many of the happiest moments of my life have been due to His Royal Highness the Duke of Edinburgh and Lord Cowdray. I have never met—I am unlikely ever to meet—Prince Philip. He is a 'prince out of my star'. And Lord Cowdray is unlikely to remember an undistinguished member of a vast luncheon-party, who hardly opened his mouth except to fill it with delicious food. For me the vitally important facts remain that without Lord Cowdray's enthusiasm and resources polo would almost certainly have vanished from the English scene after the Second German War; that without Prince Philip's patronage and vigorous personal participation polo would have had no chance to achieve anything in the nature of popular recognition.

I have never been able to understand why this popular recognition is still to some extent withheld. The fact that racing is 'the sport of kings' has not prevented its affectionate and enthusiastic adoption by all and sundry. Polo on the other hand seems fated to be 'smeared' to some extent by the label of *snobismus*. The game calls for fine horsemanship, great technical skill, a cool head, and courage. Its rules are simple in the extreme. It is played at a speed second only, I am assured, to ice-hockey. To watch, it is both thrilling and pretty. 'Polo', Sir Winston Churchill has written, 'is the prince of games, because it combines the pleasure of hitting the ball, which is the foundation of so many amusements, with all the pleasures of riding and horsemanship; and to both of these there is added that intricate loyal team-work . . . which renders a true combination so vastly superior to the individuals of which it is composed.' Sir Winston's opinion on any subject is worthy of respect. As far as polo is concerned he not only enjoyed the game and played it both in India and England with considerable success, but also admits to having appointed Admiral Beatty to the command of the Battle-Cruiser Squadron of the Grand Fleet in the First German War partly on account of the latter's reputation in the hunting-field and on the polo-ground. With other good judges he believed that the game educated the officer in dash, in quickness of reaction, and in the instinct 'to ride home'.

I believe that it is in fact the automatic association of polo with the pre-1914 Regular cavalry officer that has caused the trouble. Polo became in a way equated with privilege—and privilege is as generally damned as it is admittedly out of date. It seems to me curious that while few people object to highly-polished motor-cars, sleek chauffeurs, and other attributes of the Affluent Society, there should be a prejudice against highly-polished brown boots, sleek ponies, and grooms—most of whom are nowadays personable young women. Apparently people recall the fact that many of the officers who commanded the Somme and the Passchendaele offensives had originally belonged to cavalry regiments and played polo. Sir Douglas Haig had himself been a notable player. So was General Ismay, who was outstandingly successful as Chief Staff Officer to Sir Winston Churchill in his capacity as Minister of Defence during the Second German War. If the playing of polo was in any way responsible for the shortcomings of the former, is it not reasonable to assume a certain connection between the game and the virtues of the latter?

In fact the failure of the game to achieve any wide-spread popularity comes from a mixture of sheer ignorance on the part of the mass of game-watching enthusiasts, who cannot believe that eight men on horses can do more with a ball than twenty-two men on their own feet, and a queer snobbery in reverse on the part of people who managed to associate in their minds some connection between riders and a threat to the democratic idea; a threat presumably personified in the formidable appearance and flying moustaches of Professor Jimmy Edwards 'riding off' his opposite number with typical and infectious enthusiasm.

We shall not again experience the sight of the slow parade around the Number One ground at Hurlingham of the ponies of one Indian team: between thirty and forty matching chestnuts, each led by a scarlet-turbaned *sais*. I believe it was Lord Morrison of Lambeth who decided that the war could not be won unless that ground with its background of noble trees and its tradition of great galloping was ploughed up for allotments, so that London lost its last metropolitan polo-field and, incidentally, the recognised international head-quarters of the game. None the less, particularly on any day of bright sunshine in Cowdray Park, the watching of polo remains for me an experience compounded of matchless excitement and physical beauty: Hanut Singh going through the game like a centaur on a chestnut pony with a red martingale; Ronald Ferguson combining elegance and skill as surely as any Ouida or Ian Fleming hero; Paul Withers apostrophising heaven as one of his celebrated 'cut' shots misses the goal by inches; the brothers Gracida tempering the ultimate in professional achievement with the humour of the circus-clown. And, for a background, that fragment of Old England which was in the beginning, is now, and—with a modicum of luck and common sense—ever shall be: the tweeds and the head-scarves; the innumerable dogs; the picnic lunches; the leathery cheeks and stiff upper lips; the children so gaily and uninhibitedly stamping down divots between chukkas; the mixture of shabbiness and good breeding; the trees and the downland; and the local cricket club's match being played only a field away, supremely regardless of any rival attraction.

It was the sardonic comment of a lady, a distinguished authoress and a dear friend of mine, who gave me the title for this chapter. She ought to have known better. She too is a devotee of Kipling. Also she lives almost within sight of Cowdray Park, which makes it worse. Yet somehow the comment fails to sting, although I have been assured that croquet as a game brings out the very worst of human nature in the shape of hatred, malice and all uncharitable-ness; and that the donkey is exasperating alive and useless dead.

I prefer to think of croquet as I remember seeing it played during those summers before the First World War: a leisured, gentlemanly, unhurried manner of passing time between a luncheon of cold beef and raspberry-and-red-currant tart and a tea embellished with cucumber sandwiches: a game that implied sunlight, and very green grass, and an easy friendliness, and no thought for the morrow.

While, as for the donkey, I am content that G. K. Chesterton should have the last word.

CHAPTER FOURTEEN

Envoi

A FRIEND of mine, who was kind enough to read the typescript of this book so far, gave me a quizzical look as he put it back on my desk.

'Is that all?'

'I should have thought it was plenty. But what exactly do you mean by "all"?'

'Isn't it supposed to be a self-portrait? What about your religion? More important still in this day and age, what about your sex-life? Surely these gaps need to be filled in?'

He may have been right. It is true that I have neglected to put in all the warts, to meet the expectations of the confessional. But I do not propose to fill in those gaps, and perhaps I ought to explain why I choose not to do so.

With regard to religion I can only say that I believe this to be an intensely personal and private matter between a man and his God. I am neither a regular church-goer nor what could be called a deeply religious man; I am not the former from conviction, I am not the latter with considerable regret. I cannot believe that the thought-processes and emotional experiences which led me to these attitudes are easily explicable or particularly interesting. That I am influenced by behaviourism rather than by any conventional moralities is a matter of deep-rooted instinct; an instinct which I cannot defend and would find it hard to justify. Ritualism appeals to me. Clericalism appals me. No doubt a Church must be 'with it'— just as the Theatre must reflect contemporary trends—yet I cannot go along with clergymen who seek to fill half-empty churches by having their hymns accompanied by jazz combinations and steel guitars, any more than I could tolerate preachers at my public school who imagined that they could make their sermons acceptable by adorning them with the metaphors of the cricket-field or the boxing-ring. I fear that I find myself equally out of sympathy with the Bishop of Southwark and Archbishop Makarios. I have always felt that in the Becket case King Henry II was a much maligned man; almost as pitiable a victim of clerical propaganda as was King Richard III of Tudor malignity. But then by no means the least of my affections for Oxford arises from its tradition as the home of lost causes.

Then this business of Sex and All That. I believe that even in these days of candour and Lady Chatterley a gentleman does not kiss and tell, that it is best left to Fanny Hill and Harriet Wilson to reveal the secrets of the alcove. Should anyone be interested I have no objection to their knowing that I had the facts of life made moderately clear to me by my little playfellows at my private school, and that I don't think I should have gained very much if I had got the information embarrassedly from my parents, or scientifically from the family doctor. I was still virgin at twenty-one. I have never visited a brothel. I have always greatly enjoyed the society of women. I have been no more continent physically than *l'homme moyen sensuel*. Experience has taught me that none of the trials and difficulties of marriage can be compared with the trials and difficulties of even the most glamorous *liaison*, that the happiness of two people is no less enjoyable for being licensed. But if asked to come to cases I must, albeit a little regretfully, decline. It would be pleasantly exciting in retrospect to suffer again those ardours and endurances, those moments of torment and exultation, of apprehension and tenderness, dawns of disillusion and evenings of delight. I doubt if the real truth would emerge from any such recapitulation. Memory can lie, and romantic memory can lie damnably. Such lies are best kept to oneself.

Nor would I wish, however slightly, to hurt other people's feelings. It has always seemed to me that a physical relationship unqualified by emotion is merely brutish; that, if it is to be satisfactory, it must also imply and establish the obligations of friendship. The individual in love is at his or her most defenceless. Body and soul can—and should—be exposed without shame and without fear. Their secrets are two people's mutual trust. To expose them should be taboo. To discuss them is unpardonable. The friend who has once been a lover makes the finest friend in the world. The only love-affairs that I regret are those which were ended in circumstances of rancour preventing the renewal of the relationship on the firm foundations of knowing all and forgiving all. The rest should be silence.

'How should an old man live his days if not in dreaming of his well-spent past? ... The present he should distrust; the future shun.' So wrote John Galsworthy in *Indian Summer of a Forsyte*, which, for an avowed sentimentalist cradled in the last year of Queen Victoria's reign, is outstanding among short stories as both touching and true. I should like to be able to emulate Old Jolyon: to sit back in that armchair in Brook Street and dream of a well-spent past, or to sit back in another armchair with the view of the Downs above Glyndebourne, dropping the daily newspaper at the sound of a blackbird's song. Unfortunately—or perhaps fortunately—it can't be done. In recollection I am forced to doubt whether I spent my past particularly well. And, though I distrust the present, I decline flatly to shun the future.

Few things have depressed and irritated me more than the point of view exemplified by C.N.D.: the attitude that no belief in the future is reasonable, no conventional standards are worth preserving, because civilisation as we know it may be ended at any moment by one deadly and all-embracing bang. For the intellectually half-baked and the flabby-minded the excuse is too easy. In 1918 the life of the average infantry subaltern was computed as sixteen days from the time that he landed in France. My contemporaries continued to march to Flanders. A shamble from Aldermaston, with pop-singing accompaniment, would have seemed to them degrading and absurd. Villagers continue to live their lives on the slopes of Vesuvius and Etna, regardless of hypothetical doom. To pray for delivery from sudden death is a mark of decent humility in the face of an unknown infinite. To distrust the present and shun the future out of apprehension of that sudden death is merely to cut off one's nose to spite one's face. There was surely much to be said for those individuals who took special care concerning the dressing of their hair and the cleanliness of their linen on the mornings when they went to the guillotine. Sir Walter Ralegh made a point of dying in a clean shirt.

What our way of life has to fear, it seems to me, is not the Bomb but that all-embracing materialism which creeps upon us out of both West and East. Surely it is as dangerous and as soul-destroying to make a god of the tractor and the farming co-operative as it is to make one of the skyscraper, the top of the Hit Parade, or keeping up with John Doe? Reasonably good authority has warned us that man does not live by bread alone. I have an idea that life is not completely fulfilled even if that bread is spread with caviare, or washed down with Coca-cola to the accompaniment of long-playing jazz records in an oil-fired, centrally-heated penthouse.

It is frequently given both as explanation and excuse for the crass and rather boring behaviour of the more exhibitionist among the younger generation that they no longer see any worth-while outlets for enthusiasm and vitality: no more crusades; no more worlds to conquer in terms of exploration, colonisation, or adventure; no more great undertakings to fire the imagination and the blood. I find this baffling. Everest has been climbed, but there are still thousands of displaced persons in Middle Europe and the Middle East. Colonialism on this earth has become a dirty word, but there remains the occupation of the moon. Cancer, poverty, famine, are all still with us. Scientists are not deterred from their activities by awareness that general annihilation may be just round the corner. Is it simply that inspiration is lacking in those admirably meaning, internationally constituted bodies, with their huge staffs of earnest-looking, balding gentlemen in horn-rimmed glasses, and their arid titlings—UNRRA, UNESCO, UN, and the rest of them? Or can it be that modern education with its insistence and emphasis upon technological achievement fails to engender in the contemporary student the necessary amount of the "satiable curtiosity' of the Elephant's Child?

Personally I still find myself impenitently, even childishly, curious about the future, and thank God for it. During my fifties, as the names of people I knew—many of them no older than I— began to appear in obituary columns, I found myself compelled to think seriously for the first time about death: not as something that happened inevitably to everybody else but as something as real to myself as the day after tomorrow. I shrink from it, not being physically courageous, because of the probability of its association with pain and the gradual dissolution of the faculties which too often makes the dying a burden almost intolerable for relatives and friends to bear. But I think I am truthful when I say that my chief resentment against death is that inevitably it will mean that so many of my curiosities will be left unsatisfied. I shall read publishers' announcements of books which I shall never be able to open. I shall hear the names of a polo team which I shall never see play. There will be a kitten which I shall never see grow into a cat. There will remain the journeys I shall never take. There will be another spring.

All of which is sufficiently exasperating. None the less I remain curious, even about myself. And as long as I remain curious I shall live; I shall not merely acquiesce in the business of existing. I find in this not only consolation but active incitement. That is why I prefer to end this book looking forward to the remaining seven years of the conventional mortal span, rather than backward at memory's mirror and the ghosts that shift and fade upon its surface.

I have never cared for tomb-stones. I trust that, when the time comes, my ashes may be scattered under the open sky. I neither expect nor hope to be remembered. But I should like, should anyone find my name passing his lips, him to add—and mean it, 'He was grateful.' Perhaps fortunately it is only with the passing of the years that a man comes to realise just how many people, just how many things, he has taken for granted; how indifferent all expression of gratitude must be.

As I sit here with my books around me and Thai-Puss curled up on his cushion in the corner, it is above all things gratitude that I feel, gratitude unalloyed and overwhelming: to my parents who gave me life and love; to my brothers and sister whose affection, so often strained, was never broken; to my friends and my lovers; to all those who, in sharing work with me, made it both pleasure and privilege; to my cats and my books and many childish things; to my schools which gave me a taste of hell; to Oxford which gave meaning to the word 'heaven'; above all to one person who has taken it on herself to make one solitary place to blossom as a rose. I hope to live long enough to be able to make her fully aware of what she has done, to be able to persuade her that she has not done it quite in vain.

Barcombe. March, 1964.

INDEX